Robert Fergus

Chicago River-And-Harbor Convention

An Account of it's Origin And Proceedings

Robert Fergus

Chicago River-And-Harbor Convention
An Account of it's Origin And Proceedings

ISBN/EAN: 9783744743877

Printed in Europe, USA, Canada, Australia, Japan

Cover: Foto ©ninafisch / pixelio.de

More available books at **www.hansebooks.com**

FERGUS' HISTORICAL SERIES, No. 18.

CHICAGO
RIVER-AND-HARBOR CONVENTION

AN ACCOUNT

OF ITS

ORIGIN AND PROCEEDINGS

BY
WILLIAM MOSLEY HALL,
JOHN WENTWORTH,   SAMUEL LISLE SMITH,
HORACE GREELEY,   THURLOW WEED;

TOGETHER WITH
STATISTICS CONCERNING CHICAGO;
BY
JESSE B. THOMAS, AND JAMES L. BARTON.

COMPILED BY ROBERT FERGUS.

CHICAGO:
FERGUS PRINTING COMPANY.
1882.

Entered according to Act of Congress, in the year 1882, by
FERGUS PRINTING COMPANY,
In the office of the Librarian of Congress, at Washington, D. C.

INTRODUCTION.

IT may seem strange to the reader that the Proceedings of the River-and-Harbor Convention are published over thirty-five years after it adjourned; but the reason is a simple one: Nothing approaching a complete account of what took place during the sessions of that important body has ever been given to the public before. The mere journal was put into pamphlet form for circulation, and two or three speeches were distributed by the gentlemen who delivered them, but no one until now has undertaken the task of collecting these documents together and embodying them in a book. At the time the Convention was held the Whigs were endeavoring to supplant the Democrats. Both sought to make political capital out of the event, and to this fact is attributable the meagre official report of the work done, only such things as would glorify the Whigs, who controlled the organization, being put into the record. Democrats who participated in the deliberations were, in a great part, ignored; and, in self-protection, had printed separately the speeches they made. There have been many inquiries recently about the Convention which did so much for the Northwest, especially for Chicago, and to supply the needed information, this volume was compiled, all it contains being reliable. And in it, the originator of the Convention, William Mosley Hall, Esq., now living in Stamford, Conn., tells the story of its inception. Being a Democrat, the Whigs deprived him of the glory to which he was entitled, but, at this late day, the people of Chicago and the West will not fail to appreciate his labors and thank him for what he did.

The introduction of the newspaper articles, resolutions, etc., are intended to show the public feeling existing at that time throughout the North-West, and the deep interest taken in the subject of Internal Improvements.

Mr. Hall's Resolutions and Speech on "A National Railroad to the Pacific"—the first public speech on this subject—predict what did happen, and outline how such a road *should* have been built.

The addition of the reports of Horace Greeley, editor of the *New-York Tribune*, and Thurlow Weed, editor of the *Albany Evening Journal*, stating what they saw and heard in this vicinity; together with the statistics of Jesse B. Thomas of Chicago, and James L. Barton of Buffalo, will be appreciated by our future historians, and treasured by our old settlers and their descendants.

No little exertion has been made to correct the list of Delegates as printed in the Convention pamphlet, an 8vo. of 79 pages. To many inquiries no answers were received; and to those who responded promptly, and to other contributors, the compiler desires to express his grateful acknowledgements.

CHICAGO, *February 16, 1882.*

CORRESPONDENCE.

LETTERS FROM WM. MOSLEY HALL.

STAMFORD, Conn., Nov. 14, 1881.

My old and much esteemed Friend:

By mail of yesterday I was in receipt of a copy of "Early Chicago—Fort Dearborn," with your compliments, containing interesting information and a capital portrait of Hon. John Wentworth; for which, please accept my sincere thanks. * * *

Referring to your efforts to keep alive the early history of Chicago, I have seen nothing about the great advertisement which I rightly claim the credit of originating in 1846. The first meeting for the great River-and-Harbor Convention I called at Rathbun's Hotel, N. Y., Sept. 28th, 1846, when Wm. Duane Wilson, of Milwaukee, was called to the chair, and Robert Fergus, of Chicago, and Thomas Sherwood, of Buffalo, acted as Vice-Presidents, and William M. Hall, of Buffalo, and E. D. Burr, of Copper Harbor, were appointed Secretaries; and thus the grand scheme was launched, and the New-York and Eastern papers were unanimous in advocacy of the movement.

And now comes in a point in the history of the affair which is unknown to any but myself; as I know of no one living who was cognizent of what transpired between our meeting in New York and the decision of *where* the Convention should be held. St. Louis, Pittsburg, Detroit, Cleveland, Cincinnati, and Buffalo were all anxious for the honor. To say that liberal temptations were intimated to me, to change my original preference for Chicago, would be drawing it mild. I had traveled several thousands of miles at my own expense, and, though poor, I represented large commercial, Lake, and River interests in the West and South, and with the assurance of the Mayor and others in authority that my actual expenses (amounting to $576.00) should be paid, I continued my efforts in favor of Chicago, even after a meeting had been held in St. Louis in my absence, declaring that the Convention would be held in St. Louis. It is sufficient to say to you that I have never been in receipt of a dollar for all my outlay although the Mayors John P. Chapin and James Curtiss promised to call the matter up before the City Council, and if that failed to raise it by subscription.

The meeting of that Convention raised the value of Chicago property at once, and was the starting point of its unheard of prosperity, until overtaken by the disastrous fire of 1871. No man of intelligence, who was a citizen of Chicago at that time, and is alive there to-day, can deny this proposition, and I believe if properly presented, there is enough of the old stock left to do justice to one who cheerfully devoted his time to their common interest.

This, my old friend, is a simple statement of facts, and it grieves me to recite them. Justice demands of Chicago the prompt payment of that obligation.

Your death report of the old settlers since May 27th, 1879, includes many with whom I have enjoyed pleasant hours, which I look back upon as a fitful dream:

"And so 't will be when we are gone,
That tuneful peal will still ring on,"

and the earthworms' slimy broad will soon hold high carnival over all that remains of us! This is the unalterable decree, and we should meet it like "one who wraps the drapery of his couch about him and lies down to pleasant dreams."

My health is not good—am troubled with indigestion. Does Mrs. S. Lisle Smith still live? Please let me hear from you again.

Truly your friend,
WM. M. HALL.

To ROBERT FERGUS, Esq., Chicago, Ill.

STAMFORD, Conn., Nov. 16th, 1881.

My dear Fergus:

Yours of the 14th just received. I have not time to say more, at this time, than that I will give you what you desire as soon as I can, and will forward it—out of which you can select what is required for publication. I thought it strange that I was ignored or forgotten in your elaborate early history of Chicago.

My faithful old wife yet lives to comfort me. In haste,

I am your friend,

Deos y Libertad.—Santa Anna.   WM. M. HALL.

STAMFORD, Conn., Nov. 18th, 1881.

My esteemed Friend:

I send you to-day, by Adams Express, a package, out of which you may be able to gather some desirable information. Some of it, of course, is not pertinent to the business of the Convention, but upon the 28th page of the "Old Sailor's Story"* you will see that I had some experience before the mast on the briny deep, as well as the sterile sands of South Africa, among the Hottentots, long before I visited the prairies of Illinois, although I passed through Chicago in 1832.

You will also observe that I republished my speech at the Chicago Convention,† with other matter of National importance. It is sufficient to say that the Tehuantepec enterprise cost me $30,000. I rode over the Isthmus and returned on a "muel," and, O Moses, what a country! The wilds of Soudan is a paradise in comparison. The $2 note on the Eagle Bank of New Haven cured me of banks and banking early in life—I prize it for its

---

* "The Old Sailor's Story; or a Short Account of the Life, Adventures, and Voyages of Capt. Gurdon L. Allyn. Including Three Trips Around the World. Written by Himself, in the 79th and 80th years of his age. Norwich, Conn., 1879."

† "Speech of Wm. M. Hall of New York, in Favor of a National Railroad to the Pacific, at the Great Chicago Convention, July 7th, 1847. Also, A Review of the Tehuantepec Route; embracing the famous Garay Grant, Sloo Contract, and other Routes and Plans. New York, 1853."

antiquity only.* Indeed, every thing I send you I wish to preserve, and were it not that I feel grieved at the ingratitude I have been subjected to by those from whom I had a right to expect better treatment, and that as far as lies in your power to see me righted you will do so, I would not consent to send them.

It was my intention to make Chicago my home and my grave, but the result of my efforts for the benefit of that City determined me to leave, and, with a heavy heart, I sought another field for future labors. Thank God there is no blot upon my escutcheon, I stand *rectus in curia* before the world. Like yourself, I am not rich, but again like yourself, my conscience is void of offence, and though both may be passed by purse-proud pirates with a sneer, they may learn in time that a sneer is often the tribute that fear pays to a power born of superior intellect. "But something too much of this"—and I will pass to Serial No. 16.

I have perused it with great interest. The speech of Hon. John Wentworth in answer to the great copperhead from Ohio [Vallandigham], in 1864, when the Government was trembling in the balance for existence, was a masterly effort, and would to God the principles there presented were engraven upon the hearts of the whole people to-day, and transmitted to future generations. It fairly dwarfs such democrats as my friends W. W. Eaton, Thos. H. Seymour, James H. Gallagher, and others in this section, who at that very time were shedding crocodile tears for men who first perjured themselves, and then throttled the best Government on earth, to sustain an institution gangreened with crime, and a

---

* On one of the pages of Mr. Hall's scrap-book, sent in "package" referred to above, is pasted the note: "L 2. No. 662. The Eagle Bank of New Haven promise to pay to E. Whitney, or bearer, on demand, Two Dollars. New Haven, 4th July, 1822. Geo. Hoadly, Pres't. F. B. S. Rossiter, Cash'r."

Under the Note is written: "My dear Son,—This note is the first paper money your father ever earned. It was paid him by Deacon Samuel Barstow of Columbia, Ct., for riding horse to plow between corn, at three dollars per month, in the summer of 1822. The Bank failed, and left [your] father without shoes to attend school that winter. I feel the loss to the present day.
WM. M. HALL.

"To E. Allan Hall,
  Stamford, Ct., Nov. 14, 1869."

stench in the nostrils of the civilized world. I repeat, Mr. Wentworth, as he stated, was imbued with genuine Democracy from the Jefferson-and-Jackson school, regarded it as something which could not be bought, sold, or bartered, because the objects of a Democracy, while it secures to enterprise and talent their rewards, is to equalize the benefits of heaven to all, and the act which would avowedly confer special facilities for the amassment of enormous wealth on any body of men, is in derogation of its own comprehensive scheme. "And them's my sentiments." I cast my first vote for Gen. Jackson and last for Gen. Hancock, but when my flag was assailed, I dismissed politics. Please bear my kind regards to "Long John." That speech went to the marrow, and entitles the author to the respect of every man who is a lover of his country and law. Please acknowledge receipt of package, and believe me, your friend,

WM. MOSLEY HALL.

You state that you have sent to St. Louis for Edward Bates' speech at the Convention, I think you will fail to find it anywhere, from the fact that he had no notes when he made it, and, if my memory serves me, there were no stenographers present. Enoch E. Camp, of New York, reported for the *New-York Herald*, and I think the *New-York Tribune*. Schuyler Colfax was one of the secretaries. The Rev. Flavel Bascom, who was born within two miles of where I was born, was on the platform while I delivered my speech. Does he still live?

My faithful old forty-two-year partner sends you a present of my picture, taken during a *cold snap*, some twenty years after the River-and-Harbor Convention; she says that it is as good as John Wentworth's, but I do not—his is a capital likeness.

Does James A. Marshall still live? And Joshua L. Marsh? I again plead excuse for all mistakes in my manuscript, as I have written while suffering from indigestion, and if you have ever been thus afflicted you will know the difficulty of arranging ideas. However, you can improve it if you like. If the "wolf" was entirely out of sight, I would pocket a "hundred" and go to "Polecat." How would you like to see me walk into your sanctum?

1 *

If I was there, I could do much to aid your Serial that I can not do on paper. And what a trifling sum for a few men there that we have contributed to make rich. But let us content ourselves that "all's well that ends well," and that God is just, and retribution certain! *Au Revoir*,

W. M. H.

P. S.—I forgot to mention that my speech was the *first public speech ever made in favor of a National Railway to the Pacific.*

STAMFORD, CONN., Nov. 17th, 1881.

ROBERT FERGUS, ESQ., Chicago, Ill.

Dear Sir:—Your esteemed favor of the 14th inst. is at hand, and it affords me pleasure to respond to your request.

From 1845 to 1848, the writer was the agent, in the South and West, with headquarters at St. Louis, of the Lake Steamboat Association, running lines of steamers between Buffalo and Chicago. Connection was made by Frink & Walker's Stage-Line, and, subsequently, by packets on the Illinois-and-Michigan Canal with Illinois-River steamers to St. Louis.

At the close of the season of 1846, before leaving St. Louis for Buffalo, where I then resided, it occurred to me that inasmuch as the press of St. Louis had taken such a lively interest in the commerce of the great Lakes, it was incumbent on me, as the representative of the above-named Association, to make some appreciative recognition of its valuable services, and carried out that idea by giving an editorial dinner. At that entertainment was Col. A. B. Chambers, of the *Missouri Republican*, Col. Chas. Keemle and Joseph Field, of the *St. Louis Reveille*, and several others, whose names are now forgotten.

During the repast, the subject of river-and-harbor improvements was broached, and the Convention, previously held at Memphis, where Mr. Calhoun sought to make the Mississippi River an arm of the sea up to that place, was discussed, until finally Col. Chambers remarked that although the Democracy of the country was generally opposed to improvements of the kind desired in the

West, he thought that if a properly-directed effort was made, irrespective of politics, it would receive the endorsement of the press generally throughout the country, which would arouse Congress to favorable action. Furthermore, turning to me, he said, "there is no one that I know of better qualified to move actively in the matter than yourself; and we of St. Louis will do all we can to aid in the movement." After thanking him for the compliment, I suggested that a Convention be held somewhere in the West at a future day, which was unanimously accepted. The next day, I left for home, by the way of Chicago, where I remained two or three days, and, while there, laid the proposition before R. L. Wilson, Dr. W. B. Egan, S. Lisle Smith, and several others, who were delighted with the idea, and pledged Chicago to its support. Thus encouraged, I stopped at Detroit, and found Oliver Newberry, Capt. E. B. Ward, and many more alive to the movement, and Cleveland was no less anxious for a Convention. At Buffalo, I found Millard Filmore, E. G. Spaulding, John, William, and Robert Hollister, H. M. Kinne, Jas. L. Barton, and all the commercial men of the city, Chas. M. Reed, of Erie, included, also the press had heard of the movement and were alive to its success.

I called at Rochester, Syracuse, Utica, Albany, Springfield, and Boston, where I laid the subject before Anson Burlingame, who rendered substantial aid by giving it wings through the Boston Journals. Providence, Hartford, and New Haven received due notice of coming events, and at New York I made a stand, for the purpose of setting the ball in active motion.

There I was fortunate enough to find Wm. Duane Wilson, Robert Fergus, and a few other western gentlemen, and we held a meeting at Rathbun's Hotel, September 28th, 1846. [See the action of that meeting on page 18.]

From this time to the following summer, meetings were held throughout the Country for the appointment of delegates to a Convention. There was great anxiety manifested by several western cities to secure the Convention, and St. Louis ignored the recommendation of the New-York meeting entirely through her Chamber of Commerce by claiming the Convention for herself. This claim, however, was abandoned after several communications between Col. Chambers and myself, and *my* original plan was adopted.

When the Convention assembled, there was an effort on the part of John C. Spencer, of Albany, T. Butler King, of Georgia, and a few others, to give it a political turn, but that movement was checked at once, and Edward Bates, of Missouri, who had long before retired from politics, was chosen to preside, and most satisfactorily and eloquently did he perform the duty. (I regret to say that in consequence of a fire, I am unable to give the entire proceedings of the Convention, or the letters and documentary evidence of the temptations offered me to swerve from my original intention of holding the Convention at Chicago.)

After the River-and-Harbor business was concluded, the Convention resolved itself into Committee of the whole, with Horace Greeley in the chair; when I appeared before it, and advocated my resolutions in favor of a National Railroad to the Pacific, in opposition to Carver and Whitney's schemes. (See copy of same herewith.)

The foregoing is a plain and truthful narrative of the great River-and-Harbor Convention, held at Chicago, Ill., July 5th, 1847, which can not be successfully controverted by any human being on top of the green earth; though I am not surprised that there are men in these degenerate days who would filch honors for themselves which of right belong to another, when, at that day, men high in authority and society violated their solemn and oft-repeated pledges, which left the author of the great enterprise and their sudden advancement to wealth to seek remuneration for his labor and outlay wherever he chose to look for it! Indeed, I was looked upon by many as a "loony," and fit subject for a straight-jacket, because I contended that a railroad to the Pacific was practicable! Thank God, time has vindicated my prescient opinion, and I regret to record that not one of the pioneers of that immense work ever received a farthing, or the privilege of carrying a hod or wheeling a barrow, as a day-laborer, upon the work!

Capital, cold, grasping, unyielding capital corrupted the servants of the people, and thus secured to itself, in all the subsidies, a territory of land equal to all New England, New York, Pennsylvania, Ohio, and Illinois thrown in! Better that a line of earthquakes, topped out with burning volcanoes, ran along the entire range of the Rocky Mountains, than that such a monstrous monopoly, created by "placing money where it would do the most good," should be tolerated in the Republic. Those things will not, nor can not, come to good, and by reference to my Resolutions you will find I was of the same opinion on the 7th day of July, 1847.

Hoping that I have not wearied your patience, and that your coming serial will be as interesting and valuable as the last, I remain,

Your friend,
WM. MOSLEY HALL.*

P. S.—Bro. Fergus, you will take note that I was never six months at school in my life. There were no Gamaliels or Sheridan Knowles about when I rubbed the shell from my head, so you and your editors must not criticise too closely. Alter, shape, or arrange this communication as you deem *politic* or proper, so that you do not lose sight (of which I have no fear) of the main fact—THE ORIGINAL.

---

* Born in Hebron, Tolland Co., Ct., April 20, 1812.

COMMENTS, REPORTS, AND EXTRACTS.

VETO OF RIVER-AND-HARBOR BILL.

The following are the Lake items in the Bill that received Mr. Polk's perogative of a veto, [Aug. 3d, 1846]: If "His Excellency" should ever visit the "Northern Lake Route," these will, in all probability, be pleasant places for him to stop at and visit—*viz.:*

Port Ontario Harbor,	$10,000	Sandusky City,	$14,000
Oswego Harbor,	10,000	River Raisin,	13,000
Big-Sodus Bay, Lake Ontario,	5,000	Lake Erie, Dredge Boat,	30,000
Little-Sodus Bay,	5,000	St. Clair Flats,	40,000
Genessee River,	20,000	Grand-River Harbor, on	
Oak Orchard Harbor,	7,000	Lake Michigan,	10,000
Dredge Boat, Lake Ontario,		Mouth Kalamazoo River,	20,000
and St. Lawrence River,	20,000	St. Joseph Harbor,	10,000
Buffalo Harbor,	15,000	Michigan City Harbor,	40,000
Dunkirk Harbor,	15,000	Racine, Little Fort, South-	
Erie Harbor,	40,000	port, Milwaukee, Chicago,	
Grand-River Harbor,	10,000	Dredge Boat, in all	80,000
Ashtabula Harbor,	10,000	Hudson River, above and	
Cleveland Harbor,	20,000	below Albany,	75,000
Huron Harbor,	5,000		

"It would seem the dictate of wisdom under such circumstances to husband our means and not waste them on comparatively unimportant objects."

Thus discourses James K. Polk, in his veto message on the Harbor Bill, and the sentiment is an *insult* to the country. "Husband our means" forsooth. Are not *millions* being squandered by this same James K. Polk for the invasion of Mexico and the extension of slavery? Are not steamboats being bought and chartered daily, at enormous prices, to enrich his favorite·prodigals? Are not the Treasury doors unbarred whenever the "*open seseme*" is whispered by the slave-driver? And yet Mr. Polk outrages the intelligence of the people, his masters, by claiming, when a pittance is asked for a great Northern interest, that we must "*husband* our means!" *That the object for which we ask them is comparatively* UNIMPORTANT!

Does not Mr. Polk know that, independent of the immense wealth that is afloat upon the Northern Lakes, *human life* is risked in its care; and does he call that existence which he jeopardizes and trifles with, in his narrow-minded cringing to the South, an unimportant object? As he answers to his country for his care of the former, so let him answer to his God for the peril in which, by his acts, he places the latter—in abandoning them his protection upon the Lakes when the storm rages.

Verily he shall have his reward when he answers at the Bar.—*Chicago Daily Journal*, Aug. 12, 1846.

"Some of the objects of the appropriation, contained in this bill, are local in their character, and lie within the limits of a single State; and though in the language of the bill they are called *harbors*, they are not connected with foreign commerce, nor are they places of refuge or of shelter for our navy or commercial marine on the ocean or lake shores."

Such is the reasoning upon which James K. Polk attempts to sustain his Veto of the Harbor Bill, because appropriations are made for places, with which there is, as he asserts, no foreign commerce, and are not used as places for shelter for our navy or commercial marine. His real hostility to the Bill can not be concealed by such a shallow subterfuge. The objects of improvement lie north of Mason and Dixon's line, and would benefit the North and West, whose growing prosperity is hateful to the slave-owners of the South. The lives and property of the freemen of the North, her free laborers, sailors, and those passing to and fro upon her great Lakes and Rivers, are of no concern to the Government. They live and labor in a portion of country which is out of the pale of its care and protection. The lives of an hundred or two of hardy mariners, and a few millions of property are of no consequence in the eye of James K. Polk, when weighed against a Virginia abstraction, or that idol of the South, negro slavery. Three times already has the whole policy of this Government been changed at the command of the South, all its business broken up and deranged, because the slave-owner was jealous of the prosperity of the free States. They were rising in prosperity, growing rich in commerce, agriculture, manufactures, and great in intelligence, whilst the South, with the curse of slavery upon her, was standing still or going backward. And shutting their eyes to the real cause which produced such results, they attributed it all to what they were pleased to call partial legislation, and they have demanded a change, and every change has brought the same results, and ever will, until slavery be at an end, and the energy of free hands and minds shall raise this country to that position for which Nature intended her.

All other pretenses of objections to the Harbor Bill are idle and vain. The North can and will be no longer hoodwinked. If no measures for protection and improvement of anything North or West are to be suffered by our Southern masters, if we are to be downtrodden, and all our cherished interests crushed by them, a signal revolution will inevitably ensue. The same spirit and energy that forced emancipation for the whole country from Great Britain will throw off the Southern yoke. The North and West will look to and take care of their own interests henceforth. They will deal justly by the South, but at the same time they will see that they have equal justice, and that the power to oppress shall not again be entrusted to men who have shown themselves to be slave-holders, but not Americans.

For what was Government instituted, if not to protect the lives and property of the governed? And because a portion of the governed happen to live in a part of the Union where every man is free, where the chain and the slave-driver are unknown, are their lives and property to be left to the merciless fury of the winds and the waves? We shall see. The spirit of freedom yet lingers around Bunker Hill, Bennington, and Saratoga, and there are children, yet living, of the fathers whose bones are bleaching there. They have ever been willing to allow more than justice to their Southern brethren, but they will not allow them to be their masters—they will have justice. The fiat has gone forth—Southern rule is at an end.—*Chicago Daily Journal*, Aug. 19, 1846.

THE LAKE COUNTRY.—In a few years the trade and commerce of the Lake Country will nearly equal that of the Atlantic. When the various arteries to the main channel shall have been opened —especially when the boundless West shall have poured in her tribute through the Illinois-and-Michigan Canal, the increase in the amount of produce will be immense, and the tonnage on the Lakes will increase in proportion. Through this channel, most probably, the States and territories bordering on Lakes Michigan, Huron, and Superior, including the copper region, will be supplied with the necessaries and luxuries of life from the tropical regions; thus creating an entirely new era in the commerce of the West.

At the present moment, the commerce of the Lakes exhibits evidence of a gigantic increase. It is known, says the *Cleveland Plain Dealer*, that the first steamboat which reached Mackinac was in 1819; and in 1826, steamboats navigated Lake Michigan. In 1833, there were on the Lakes 11 steamers, which cost $360,000, and which conveyed, to and from the Lake ports, 61,485 passengers. In 1834, there were 18 steamboats in the trade, which cost $600,000. In 1845, the following vessels navigated the Lakes, above the Falls of Niagara: steamboats, 52, 29,500 tons; propellers, 8, 2500 tons; brigs, 50, 11,000 tons; schooners, 270, 42,000 tons. Total, 380; 76,000 tons. The cost of the

construction of these vessels was $4,600,000. In the same year there were on Lake Ontario 7 steamboats, 8 large propellers, and 100 brigs and schooners. The tonnage is estimated at 8000 tons.
The navigation of the Lakes is critical, and requires a great improvement in light-houses, beacons, buoys, harbors, etc. During the last five years, more than four hundred lives have been lost, and last fall, during the boisterous weather, 60 lives were lost, 36 vessels were driven ashore, 20 became total wrecks, 4 foundered, the loss of property was estimated at $200,000. In 1845, not less than 1,500,000 barrels of flour passed over the Lakes, and 250,000 passengers. At the present time, the commerce of the Lakes may be fairly estimated at $100,000,000 per annum. This is an evidence of what the commerce will be which is now in its infancy, and which calls for the fostering hand of Government for its protection. The Lakes, from their peculiar position, require not the presence of armed agents of Government for the protection of the commerce that is borne upon their surfaces. All they require is a shelter for the mariner from the effects of the strife of the natural elements, not from the ill effects that too generally succeed a wrangling among nations. But even this boon has been denied by the enlightened! statesmanship of James K. Polk, who interposes his *Veto* to the construction of that shelter, because he wants the money for the Mexican War! Justice in such cases may well turn aside and weep for the neglect.—*Chicago Daily Journal*, Aug. 31, 1846.

From *Chicago Daily Journal*, Sept. 17, 1846.

☞ Who is James K. Polk? Answer ye 54°- 40″ Crusaders. Answer ye, betrayed and insulted Pennsylvanians. Answer ye, friends of internal improvements. Answer ye, long-suffering claimants of National Justice. Answer ye, Hard-Currency "Democrats." Answer ye, advocates of Freedom. Answer ye, friends of peace. WHO IS JAMES K. POLK?—*Portland Argus*.

THE CALL FOR NEW-YORK MEETING.

NORTH-WESTERN LAKES AND RIVERS.—A meeting of all those who reside on the borders of the North-Western Lakes, now in this City, and others interested in the improvements of the harbors on those Lakes, will be held this evening at Rathbun's Hotel, at 7½ o'clock. It is hoped that Western men, particularly, will attend without fail, as matters of great importance will be brought up for consideration.—*N.-Y. Herald, Sept. 28, 1846.*

PRELIMINARY MEETING IN NEW YORK.

[From the *New-York Herald*, Tuesday, Sept. 29, 1846.]
NORTH-WESTERN LAKES AND RIVERS.

A respectable and influential meeting of leading Western men, and others interested in the improvement of the harbors on the above-named Lakes and Rivers, was held last evening at Rathbun's House [Broadway], and was numerously attended.

At 7½ o'clock, WM. DUANE WILSON, Esq., of Milwaukee, was called to the chair, and ROBERT FERGUS, Esq., of Chicago, and THOMAS SHERWOOD, Esq., of Buffalo, acted as Vice-Presidents. WM. MOSLEY HALL, Esq., of Buffalo, and E. D. BURR, Esq., of Copper Harbor, were appointed Secretaries.

THE CHAIRMAN, on taking the chair, said he would call the attention of the meeting to the following article, from the *Chicago Daily Journal*, [Tuesday, Sept. 15, 1846]:

["THE LAKES AND WESTERN RIVERS:—The *St. Louis Republican*, in commenting upon the expression of public feeling in the West on the subject of the President's last veto of the River-and-Harbor Bill, takes the ground that the men in office should be convinced by the moral force of the popular will that this Government was framed *for the benefit of the people*—that the benefits and assistance they have a right to expect they *will exact* from their agents, and, after reviewing in an able manner the whole ground, makes the following suggestions, to which] we call the especial attention of those in the Lake interest, as a matter of the first importance to their commercial welfare, and worthy of their most attentive consideration.

"The press, in States bordering upon the Lakes, will, of course, speak out on this subject:

"'With due deference to the opinions of others, as to the most effective means of obtaining and embodying the opinions of the great mass of the people residing within the valley of the Mississippi and the basin of the Lakes, on this subject, we venture to make the following suggestion, and ask for it a candid consideration, and the attention of the press throughout the country—

"'That a Convention of delegates from every State, county, and district within the country designated, be held at some convenient point, say at St. Louis, to embody and express the views of the mass on this subject, as well as to consider and act upon any other subjects legitimately connected with it.

"'We have not the space to-day to pursue the subject as well as we desire, and to show why we prefer this to any other method proposed. We, therefore, content ourselves at this time, with submitting the proposition, and hereafter shall state some of the reasons which influence us in favor of it. It may, however, be proper to remark that the proposition is made at the suggestion of many citizens of the West, of this vicinity and other places; and if favorably received by the people to whom it is addressed, and St. Louis should be selected as the place of holding the Convention, nothing will be wanting which can contribute to the comfort of the delegates in attendance, or to a careful consideration of the subject. As to the proper time for the meeting of the Convention, various opinions have been expressed.

"'Some are in favor of holding it during this fall; others at an early day next spring. Individually, we prefer the latter proposition. If held in the spring, after the navigation of the Lakes and Rivers is fairly opened, the facilities for traveling would be greater, and the delegates from all quarters would have the means of seeing and forming some idea of the vastness of the commerce and the interests involved. No one who has not seen something of the carrying-trade of the Lakes and of the Mississippi, in the full tide of its spring flood, can form a correct conclusion as to its extent. This evidence would be furnished to all the delegates who might travel to this point by water. As to the time, however, we should be glad to hear the suggestions of others.'"

"We fully concur with the St. Louis *Republican*, in reference to 'the most effective means of obtaining and embodying the opinions of the great mass of the people,' on this interesting and important subject. Such a Convention, representing the varied and mighty interests of the great valley of the West, will undoubtedly be productive of the most beneficial results. The only danger to be apprehended is, that aspiring demagogues, or hackneyed politicians, may endeavor to give a *political* bias to the deliberations of that body, or may attempt to shape its action in such a manner as to secure some *ulterior political advantage*. Such an assemblage of men should be free from any political bias —it should be a union of all those interested in this most important subject, who, although differing fundamentally on the other great political topics of the day, agree on the absorbing question of *future justice to the West*. Its only aim should be, not to obtain or secure political capital for either of the great political parties that divide our country, but fearlessly to set forth those *cardinal principles of public policy*, in reference to appropriations for our Rivers and Harbors, in support of which the united West will rally with ardent enthusiasm. Every attempt, therefore, to give to the action of the Convention a political direction, will defeat the great object in contemplation, and, therefore, should be indignantly frowned upon. Let such a Convention be held, and let that Convention proclaim, not mere general principles, which astute politicians can when necessary qualify or evade, but let it set forth in detail, certain *definite and specific* appropriations, which that body, representing the varied interests at stake, shall deem necessary for the present security and future prosperity of the West; and let each of the delegates pledge themselves hereafter, to support no man for the Presidency or for member of Congress, who will not unreservedly commit himself in favor of these measures, and the work is done. Neither of the great political parties will [*dare* to] nominate a candidate for the Presidency or for member of Congress, against whom will be arrayed such a moral power of united and enlightened public opinion, [and we shall hear no more of 'vetoes,' or of such hair-splitting obstructions as the difference between 'salt water and fresh,' in reference to appropriations absolutely necessary for the protection of our rapidly-increasing commerce.]

"In reference to 'time,' we should think the 4th of July, A. D. 1847, a sufficiently early day, and whilst we have no disposition to be captious about the 'place' of holding the Convention, we think Chicago has claims that can not with propriety be overlooked. Its central position at the head of the vast Lake-trade, and its intimate connection with the Lake-and-River interests, seems to point it out as the most convenient and appropriate place. It stands a connecting link between the different channels of communication, and we believe that more of the interests involved will be accommodated by the selection of Chicago, than in the choice of any other place with which we are acquainted. We are willing that a *majority* of those interested should decide this question, at the same time promising in advance, that if *Chicago* is honored by the selection, every effort will be made by her citizens, to extend to the delegates from abroad a *hearty Western welcome*.

"What say our friends of Milwaukee, Detroit, Toledo, Cleveland, Oswego, Buffalo, and other places in interest upon the Lakes, to our suggestions?"

The following were appointed a committee:—John A. Brown, of Milwaukee, Morgan Bates, of Detroit, G. M. Atwater, of Cleveland, Geo. R. Babcock, of Buffalo, and A. Haraszythy, of Wisconsin, who retired and drafted resolutions—pending which

Colonel CHARLES KING, being called upon, addressed the meeting, and stated that the important question before the meeting was one which should not be viewed as a party question—God had done everything in those harbors, and little was left for man to do. Mr. King, after glancing cursorily at the great natural advantages which are presented in the rivers and lakes in the North-West, went on to say that the improvements which had hitherto been made, were dealt out with a niggard hand. The Constitution contained no provision to restrict an improvement in the rivers and harbors, and he felt thoroughly convinced that if a convention of delegates, uninfluenced by politics, should meet some time next summer at Chicago, or in some other Western city, no doubt existed but they could accomplish an object which was so desirable, and in which all should feel a deep interest. The trade of the great inland Lakes, they saw was carried to the salt water, solely by means of British enterprise, and internal colonial improvement. He did not mean to derogate from the British in having made such efforts; but he complained of the absurd dealings in abstractions and scruples, which it would seem influenced themselves at home. After detailing the innumerable advantages to be derived from such a project as contemplated by the meeting—

The Committee here reported the following resolutions:

WHEREAS, the great and rapidly-increasing trade and commerce of the Western Lakes and Rivers, which at the present moment are more than one-half of the foreign commerce of the country, and fully equal in amount to our coasting-trade, should command the protection of our National government; And whereas, it is of the first importance to have a concert of action of the friends of this great interest in order to present it to our National legislature in a proper light. Therefore,

Resolved, That we heartily approve of the recommendation of the Western press, for a Convention of all the interests involved in Lake-and-River navigation, proposed to be held in the summer of 1847.

Resolved, That we recommend Chicago as the most suitable point for holding said Convention, and the 17th of June next as the most favorable time.

Resolved, That we view the commercial interests of this great State, and the Atlantic States generally, closely identified with those of the Western Lakes and Rivers, and we cordially invite their coöperation, expecting to see them all fully represented in the proposed Convention.

Resolved, That we view with the highest gratification the interest already manifested in this City favorable to the proposed Convention; and that we hope soon to see a hearty response by them to this important movement.

Resolved, That we pledge our individual exertions to secure a general attendance and representation of interest in this Convention, from the communities where we severally reside.

Resolved, That we tender our thanks to those of the press of this City who have lent their columns to favor the objects of this meeting; and we earnestly call upon the press generally to keep this subject before their readers, and to publish the proceedings of this meeting entire.

MORTIMER M. MOWBRAY, Esq., (late Attorney-General of Wisconsin), seconded the resolutions, and trusted that the subject would be made a question for the ballot-box. After briefly advocating the objects of the meeting, he concluded.

A committee was here appointed to carry out the objects of the meeting. The following are the names of the committee:—

Chicago—Wm. B. Ogden, S. Lisle Smith, Geo. W. Dole. Milwaukee—Byron Kilbourne, W. D. Wilson. Detroit—Augustus J. Porter. Cleveland—J. W. Allen. Buffalo—James L. Barton. St. Louis—David Chambers.

The following resolution, offered by Mr. Burr, was then put and carried:—

Resolved, That the thanks of this meeting be tendered our worthy host, who, ever alive to Western interests, in his usual spirit of accommodation, has obligingly furnished us the gratuitous use of his rooms.

The meeting adjourned.

[From the *Chicago Daily Journal*, Tuesday, November 10, 1846].

MEETING OF THE CITIZENS OF CHICAGO, FOR THE PURPOSE OF MAKING ARRANGEMENTS FOR THE WESTERN CONVENTION: —The undersigned committee, appointed by a meeting of Western men, held in the City of New York, for the purpose of making arrangements for the North-Western Convention, to be held in the City of Chicago, on the 17th day of June, A.D. 1847, respectfully request a meeting of the citizens of Chicago, at the Court-House, on Friday evening, Nov. 13, at 7½ o'clock, for the purpose of making suitable arrangement for the appointment of the necessary committees of arrangements, correspondence, etc.

As Chicago has, with great unanimity, been selected as the place for the assembling of this important body of Western men, it is hoped that every effort will be made on the part of her citizens to have the Convention fulfil the great objects for which it will be convened.

Wm. B. Ogden,
S. Lisle Smith, } Committee.
Geo. W. Dole,

[From the *Chicago Journal*, Monday, Nov. 16, 1846.]

NORTH-WESTERN HARBOR-AND-RIVER CONVENTION.

At a public meeting of the citizens of Chicago, held at the Court-House on the evening of the 13th instant, pursuant to a call made by the Committee appointed at a meeting in New York, for that purpose, to make the preliminary arrangements for holding the above Convention in this City, the coming season, on motion of WILLIAM B. OGDEN, Esq., the meeting was organized as follows:

MARK SKINNER, Esq, President.

Eli B. Williams, Benj. W. Raymond, Vice-Presidents.

Geo. W. Meeker, Mahlon D. Ogden, Secretaries.

S. Lisle Smith, Esq., on behalf of the Committee appointed by a meeting in New York, to make arrangements for a North-Western Convention, to be held at Chicago, stated the objects of the meeting, Whereupon, on motion of J. Young Scammon, Esq., the following Committee was appointed to report upon Resolutions:

J. Young Scammon, Isaac N. Arnold, Norman B. Judd, who reported the following, which, on motion of Hon. David L. Gregg, were unanimously adopted:

Whereas, The subject of a great North-Western Convention, for the purpose of uniting interests in reference to the widely-increasing commerce of the Northern Lakes and Western Rivers, and declaring the opinions of the public, and diffusing information in regard to the necessary appropriations for the protection of lake-and-river commerce, has been agitated by the public press throughout the country; and whereas Chicago has been with great unanimity designated as the proper place for holding such Convention, therefore be it

1. *Resolved*, That the citizens of Chicago, feeling deeply interested in the subject of appropriations by the General Government

for the improvement of the navigation of Western Lakes and Rivers, and in the advancement and protection of Internal commerce, will most cordially coöperate in all proper and suitable measures for the attainment of these objects.

2. *Resolved*, That we are greatly indebted to the press throughout the country, for the unanimity with which, unsolicited by us, they have designated Chicago as the place for holding the proposed Convention, and that we will endeavor to manifest our appreciation of the honor thus conferred, by our zeal and efforts to advance the patriotic purposes for which the Convention will be convened.

3. *Resolved*, That the peculiar location of Chicago, at the terminus of lake navigation and at its nearest point of junction with the river commerce, points to it as the natural place for the holding of a Convention, affecting the interests of both the Lakes and Rivers; and that it might be impracticable to comply with the request of the St. Louis Chamber of Commerce, that the said Convention be holden at the latter City on the 10th of May next, for the reason that the navigation of the Lakes does not always open in season to enable those gentlemen who would be desirous of traveling by the lake route, to the Convention, to avail themselves of it for this purpose.

4. *Resolved*, That we sincerely regret the action of the St. Louis Chamber of Commerce in reference to the subject of the proposed Convention, believing that the almost unanimous expression of the press in favor of Chicago, and the action of the meeting in New York, should determine the question in favor of this City, especially as the South-West have already held a Convention (at Memphis) to advance river and peculiarly *South-Western interests;* and we deem it but just that the NORTH-WEST should assert its claim, free from all prejudice, to have this Convention held within North-Western borders, at the same time trusting that St. Louis, having with us a unity of interests, will see nothing unreasonable in this determination.

5. *Resolved*, That a North-Western Convention, having in view the improvement of the navigation of Western rivers and the advancement of Internal commerce by the General Government, be held at Chicago, on Monday, the 5th day of July, A.D. 1847; the Committee, appointed at the meeting in New-York City, having learned from the corresponding members elsewhere that the day designated at said meeting is too early, and that the day above designated meets their approval.

6. *Resolved*, That we consider the exigencies which have called this Convention as of no trifling import; bounded by no sectional

prejudices or partizan predilections; and in view of the object for which we are convened, it is with the utmost confidence that we call upon the People, and States, Counties, Cities, and Towns interested in Lake-and-River commerce to second our efforts in this behalf by such decided action in the premises as will secure for the Convention a general attendance.

7. *Resolved*, That a cordial invitation is hereby extended to all, without distinction of party, who feel interested in the improvement of River and Lake navigation and in the advancement of the Internal Commerce of the country, to assemble in our City on the first Monday of July, A.D. 1847, to consult upon the best means to secure those appropriations absolutely necessary for their development.

8. *Resolved*, That a Committee of seven be appointed by the Chair as a Committee of Correspondence.

9. *Resolved*, That a Committee of seven be appointed to prepare a call for the Convention, and an address to the people.

10. *Resolved*, That the chair appoint a Committee of one hundred to act as a general Committee of Arrangements.

11. *Resolved*, That the proceedings of this meeting be published in the Chicago papers, and that the editors of all papers who are in favor of the objects of the proposed Convention be requested to copy the same; and that the Committee of Correspondence be requested to publish the same in circular form, for distribution.

The following is the appointment of Committees under the resolutions:

ON THE ADDRESS.

JOHN WENTWORTH, PAT'K BALLINGALL, GRANT GOODRICH. J. YOUNG SCAMMON, GEORGE MANIERRE, ISAAC N. ARNOLD. RICHARD L. WILSON.

OF CORRESPONDENCE.

NORMAN B. JUDD, SAMUEL J. LOWE, WM. L. WHITING. GEO. W. MEEKER, THOMAS HOYNE, ELISHA W. TRACY. WILLIAM B. OGDEN.

MARK SKINNER, President.
ELI B. WILLIAMS, BENJ. W. RAYMOND, Vice-Presidents.
GEO. W. MEEKER, MAHLON D. OGDEN, Secretaries.

COMMITTEE OF ARRANGEMENTS.

Wm. B. Ogden, Zebina Eastman, John Murphy,
Benj. W. Raymond, Wm. Rounseville, Joseph E. Brown,

Chas. Walker,
John H. Kinzie,
Francis C. Sherman,
John P. Chapin,
Alexander Loyd,
Walter L. Newberry,
Alanson S. Sherman,
Justin Butterfield,
Augustus Garrett,
Geo. W. Dole,
Jesse B. Thomas,
James H. Rees,
Laurin P. Hilliard,
Edward H. Hadduck,
Elisha S. Wadsworth,
Robert C. Bristol,
Almon Walker,
Hibbard Porter,
Dr. Philip Maxwell,
Gurdon S. Hubbard,
Chas. McDonnell,
Geo. A. Gibbs,
Jas. H. Rochester,
Joel C. Walter,
James Peck,
James Carney,
Theron Pardee,
Eli B. Hulburt,
David Humphreys,
Albert Neely,
Hiram J. Winslow,
Thomas A. Robb,
George F. Foster,
Allen Robbins,
John S. Wright,

David M. Bradley,
Nathan C. Geer,
Marcus C. Stearns,
Asher Rossetter,
John King, Jr.,
Ira Couch,
Wm. L. Whiting,
Walter S. Gurnee,
Cyrenius Beers,
Jabez K. Botsford,
Stephen F. Gale,
Chas. E. Peck,
Valentine A. Boyer,
Jacob D. Merritt,
Albert G. Hobbie,
Patrick Duffy,
Haines H. Magee,
Anton Getzler,
William Jones,
William E. Jones,
Leroy M. Boyce,
Isaac H. Burch,
George Smith,
Alexander Brand,
John H. Dunham,
John B. F. Russell,
Nelson C. Walton,
Chas. Follansbee,
Alonzo Huntington,
James H. Collins,
Henry L. Rucker,
Henry Brown,
Richard K. Swift,
Wm. H. Brown,
Henry W. Clarke,

Philip F. W. Peck,
Anthony Johnston,
Jason Gurley,
John Frink,
Alfred Cowles,
Martin O. Walker,
Hamilton Barnes,
Chas. M. Gray,
Peter L. Updike,
Peter Page,
Jacob R. Bates,
John Gray,
John Gage,
Samuel Hoard,
George Davis,
Wm. B. Egan,
James Curtiss,
Chas. H. Larrabee,
Joseph H. Gray,
Lewis C. Kercheval,
Dr. John W. Eldridge,
Dr. Levi D. Boone,
Jas. H. Woodworth,
Horatio G. Loomis,
Dr. Daniel Brainard,
John Calhoun,
Lewis W. Clark,
James Fennerty,
Capt. A. H. Squier,
Wm. Rickcords,
John Rogers,
Robert D. Sherman,
Silas B. Cobb,
Azel Peck.

ADDRESS OF THE CHICAGO COMMITTEE.

The high prices of freight, taken in connection with the loss of life and property upon the Western waters last season, caused several public meetings to be held in various sections of the country, for the purpose of devising the best means of remedying those and other evils of which the great mass of the people interested in commerce were complaining. At all these meetings, the propriety of holding a convention at some convenient point was discussed and universally concurred in.

In consequence of Chicago having been generally named as the proper point, its citizens called a meeting, named the fifth of July as the appropriate time, and chose the undersigned a committee to draft an address, setting forth the objects of the Convention.

The movers in this matter have been, from the first, like the undersigned, of entirely different politics, and, so far from there being, even in the remotest degree, any political design in the contemplated Convention, one of the chief objects of it is to call together for a common object the men of all parties, and to convince the people every where that the improvements desired are not now, never have been, and never should be, connected with '*party politics,*' in the ordinary use of that term. Such a connection would, in the minds of all interested, have a very deleterious tendency. It can not be denied that there is a predisposition among all politicians to support the measures of a chief magistrate of their own party, and hence we have seen Western representatives, originally supporting harbor and river improvements, and elected upon express pledges to do so, finally vote to support a *veto* of bills providing for that purpose, and assigning as a reason therefor that it was their duty to sustain an executive of their own selection, even though it be in express opposition to the wishes and interests of their constituents. Repeated instances of this kind must eventually give this question somewhat of a political cast, which the undersigned and all who coöperate with them would seriously regret.

The construction of *harbors* upon our Northern Lakes, as well as upon the Atlantic, with the improvement of our great rivers, where commerce is of a national character, necessarily involves no questions of party difference. They are matters that must interest all parties, as they do all classes, alike, and harbor and river bills have been supported by the ablest men of both the great political parties which divide this country. This subject has never entered into any presidential canvass, since each party has always taken it for granted that the candidate of the other was above suspicion upon a matter of such preëminent importance. The first Congress that ever assembled under the present Constitution, many of whose members helped to frame it, passed a law defraying all expenses which should accrue after the 15th of August, 1789, in the necessary support, maintenance, and repairs of all light-houses, beacons, buoys, and public piers, erected, placed, or sunk, before the passage of this act, at the entrance of, or within any bay, inlet, *harbor*, or ports of the United States, *for rendering the navigation thereof easy and safe.* General Washington signed this bill; and bills for the continuance of such works were also successively signed by Presidents the elder Adams, Jefferson, and Madison. The first *Lake Harbor* Bill was signed by Mr. Monroe. He never raised the constitutional question, nor do the Congressional debates of those days show that any members of either branch of Congress made any distinction between *salt* and *fresh* water improvements, or between foreign and domestic commerce. All at that time were acknowledged alike deserving the fostering care of the General Government, as they also were during the administrations of the younger Adams, General Jackson, and Mr. Van Buren. Though remarkably scrupulous as to the extent to which the power to construct works of internal improvement should be exercised, General Jackson and Mr. Van Buren signed bills for the improvement of rivers and construction of harbors to the amount of $7,800,000, and the two bills signed by General Jackson in 1836, contained no less than eighty-nine items, and the bill of 1837, no less than fifty-nine. After the General Government has expended upward of seventeen millions of dollars for works of internal improvement, and mostly in the old States, by the consent and support of the very framers of the Constitution and their cotemporaries, and by men, too, of all political parties, there can now be but little consideration due the cry that 'it is unconstitutional,' or the plan of a single political party to extend the advantages of such works to the new States, and to such portions of the old States as have thus far been neglected.

Thus disposing of the constitutional and the political question, the friends of harbor and river improvements arrive at the only one which can rightfully be raised, and that is merely the question of necessity. Is IT NECESSARY to protect our domestic as well as our foreign commerce? Shall we protect the *lesser* and neglect the greater? For the past three years, petitions have been presented to Congress in vain: senators and representatives in Congress have spoken in vain. The present Secretary of War, in his official reports, has recommended in vain; and the whole topographical corps has estimated in vain. Our bills have invariably been vetoed, and we have been unable to secure two-thirds of the popular branch. Confident that there is wanting a knowledge of the necessity of these improvements among the people or their representatives, since all efforts at success have failed, it has been thought that a *general convention* and consultation, with personal observation, might do much for us. There is not a State in the Confederacy but that touches the lakes, the ocean, or the great rivers of the West. The lakes line almost our entire northern frontier, and separate us from a foreign country; and the rivers, like arteries, run through the whole country, constituting an extent of navigation sufficient to reach round the globe.

These great waters, for whose safe navigation this Convention is called, are soon to be united by the completion of the Illinois and Michigan Canal. The commerce of Boston, of Philadelphia. of Baltimore, of New York, of New Orleans, Cincinnati, St. Louis, and, indeed, of the whole country, thence becomes in a great measure connected. It has a common interest, and no injury *could*, and the greatest advantages *might* rise from a common consultation. It is a notorious fact that statements, during the pendency of harbor and river bills before Congress, are made on the highest personal authority, which never would be made if the authors had any personal observation of the great inland waters of this country, or could realize the necessity of the millions whose lives and property are jeoparded by them. Delegates in attendance will not only have the advantages of their own observation to take back with them, but they can profit others meeting them here by a consultation as to the best means of redressing existing wrongs. Having done this, they can impart the proper feelings to their neighbors, and thus aid in arousing the people to take this matter into their own hands, and see that their chief interests are no longer neglected. It is confidently hoped that a more intimate acquaintance with the claims of these great waters, formed by men congregated for this special purpose from all parts of the Union, will result in sufficiently convicting and awakening the public mind to secure the constitutional majority, should a harbor bill ever again be vetoed. This Convention is designed to be one of free discussion, and it is hoped that the *opponents* as well as the *friends* of lake and river improvements will attend, and more especially since it is generally believed that they have only to see for themselves in order to be convinced that these demands, coming from all our great waters, are founded in justice.

Although the construction of harbors and the improvement of rivers will be the prominent subject before the Convention, yet, whatever matters appertain to the prosperity of the West, and to the development of its resources, will come properly before it, and all plans and suggestions will be freely entertained. The committee invite a general attendance from all sections of the Union, and tender, in behalf of their fellow-citizens, the hospitalities of the City of Chicago to such as, impelled by a common interest, see fit to honor them by their presence on the occasion.

JOHN WENTWORTH,
GEORGE MANIERRE,
J. YOUNG SCAMMON, } *Committee.*
I. N. ARNOLD,
GRANT GOODRICH,

[From the *Buffalo Express*, March 22, 1847.]
[BUFFALO] RIVER-AND-HARBOR MEETING.

On Saturday evening, a meeting of the Citizens of Buffalo was held for the appointment of Delegates to the Convention to be holden at Chicago, on the 5th day of July next. The night was exceedingly rainy and inclement, but notwithstanding the weather, the Court-House was well filled, and a deep interest in the subject manifested. The meeting organized by calling the Hon. E. G. SPAULDING to the chair, and appointing S. T. ATWATER and H. M. KINNE, Esqrs., Secretaries.

The Chairman returned thanks to the meeting for the honor conferred upon him by making him chairman of so respectable and so important a meeting of the citizens of Buffalo. He did not deem it necessary to make any extended remarks in the way of explaining the objects for which the meeting was assembled, as it was well and generally understood throughout this City. He said that the large attendance, under the circumstances, gave certain evidence that a deep feeling of interest prevaded the citizens of Buffalo upon the subject of River-and-Harbor improvements. He had no doubt that all felt the necessity of some prompt and decided action in regard to the measure, and that the Convention proposed to be held at Chicago would be well attended. For the purpose of securing that object, this meeting had been convened.

The Hon. N. K. HALL moved that a committee of five be appointed to draft resolutions expressive of the sense of this meeting. The Chair announced Messrs. N. K. HALL, F. P. STEVENS, O. G. STEELE, T. M. FOOTE, and O. H. MARSHALL as said committee.

H. P. DARROW, Esq., then moved that a committee of five be appointed to select persons to represent this City in the Convention at Chicago on the 5th day of July next.

CLARK ROBINSON, Esq., then moved that the number be fixed at fifty.

Gen. H. B. POTTER thought that twenty-five would be as many

as would be likely to attend.—He stated that Rochester only sent that number.

Mr. ROBINSON thought that fifty here to twenty-five at Rochester, was scarcely a full proportion, in regard to the size, commerce, and interest of the two cities. He thought the number should be increased instead of diminished.

The Hon. MILLARD FILLMORE thought the proposed number none too large, but he would prefer that only those should be appointed who would probably attend. He would rather see a full attendance at Chicago, than a large array of names on paper with a small attendance there.

J. McKAY, Esq., could not see the force of the objections urged by the gentleman opposing the large number proposed. It was important that Buffalo should be fully and ably represented in the Convention. She had a deep interest in the subject, and should be promptly represented.

The Hon. E. G. SPAULDING was of opinion, from what he understood of the feeling abroad in this City, that more than fifty persons were not only willing, but desirous to attend the Convention, and he thought all who desired to attend should be allowed the opportunity.

The resolution was then passed fixing the number of delegates at fifty.

Messrs. H. P. DARROW, H. B. POTTER, CLARK ROBINSON, E. A. MAYNARD, and RICHARD SEARS were then appointed the committee to nominate delegates.

The Hon. M. FILLMORE was then called for, and addressed the meeting in a very appropriate manner. He urged upon the meeting the importance of prompt and efficient action in behalf of the cause of our inland harbors and rivers. We had designed giving his remarks at greater length, but have been induced against our wishes to desist. He gave way that the committee on resolutions might make their report.

The Hon. N. K. HALL, from the committee on resolutions, moved the following report:

Resolved, That the commerce and navigation of the great North-Western Lakes and Western Rivers eminently deserve the attention, encouragement, and protection of the National government. That the commerce of the Lakes, now nearly equal to the export trade of the United States, will soon, by its rapid increase, equal the entire foreign trade of the Union, while that of the Western Rivers already surpasses our foreign commerce; and that this inland commerce, by its importance, value, and extent, and the number interested in its prosecution, will soon force upon the general government the performance of its constitutional duty to provide for the improvement of the navigation of our great lakes and rivers, and the construction of safe and capacious harbors on our great inland seas.

Resolved, That while more than six millions of dollars are annually appropriated for the construction of light-houses, breakwaters, and harbors on the Atlantic coast, and the maintenance of a navy for the security and protection of our foreign commerce, it is neither wise nor just to refuse moderate appropriations for the protection of the commerce of our rivers and lakes, and the preservation of the lives of the hardy mariners who navigate these waters.

Resolved, That the commerce and navigation of the great lakes and their connecting rivers, and of the Mississippi and its principal tributaries, are equally deserving the fostering care and protection of our government. That we regard these great channels of communication, extending for thousands of miles into the interior of the country, bordering on more than half the States of the Union, affording an easy and cheap communication to millions of acres of land belonging to the general government, and thus adding immensely to the value of our national domain, as so entirely national in their character and benefits, as to put forever at rest all questions in regard to the constitutional power and duty of Congress to make appropriations for their improvement.

Resolved, That we can not appreciate the force of the arguments advanced by those who admit the right to make unlimited appropriations for the protection of our foreign commerce, and yet deny the power of Congress to make appropriations for the protection of the commerce between the States, especially as the Constitution, in the same sentence, gives to Congress the power to regulate commerce with foreign nations *and among the several States*, and also gives the power to provide for the common defence and general welfare of the United States: That while these great lakes and their connecting rivers separate us from the territories of Great Britain—while we have upon them not only the merchant vessels of our own and foreign merchants, but the national vessels and revenue cutters of our own and a foreign government—with ports of entry, collection districts, custom houses, and collectors, and while the courts of admiralty extend their jurisdiction over these Lakes and those employed in their navigation, we can see no ground for distinguishing between the commerce of the Ocean and that of the Lakes.

Resolved, That the thanks of the millions more directly interested in our inland commerce, and of the whole country, are due to those members of Congress who, by their votes, have twice passed bills making appropriations for harbor and river improvements.

Resolved, That to secure to those interested in the commerce and navigation of the Great Lakes and Western Rivers their just share of the annual appropriations for the protection of commerce and navigation, it is only necessary that they should unite in purpose and effort in favor of such appropriations as are not only dictated by a wise policy, but required to distribute equally to the North and West as well as to the South, the benefits conferred by the action of the government of the Union.

Resolved, That in view of its tendency to promote united and systematic action on the part of those interested in the commerce of the Lakes and Rivers of the North and West, we heartily approve of the call for the Convention, to be held at Chicago on the 5th day of July next, and deem it expedient for the citizens of Buffalo to send delegates to that Convention.

Resolved, That a Committee of Correspondence, to consist of seven members, be appointed by the Chair, whose duty it shall be to correspond with persons in Albany, New York, Boston, and other cities and sections of the country, and invite the attendance of delegates at the said Convention.

Resolved, That the said committee be also authorized, in behalf of the citizens of Buffalo, to invite the State Officers and Canal Commissioners of the State of New York to attend that Convention; and that it shall also be the duty of such committee to act as an Executive committee to make arrangements to secure for such officers and the delegates to such Convention, suitable passages, berths, and accommodations on board the steamboats from this City to Chicago at the most reasonable rates at which they can be procured.

Mr. DARROW, from the Committee on Delegates, reported the following names:

Millard Fillmore,	Isaac Sherman,	S. S. Jewett,
Wm. A. Moseley,	Orlando Allen,	J. O. Brayman,
Heman B. Potter,	Geo. R. Babcock,	R. C. Palmer,
Samuel Wilkeson,	Philo Durfee,	Thos. C. Love.
John Hollister,	Geo. Coit,	James McKay,
James L. Barton,	Geo. W. Tift,	Wm. T. Miller,
E. G. Spaulding,	Isaac S. Smith,	Elijah Ford,
Nathan K. Hall,	Thos. M. Foote,	Geo. C. White,
John L. Kimberley,	Samuel T. Atwater.	A. D. Patchin,
Henry M. Kinne,	C. C. Bristol,	Benjamin Bidwell,
Geo. P. Barker,	E. A. Maynard,	Geo. B. Walbridge,

Sheldon Thompson, Silas Sawin, I. T. Hatch,
Geo. B. Webster, Horatio J. Stow, M. Kingman,
George Palmer, Oliver Bugbee, R. H. Heywood,
Jas. C. Evans, O. G. Steele, Dean Richmond,
John M. Griffith, H. K. Smith, F. P. Stevens,
Clark Robinson, Wm. Williams, I. A. Blossom,
Bela D. Coe, Wm. Ketchum, Peter Curtiss,
Wm. M. Hall, Seth C. Hawley, T. T. Sherwood.
R. H. Maynard,

J. McKAY, Esq., moved that the delegates be authorized to add to their number and appoint substitutes.

Mr. G. W. BULL solicited aid from the meeting to pay a balance due the printers for printing the work of JAMES L. BARTON, Esq., relating to the commerce of the Lakes. This, of course, had the usual effect of such things, and the people began to move off, but about $20 was received, which still leaves a balance of some $70 yet due.

Mr. WM. M. HALL then addressed the meeting upon the subject before it, and closed by offering the following:

Resolved, That the Executive Committee be requested to invite the citizens of St. Louis and Cincinnati, as well as the citizens of all other cities and towns on the Mississippi and its tributaries, to meet us in Convention, at Chicago, on the 5th day of July next.

On motion of T. C. LOVE, Esq., who appeared a little impatient, the meeting then adjourned *sine die*.

[From the *Laporte-County Whig* (Michigan City, Ind.), April 30, 1847.]

RIVER-AND-HARBOR MEETING.

At a meeting of the citizens of Michigan City, held at the Common Council Room, on Wednesday, the 7th of April, for the purpose of appointing delegates to the Chicago River-and-Harbor Convention, and for the transaction of such other business as might be deemed expedient. John Francis, Esq. was appointed President and Thomas Jernegan, Secretary.

On motion it was voted to raise a Committee of seven to draft resolutions expressive of the sense of the meeting, and report the same at an adjourned meeting:—and J. G. Sleight, T. Jernegan, W. H. Goodhue, C. B. Blair, E. Folsom, W. W. Higgins, and J. R. Wells were appointed.

On motion the meeting adjourned to meet again on Thursday, the 29th April.

Pursuant to adjournment, an adjourned River-and-Harbor

Meeting was held at the Common Council Room, on Wednesday, the 29th of April, and was called to order by the Chairman, and the proceedings of the last meeting read. Mr. Jernegan, from the Committee on Resolutions, then reported the following Preamble and Resolutions.

Whereas Congress has power, under the Constitution, to "regulate commerce with foreign nations and among the several States; and, as one of its first acts in 1789, made provisions for the lighthouses, beacons, buoys, piers, and other public works on the harbors, bays, inlets, and navigable waters of the United States;— and whereas the several States, in forming our Constitution, deprived themselves of this power for the express purpose of conferring it upon, and making its exercise the duty of Congress; and whereas the construction of such works is beyond individual ability; and whereas a large majority of the people, every Congress and each President (except John Tyler and James K. Polk), have unhesitatingly believed in the constitutionality and expediency of constructing such improvements; and whereas the General Government has derived a very large portion of its revenue from public land situated on or about the Lakes and Rivers, deriving their value and being readily sold from the fact of Government having commenced, and a belief that she would complete the public works upon our inland 'Mediterraneans,' and the great arteries of commerce; and whereas the commerce of these great waters already doubles our foreign imports and exports—furnishing a great portion of the latter, thereby replenishing the national treasury and conducing largely to the general prosperity of the Nation, and, hence, equally entitled to the governmental protection extended to other works of general and national importance; and whereas the people of the North-western, Western, and Southwestern States, composing a majority of the States of this Union, can not be equal participants of the disbursements, protection, and benefits of government, without the construction, improvement, and repairs of public works upon the Lakes and Rivers, therefore—

Resolved, That we have witnessed, with surprise and regret, the will of the people, the decisions of Congress, and the principles and practice of every President, from Washington to Harrison, thrust aside by the arbitrary and unjust use of the veto power.

Resolved, That we consider the veto of River-and-Harbor bills, upon mere grounds of expediency, and in opposition to almost unanimous votes in the Senate and large majorities in the House, as neither in accordance with a courteous regard for the opinions of the coördinate branches of government, with the genius of our institutions, or the doctrine of equal rights, which, like the dews of heaven, dispense its blessings equally upon all.

Resolved, That, believing the construction and improvements of harbors on the seaboard and lakes, and the removal of obstructions to the navigation of our rivers to be, permanently, works of general and national importance—indispensable for the protection of our immense commerce—as harbors of refuge to the storm-driven mariner, and an ark of safety to those who 'go down to the sea in ships,' and important in providing a nursery for the hardy seamen who may at any time be called upon to defend our 2500 miles of lake coast from the attack of a foreign foe—we deem it the duty of the people to unite in the adoption of such measures as will secure appropriations for these great objects.

Resolved, That without these improvements, the people of the Lakes and Rivers are unjustly deprived of an equal participation in the protection and benefits of Government.

Resolved, That the paramount importance of this subject demands the union of all political parties to assist in obtaining by all suitable means, justice to these great interests; and that we deprecate the mingling up of this great question in any way with the issues of the two great political parties, not only as untrue issues in fact, but as directly calculated to defeat the very objects we are striving to obtain.

Resolved, That we are opposed to the election of any man, for President or Vice-President of the United States, who does not in some satisfactory manner frankly avow himself in favor of signing such River-and-Harbor bills as do not overstep the landmarks of the Constitution, and have been sustained, or their principles sanctioned, by our Congress, our Presidents, and the People.

Resolved, That we will vote for no man as Representative in Congress who does not approve of such bills.

Resolved, That we cordially approve of the call for a River-and-Harbor Convention at Chicago, on the 5th of July next, and believe that the union there of men of all parties, sacrificing all party feelings on the altar of the public good, and seeking by all constitutional, just, and expedient means to secure to the great West those objects which her rapidly-increasing numbers will soon enable her constitutionally to obtain, must speedily result in accomplishing, or, at least, hastening the period when our birthright to equal privileges and protection shall be fully restored.

On motion, the above resolutions were unanimously adopted.

The Hon. C. W. Cathcart, who was present, was then called upon, and in a short speech, gave a concise history of the proceedings of the friends of River-and-Harbor improvements during the two last sessions of Congress, showing that every effort had been made to induce the President to sign the bill. The speaker remarked that no appropriations could be expected during the present administration and thought there was but little probability of a two-thirds' vote in the House. He closed his remarks by suggesting a remedy for this evil.

On motion, it was voted to choose delegates to the Chicago Convention; and

J. R. Wells,	Edward D. Taylor,	J. Francis,
E. Folsom,	J. S. Carter,	J. R. Bowes,
E. H. Noyes,	W. H. Goodhue,	J. Wendover,
C. B. Blair,	J. G. Sleight,	Jonathan Burr,
W. R. Bowes,	Thomas Jernegan,	J. Barker,

were chosen.

It was then moved and carried, that said Committee have power to fill vacancies.

On motion, E. Folsom, G. Ames, J. R. Wells, J. G. Sleight, C. B. Blair, J. S. Carter, W. R. Bowes, T. Jernegan, and J. Francis, were appointed delegates to the LaPorte-County River-and-Harbor Meeting, to be held at Laporte, on the 12th of June next, and report the proceedings of this Meeting.

Voted, That the proceedings of this meeting be published in the *Michigan-City News* and *Laporte-County Whig*.

On motion, the Meeting then adjourned.

JOHN FRANCIS, *President*.

THOMAS JERNEGAN, *Secretary*.

Michigan City, April 29, 1847.

[*Chicago Evening Journal*, Friday, July 9, 1847.]

A LETTER TO HON. DAN'L WEBSTER, FROM SOME OF HIS PERSONAL FRIENDS IN CHICAGO.

CHICAGO, *May 10th, 1847.*

HON. DANIEL WEBSTER—*Dear Sir:* We have lately seen it announced, in the *National Intelligencer*, that it is your intention to return home, from your "long-projected tour through the Southern States, by way of the Great Lakes," and we avail ourselves of this opportunity to express to you our hope that you will honor this City by a visit.

Whilst it ever affords our citizens sincere pleasure to welcome distinguished citizens of other States, who may honor them with their presence, rest assured, dear Sir, that to no one will a more sincere and hearty welcome be extended, than to the "Great Defender of the Constitution."

A large portion of our inhabitants claim New England as their birthplace, and have ever been taught to honor and revere New-England's most gifted son. They feel proud of that name and fame that have shed a halo of glory around our common country, and they are anxious to testify, in a suitable manner, their respect and gratitude for those faithful and laborious services, rendered in the Nation's Council during a long life of untiring devotion to the public good. To recapitulate those services would be but to recite the history of the country for the last thirty years, so intimately have they been connected with the welfare and true interests of our people.

In you, Sir, the Great West has ever found a faithful friend. Your comprehensive patriotism, bounded by no narrow horizon, has ever been devoted to the prosecution of measures tending to develop the resources of this young and growing section of our land. No illiberal jealousy—no contracted sectional feeling—has ever actuated you in the discharge of your public duty. "The country—the whole country—and nothing but the country," has ever been your motto; and the interests of this young, free West, have ever been the objects of your constant care.

An opportunity will be presented to you to witness the growth of our State, since you last honored us with a visit in 1837. Ten years, which effect but few changes in the Old World, completely alter the face of a new country. Since your last visit, our population has nearly quadrupled; our commerce has greatly increased; the various branches of mercantile and mechanical business have been vastly augmented; and our borders have been filled with thousands of the honest tillers of the soil, who, by their industry, have improved and adorned this Prairie Land. To you it will doubtless be gratifying to view this magical change.

Beside, on the 5th of July, a Convention of Western men assemble in our City to deliberate on the interests of this young empire—interests which have been wantonly sacrificed by the hair-splitting abstractions of the Southern politician, now, unfortunately for us, at the head of our government. In such a council we desire to hear your voice. Your enlarged experience, your profound statesmanship, your gigantic intellect, your high-toned patriotism, will do much to aid us in our consultations and efforts; and may we not hope that they will be devoted, on that occasion, to the advancement of our prosperity? The West is not ungrateful, and will surely remember any sacrifices made in her behalf.

DANIEL WEBSTER'S CHICAGO FRIENDS.

Again assuring you of a hearty Western welcome, and with the tender of our sincere personal regards, we remain, with sentiments of profound respect,
Yours, etc.

Samuel Lisle Smith,
Justin Butterfield,
Isaac H. Burch,
James M. Adsit,
Elisha W. Willard,
James A. Smith,
Wm. W. Saltonstall,
John P. Chapin,
Silas B. Cobb,
James E. Bishop,
William Blair,
Richard L. Wilson,
Edward H. Hadduck,
Charles E. Avery,
Henry R. Payson,
George A. Robb,
C. W. Appleby,
James Peck & Co.,
George C. Drew,
John H. Dunham,
Tarleton Jones,
Joseph W. Shoemaker,
R. Hamlin,
Nathan C. Geer,
John Filkins,
Charles L. Wilson,
John B. F. Russell,
Arthur G. Burley,
Michael A. Neff,
John King, Jr.,
Nathaniel P. Wilder,
Charles Burley,
Lewis W. Clark,
George W. Dole,
Samuel N. Stebbins,

William E. Stimson,
W. S. Harkinson,
Edward K. Rogers,
John C. Williams,
Samuel W. Goss,
Arche Kasson,
Haines H. Magie & Co.,
James W. Steele,
Giles Spring,
Sidney Sawyer,
Joseph W. Hooker,
Justin Butterfield, Jr..
John A. Brown,
Buckner S. Morris,
David Humphreys,
Theron Pardee,
Wm. Hull Clarke,
George W. Meeker,
George Steel,
Augustus L. Jacobus,
Charles R. Vandercook,
Allen Robbins,
Leroy M. Boyce,
H. C. Lawrence,
Ephraim C. Stowell,
Asher Rossiter,
John S. Wright,
David S. Lee,
Robert Stuart,
Isaac Hardy,
Samuel Edward Davis,
Wm. Gooding,
Joseph Keen, Jr.,
Wm. H. Brown,
Alfred Cowles,

Raymond, Gibbs & Co.,
Thos. B. Carter & Co.,
Benjamin F. Taylor,
Archibald Clybourn,
John Parker,
Cyrenius Beers,
Wm. L. Whiting,
Samuel Nickerson,
Charles G. Archer,
Joseph T. Ryerson,
Andrew Blaikie,
George W. Taylor,
Chas. B. King,
E. H. Burdsall,
John Rogers,
John H. Kinzie,
John W. Ransom,
Henry Stecker,
Edward I. Tinkham,
John Brinkerhoff,
Thomas B. Penton,
Smith J. Sherwood,
Samuel B. Collins & Co.,
Thomas Whitlock,
Samuel J. Surdam,
W. Wait Smith,
Alfred Dutch,
J. P. Brittain, Jr.,
Thomas Church,
Jacob Russell,
Stephen F. Gale,
Alexander Brand,
Aaron Gibbs,
Adoniram Judson
Woodbury.

[*Chicago Evening Journal*, Monday, July 5, 1847.]

DELEGATE MEETINGS. At 8 o'clock this morning:—The Illinois Delegations meet at the Tent on the Public Square; the New-York Delegations at the Court-House; the Missouri Delegations at 100 Lake Street, Peck & McDougall's office (up stairs); the Ohio Delegations at the Sherman House.

DELEGATES TO THE CONVENTION.—The different Delegations will form for the procession with the New-England States on the right, and by seniority in order, with the Territories on the extrême left, being designated as follows, by order P. Maxwell, *Marshal:* Maine, yellow; New Hampshire, white; Vermont, green; Massachusetts, red: Rhode Island, purple; Connecticut, scarlet; New York, crimson; New Jersey, pink; Delaware, blue; Maryland, lilac; Virginia, brown; Pennslyvania, Drab; North Carolina, orange; Ohio, red and white; Michigan, blue and white; Illinois, red, white, and blue; Wisconsin, yellow, white, and Green; Iowa, blue, scarlet, and brown; Missouri, white and scarlet; Kentucky, white and green; Tennessee, crimson and yellow; Georgia, orange and lilac; Indiana, brown and red; Florida, yellow, drab, and pink; Mississippi, purple and white; Louisiana, blue and yellow; Arkansas, green and orange; South Carolina, brown and pink; Texas, scarlet, blue, and green.   *   *   *   Delegates will find a member of the Committee of Arrangements in attendance at the Sherman House to furnish them with badges.

ORDER OF THE DAY FOR 5TH OF JULY.—Marshal of the day—Band—Cleveland Artillery—Other Military—Marshal—Band—Mariners—Marshal—Band—Fire Department—Marshal—Judiciary and Civil Officers—Clergy—Mayor and Common Council—Ex-Mayors—Marshal—General Committee—Committee of Arrangements—Committee of Reception—Societies and Orders of Chicago—Marshal—Band—Illinois Delegations.

The procession of escort will assemble and form as follows, precisely at 9½ o'clock, at the signal of a gun. Cleveland Artillery and other Military, Sailors, and Mariners, in Water Street, right resting on Michigan Ave.; Fire Department in Lake Street; Judiciary and Civil Officers, Clergy, Mayor and Common Council, Ex-Mayors, and Committees, on Randolph Street; Societies and Orders of Chicago, on Washington Street; Illinois Delegation on Madison Street. The Marshals will assemble on the old Garrison Ground.

The procession will move at 10 o'clock, at the signal of a gun, filing into a line on Michigan Avenue; pass through Monroe St. to Wells, through Wells to Lake St., through Lake to Michigan Ave., resting at the Public Square, to take in escort the foreign delegations, then proceed west upon Madison to State St., north on State to Lake St., west on Lake to Clark St., south on Clark to Public Square.

The foreign delegates are requested to assemble at Public Square [Dearborn Park], on Michigan Ave., at 10 o'clock, or before the return of the procession of escort, and form by States.

PHILIP MAXWELL, *Marshal.*

[From the *Chicago Evening Journal*, Tuesday, July 6, 1847.]
FIFTH OF JULY.

A GREAT, a glorious day has gone down—a day which children's children will remember, when the actors that took part, and the hands that indited, are cold and motionless; as a day when party predilections were obliterated; when sectional interests were forgotten; when from eighteen free and independent Sovereignties, men came up to the achievement of a noble work, united their voices in one grand harmony, for the promotion of an object demanded alike by the most enlightened self-interest, the most liberal view, and indeed by common humanity.

The scenes which have lightened the eyes and gladdened the hearts of our citizens, are no idle pageant that shall vanish with the day, and leave no trace behind—no gathering for political or temporary effect—no indignant convocation for the mere indulgence in invective—no effervescence of feeling, that shall expend itself in empty resolves, be the wonder of the hour and then forgotten, but an occasion upon which great and startling facts—facts embodied in figures that can not lie, are to be presented—facts in which the farmer, the artizan, and the merchant, the manufacturer, and the operative, the capitalist in Boston, the sailor before the mast, and his family at home, are all proportionably and deeply interested—facts involving the history of the country, from that hour when the hardy pioneers left New York behind them, or crossed the heights, and pierced the dense forests of Pennsylvania in quest of "the better land" that was at last disclosed to them all cleared and ready for the furrow.

A demonstration like that which we have witnessed today, causes us to think better of our race than we were wont—to rejoice that there *are* questions upon which men of every political bias and of every sectional interest can meet as one great brotherhood, speak with one harmonious voice, and act as one man. But to the pageant. At an early hour, the streets were thronged with strangers, the gray-haired and the young, the matron and the maid, the hope and promise of a coming day, and the veteran of his three score and ten; flags were flying from every steamer and sail-vessel in port, blasts of martial music swelled ever and anon upon the air, and the deep notes of artillery boomed over the prairie and the Lake. Joyous faces were everywhere, and heaven itself smiled upon the scene. At nine o'clock, the roar of cannon and the roll of drums announced the hour for the formation of the procession. The Fort, Water, Lake, and Washington Streets were alive with the military, the fire-companies, and the civic procession. Column after column and line after line, away they moved to the rendezvous; banner after banner, band after band, host after host. It was a glorious, almost a sublime spectacle; worthy the times ere Babel left the world. — Five thousand men— *five* thousand *free*men in solid column moving on, not to carnage, but to the expression of a great truth, the pleading of a great necessity, the arguing of a great cause.

Never was the birthday of our National Independence more befittingly celebrated than on this day—to give freedom and tone to the pulse of commerce—to cheer the mariner on his airy shrouds—to brighten the homes and the hopes of thousands. Is there, *can* there be a nobler cause under which freemen can rally in behalf of the State? That vessel with sails all set, and signals flying to the breeze, drawn by eight horses and manned throughout by sailors, bore a banner eloquent of the object of this Convention. It was a sea roughened by storms, that lifted the waves to the very heaven in the distance, but hard by was a Harbor where "the winds and the waves lay together asleep," and a lighthouse lifting its star of joy and hope upon the rocky cliffs. Over all was inscribed the significant words, "What we want." Ah! that ship "Convention" had a speech and an argument that appealed to the eye and reached even to the heart; and we are sure that it will not be the fault of the body of Delegates now assembled, if many a gallant craft does not plough these inland seas and nobly breast the storm, in the good hope of a light to guide it, and a safe harbor at last.

First in the procession and immediately following the Marshals, were a part of the Cleveland Light Artillery, a soldierlike, splendid corps, and an honor to the "Buckeye State." They were followed by the Montgomery Guards, a fine company of forty-five, composed of our own citizens, tastefully uniformed, and indebted in a great degree to the energy and perseverance of Capt. Wm. B. Snowhook for their organization. The Guards were followed by the company of horse under the command of Richard K. Swift. Then came the good ship "Convention," under a cloud of canvas, drawn by eight horses and completely manned. Then the Chief Engineer, Stephen F. Gale, Esq., accompanied by his assistants and succeeding them, a train that would do honor to an older city than our own Chicago. A beautiful banner of silk preceded them, bearing the expressive motto, "Protect our Commerce and we will protect your dwellings." On they came— "Hope" Hose, Number one, and forty in number, uniformed and with banners—"Rough-and-Ready," Bucket Co., 30 strong—lo! a banner, "Stay the destroyer" its watchword—Hook-and-Ladder

Company, No. 1 came glittering on, full forty more. A band of music, and the "Fire King" [Engine Co., No. 1,] wheels into view. A broad and carpeted platform, elegantly ornamented, bore the engine. Wreaths of flowers decked the polished shafts and a bower of evergreen in front, a sort of miniature Eden, was graced by the presence of three young ladies arrayed in white. The occupants of this beautiful structure, though not the *queens* of fire, might well have been mistresses of a gentler flame. Six horses, gorgeously caparisoned, were attached to this elegant vehicle, and the Company, fifty-six in number, filed on in its wake. Still on they came—"Metamora," No. 2, full fifty strong, with white waving plumes and banners, their engine drawn by six horses. Their fine uniforms, blue frocks fringed with red, forming a beautiful contrast with the white array of the company of the "Fire King." And yet "the long line comes gleaming on"—the Spartan phalanx [Niagara,] No. 3, in full force, admirably uniformed and equipped to do good service against the Destroyer. "Red Jacket," [No. 4,] fifty in number, their engine decked with festoons of flowers and silken banners, drawn by twelve gray horses, caparisoned with crimson trappings and guided by twelve blacks, in the gay turbans and full costume of the land of harems and song.

Now a brass band immediately preceding the Fire Wardens and Aldermen with their appropriate badges. Again music, followed by the Illinois Delegations, 600 strong, with banners. The 'Blue,' the 'Red,' the 'Red and White,' Delaware, the old Bay, and the Buckeye State wheel into line. The good old land of rocks and hills and 'steady habits,' the Empire State, and the woods of the old Quaker sent up their representatives to swell the host. Indiana, the 'Peninsula,' Iowa, and the 'orange and lilac' followed on and so they came, from eighteen sovereignties, full five-thousand strong.

It was a noble, a soul-inspiring spectacle, and as it thronged our streets and filed into our public square, it was a glorious exemplification of the great truth that the hope of our republic, a holier order of liberty than the Gothic or old Corinthian, an order of heaven's own architecture, lies with a free, intelligent, and independent people.

It was a display, such as the West has never before beheld, but we value it not for the badges, and banners, and pageantry—not for its array of military or its blasts of music, but for the community of interest and of feeling that it indicated, thus gathering from every quarter of a Republic, wide as the New World and comprehended by two oceans—gathering here at the hithermost extremity of the great Lake chain, the trading-post, the very outpost of civilization—no, no, not that, for that was Chicago of 1812—but at the city of sixteen thousand, the Chicago of today, in itself a glorious exponent of the triumph of enterprise, but at a sacrifice how fearful, over the perils incident to our River-and-Lake navigation, in seas without harbors, in rivers fretful as the porcupine, with dangers—befitting monuments of the fortunes, and the lives that have perished upon and now lie beneath them —a triumph over influences constantly retarding and impairing honest and honorable enterprise—over dangers more imminent, and necessity more imperative, which each returning year has brought with it—and yet, notwithstanding all these influences, extending as they do, back through what of the West has become matter of history, and binding, as they do, with links of iron, the free scope of enterprise, chilling with their manacle touch, every department of our internal Commerce, and by the loss of life through the dangers that throng our waters, and rise like the mists from their surface, *festering* in many a living heart, yet it has become what it now is, the pride and the mart of Northern Illinois, but at what a sacrifice of treasure and of life!

These counteracting influences are the data upon which, we suppose, the Convention will be called to act—we say to *act*, for words are not always but "empty air," and the united voice of such an assemblage, going forth to the world, and reaching the ears of Government, the articulate "voice of many waters," *is* a great act, and will not, can not be disregarded. It is for this, we say, that the far-reaching and radiant influences of this meeting can neither be traced nor estimated, nor the responsibility of its actors too carefully weighed. While in every respect it is an important trust committed to the Delegates, demanding decision and energy tempered with prudence, guided by judgment, enlightened by experience, and hallowed by a true devotion to the best interests of the whole country, in one respect it is a solemn trust.

We are not about to speak of the wail of orphanage rising like the dirge of complaining waters; or the weeds of mourning, that would, if recalled from the past, sadden and darken the noonday —we are not about to specify a single one of the thousand interests involving human happiness, that are interwoven with this great but simple question, the *improvement of our Harbors and Rivers*, but feebly to comprehend them all in the words of another: "It is a solemn occasion, because the deeds of today are *not* the deeds of today."

The questions to be brought before the Convention, then, are momentous but by no means intricate. As was truthfully and beautifully said of England's great architect, in speaking of the numerous and noble monuments he had left to perpetuate his name, "would you see the tokens of his fame—*look around!*" so with equal truth it may be said, that through the last thousand miles of their journey hither, the Delegates to this Convention, from whatever quarter they came, had but to '*look around*' to behold the theme of their deliberations stretching away, far as the eye could reach—everywhere the Lakes, everywhere the Rivers, and everywhere the West.

While we were penning this last sentence the fire companies of Chicago were promenading our streets in a torch-light procession. Beautifully emblematic of the hopes of the great West, which, if it ever achieves a triumph, must *conquer by water*, and only then, when the true relations of that West to the whole Union, are clearly revealed in the full and unclouded light.

CHICAGO IN JULY, 1847.—POPULATION, 16,000.

CITY OFFICERS.—*Mayor*, James Curtiss; *Aldermen*, 1st Ward: James H. Woodworth, Peter L. Updike; 2d Ward: Dr. Levi D. Boone, Isaac Speer; 3d Ward: Benj. W. Raymond, Dr. John Brinkerhoff; 4th Ward: Robert H. Foss, Chas. McDonnell; 5th Ward: Jas. Sherriffs; 6th Ward: Asahel Pierce, Andrew Smith; 7th Ward: Elihu Granger, Charles Sloan; 8th Ward: Wm. B. Snowhook, James Lane; 9th Ward: Wm. B. Ogden, Michael McDonald; *City Clerk*, Henry B. Clarke; *Attorney*, Patrick Ballingall.

PUBLIC SCHOOLS.—*Agent*, Wm. H. Brown. *Inspectors*, Wm. H. Brown, George W. Meeker, Wm. Jones, Wm. E. Jones, Dr. E. McArthur, Charles McDonnell, Samuel Hoard. *Clerk*, George W. Meeker.

SCHOOLS.—District No. 1 and 2, "Dearborn," Madison St., bet. State and Dearborn, built in 1844. Principal, Albert W. Ingalls; Assts., Miss H. B. Rossetter, Miss Ferguson, Miss M. C. Durant, Miss A. M. Day. 600 scholars.

District No. 3, "Scammon," West Madison Street, bet. Union and Halsted, built in 1846. Mr. and Mrs. C. J. Ballard, Teachers. 300 scholars.

District No. 4, "Kinzie," Ohio Street, cor. N. LaSalle; built in 1845. Principal, Alden G. Wilder; Assistants, Miss Mary A. Kent, Mrs. Mary E. Warner, Mrs. Lamb. 500 scholars.

CHURCHES.—Bethel (Sailors'), N. Dearborn St., Rev. T. Wilcox, Pastor.

Church of the Evangelical Association (German), Wabash Avenue, N.-E. corner Monroe Street; Rev. Jacob Cobb, Pastor.

First Baptist, Washington Street, S.-E. corner LaSalle.

First Methodist, Washington St., S.-E. cor. Clark; Rev. C. Hobart, Pastor.

First Presbyterian, Clark St., S. of Wash'ton; Rev. Flavel Bascom, Pastor.

German Lutheran, Indiana St., near N. Wells; Rev. Augustus Selle, Past'r.

New Jerusalem (Swedenborgian), worship in old Common-Council Room, Saloon Bldg, S.-E. cor. Clark and Lake Sts.; Rev. Joseph K. C. Forrest, Past'r.

Tabernacle Baptist, LaSalle, bet. Rand. and Wash., Rev. Wm. H. Rice, Pastor.

Second Methodist, Canal, bet. W. Rand. and Wash.; Rev. S. Bowles, Pastor.

Second Presbyterian, Randolph St., bet. Clark and Dearborn; Rev. Robt. W. Patterson, Pastor.

St. Mary's (Catholic), Wabash Ave., S.-W. corner Madison; Very Rev. Bishop Wm. Quarter, V.G., Rector.

St. James Episcopal, Cass, nr S.-W. cor. Ill.; Rev. Ezra B. Kellogg, Rector.
Trinity (Episcopal), Madison Street, near and west of Clark.
Unitarian, Washington St., bet. Clark and Dearborn; Rev. Wm. Adam, P'r.
Universalist, Washington St., bet. Clark and Dearborn, (opposite the Unitarian, and east of the First Methodist); Rev. Samuel P. Skinner, Pastor.
FIRE DEPARTMENT.—Chief Engineer, Stephen F. Gale; 1st Asst., Chas. E. Peck; 2d Asst., John H. Kinzie.
"Fire-King" Engine Co., No. 1; Motto, *Pro bono Publico*. Organized Dec. 12, 1835. Foreman, Cyrus P. Bradley; Asst., Ashley Gilbert; Clerk and Treasurer, George R. Bills; Steward, Joel C. Walter.
"Metamora" Engine Co., No. 2. Organized Dec. 14, 1837. Forman, Sandford Johnson; Asst., Clerk, and Treasurer, Peter L. Yoe.
"Niagara" Engine Co., No. 3; Motto, *Semper Promptus*. Organized Nov. 24, 1844. Foreman, Gurdon S. Hubbard; Asst., George F. Rumsey; Clerk, Geo. H. Rankin; Treasurer, Benj. L. T. Bourland; Steward, Geo. F. Foster.
"Red-Jacket" Engine Co., No. 4. Organized Nov. 23, 1846. Foreman, Francis T. Sherman; Asst., Delos N. Chappel; Clerk, Oscar F. Lowe; Treasurer, James J. Langdon; Steward, Charles V. Dodge.
"Excelsior" Engine Co., No. 5. Organized Nov. 23, 1846. Foreman, Alanson S. Sherman; Asst., Charles Morton; Clerk, John Link.
."Philadelphia" Hose Company, No. 1; Motto, We strive to save. Organized Jan. 30, 1845. Foreman, J. K. Webster; Asst., Wm. O. Snell; Clerk, Ebenezer M. Gustine; Treas., J. Johnson; Steward, Thomas Cann.
"Rough-and-Ready" Bucket Company. Organized Sept. 7, 1841. Foreman, John Atkinson; Asst., Charles S. Perry; Clerk, Wm. T. West.
INSTITUTIONS.—Chicago Lyceum. Constitution adopted Dec. 22, 1835.
Young Men's Association. Organized Feb. 6, 1842.
Mechanics' Institute. Incorporated Feb. 23, 1842.
Rush Medical College. Pres., Wm. B. Ogden; Sec'y, Grant Goodrich; Treas., Mark Skinner. Chartered 1837; erected 1844 N. Dearb. and S. of Ind. Sts.
University of St. Mary's of the Lake, Superior St., bet. Wolcott and Cass; buildings erected in 1845-6, cost $12,000. Rev. Jeremiah A. Kinsella, Prest.
NEWSPAPERS AND PERIODICALS.—*Chicago Democrat*, (Democratic), morning, daily and weekly (Tuesday). Hon. John Wentworth, editor and proprietor; 107 Lake St., (building new office at 45 LaSalle St., "Jackson Hall.")
Chicago Evening Journal, (Whig), daily and weekly (Monday). Richard L. Wilson and Nathan C. Geer, Sal'n Bldg, S.-E. cor. Lake and Clark Sts., 3d floor.
Commercial Advertiser, (Whig), morning, daily and weekly (Wednesday). Alfred Dutch, editor and proprietor; 98 Lake Street.
Chicago Tribune, (neutral), morning, daily. James Kelly, John E. Wheeler, and Joseph K. C. Forrest, editors and proprietors; 159 Lake St.
Gem of the Prairie, (neutral), weekly (Saturday). Published by *Tribune*.
Better Covenant, Universalist, weekly (Thursday).
Herald of the Prairies, Presbyterian, weekly. Rev. James B. Walker and Benj. F. and Wm. Worrall; Wells Street, north of and near Randolph.
People's Friend, German, weekly. Robert B. Hoeffgen and —— Mueller; 43 LaSalle Street.
Western Citizen, (Liberty), weekly. Zebina Eastman, 63 Lake Street.
Liberty Tree, (Abolition), monthly. Zebina Eastman, 63 Lake Street.
Prairie Farmer, Agricultural, monthly. John S. Wright and J. Ambrose Wight, editors and proprietors; 171 Lake Street.
Illinois Medical and Surgical Journal, bi-monthly. Drs. Jas. V. Z. Blaney, Daniel Brainard, and John Evans, editors. Robert Fergus, publisher, 37 Clark Street, Saloon Building.
POST-OFFICE.—50 Clark Street, Hart L. Stewart, Postmaster.

PROCEEDINGS

OF THE

CHICAGO RIVER-AND-HARBOR CONVENTION,

MONDAY, JULY 5TH, 1847.

AT a meeting of the Delegations from different parts of the Union, to a Convention held at Chicago, pursuant to public notice, on July 5th, 1847, for the purposes named in the Call of said River-and-Harbor Convention, the following proceedings were had:

The several Delegations having assembled in the Public Square [Dearborn Park] on Michigan Avenue, were escorted by a procession composed of the Volunteer Military and Fire Departments and citizens to the Pavilion prepared for their reception, in the Court-House Square. Upon their arrival, they were [called to order by Dr. Philip Maxwell, Marshal of the day, and] welcomed by the Hon. Jas. Curtiss, Mayor of the City of Chicago.

In conformity to the instructions of the General Committee of nine, consisting of

    JAMES L. BARTON of Buffalo,
    JOHN W. ALLEN of Cleveland,
    AUGUSTUS S. PORTER of Detroit,
    WM. DUANE WILSON of Milwaukee,
    BYRON KILBOURNE   "
    WILLIAM B. OGDEN of Chicago,
    SAMUEL LISLE SMITH   "
    GEORGE W. DOLE   "
    A. B. CHAMBERS of St. Louis,

appointed by a meeting of citizens from several of the Western and North-Western States, held at Rathbun's Hotel, in the City of New York, on the 28th day of September, 1846, William B. Ogden of Chicago, Chairman of said Committee, and on their behalf, moved that James L. Barton of Buffalo, take the Chair temporarily, for the purpose of organizing the Convention, which was carried by acclamation.

On his further motion, A. B. Chambers of St. Louis, and Hans Crocker of Milwaukee, were appointed Secretaries *pro tem.*

Mr. Barton, on taking the Chair, returned thanks for the honor conferred upon him, in calling him to preside temporarily over the deliberations of the Convention.

By request of the President, the Rev. Dr. William Allen of Northampton, Mass., opened the Convention with prayer.

RULES FOR ORGANIZING AND VOTING.

S. Lisle Smith of Chicago, on behalf of the General Committee, laid before the Convention the following propositions, for their consideration and decision — said propositions being recommended by said Committee:

"1st. The States shall be called over, and the Delegations, through one of their number, shall report a written list of the names of the Delegates in attendance from each State and Territory, giving their locality as far as practicable.

"2d. A Committee of one from each State and Territory (to be designated by the Delegation,) shall be appointed to report to the Convention, officers for its government, rules for its conduct, and the order of its business.

"3d. Upon a division being called for, on any question, the Delegation of each State and Territory shall be entitled to cast the vote of the State or Territory, according to its representation in the Federal Government—Territories to be entitled to four votes.

"4th. Each Delegation is requested to appoint one of their number, to respond to the Chair, in casting the vote of their State or Territory."

The question being propounded by the Chair, "Shall the recommendation of the Committee be adopted by the Convention," David Dudley Field of New York, moved to amend the third proposition, by adding thereto the following:

"And the vote of each Delegation shall be taken by Ayes and Noes; and in reporting the same to the president, the person announcing it shall announce, also, the state of the vote."

A division having been called for, the vote was first taken on the first proposition, and it was adopted.

The second proposition was also adopted.

The third proposition coming up, Mr. Field's amendment was carried, and the proposition, as thus amended, was adopted.

The fourth proposition was also adopted.

On motion of Solon Robinson of Indiana, the reports of Delegates were postponed until after the permanent organization of the Convention.

COMMITTEE TO NOMINATE PERMANENT OFFICERS.

The States were then called over alphabetically, to designate the Delegate who should represent them on the committee to nominate permanent officers for this Convention, and to recommend rules, etc.

The following States answered, and named committee-men, as follows:

Connecticut—John A. Rockwell, Michigan—John Biddle,
Florida—John G. Camp, Missouri—Albert Jackson,
Georgia—Thos. Butler King, New Hamp.—Francis S. Fiske,
Indiana—Samuel C. Sample, New York—John C. Spencer,
Illinois—Robert Smith, N. J.—Littleton Kirkpatrick,
Iowa—N. L. Stout, Ohio—Robert C. Schenck,
Kentucky—T. H. Crawford, Pennsylvania—A. G. Ralston,
Maine—M. A. Chandler, Rhode Island—Edw'd Seagrave,
Massachusetts—Artemas Lee, S. C.—Thos. L. Halsey Cross,
Wisconsin—Marshall M. Strong.

On motion of John C. Spencer of New York, this Committee were required to meet at the Court-House, for the performance of their duties, at 3 P.M., this day.

On motion [of H. N. Wells of Wisconsin,] the Convention adjourned, to meet at 4 P.M.

AFTERNOON SESSION—4 P.M.

The Convention met pursuant to adjournment, James L. Barton, president *pro tem.*, in the Chair.

The Committee to nominate permanent officers, prepare rules, etc., not being prepared to report, Rev. Wm. Allen of Massachusetts, Hon. Thomas Corwin of Ohio, and Horace Greeley of New York, responded, in brief addresses, to the calls made upon them by the Convention.

REPORT OF COMMITTEE ON OFFICERS, ETC.

John Biddle of Michigan, from the Committee appointed to report the names of permanent officers of the Convention, prepare rules of conduct, and report the order of business to be observed, made the following report:

Your Committee met at the Court-House at 3 P.M., and appointed John Biddle of Michigan, chairman, and A. G. Ralston of Pennsylvania, secretary. The roll being called, the members were found to be present.

On motion, it was resolved that

EDWARD BATES of Missouri,
be nominated to the Convention, for its presiding officer.

VICE-PRESIDENTS:

JOHN H. BROCKWAY of Conn., WM. WOODBRIDGE of Michigan,
JOHN G. CAMP of Florida., N. W. WATKINS of Missouri,
THOS. BUTLER KING of Ga., ERASTUS CORNING of N. Y.,
E. W. H. ELLIS of Indiana, LITTLETON KIRKPATRICK of N. J.
CHAS. S. HEMPSTEAD of Ill., FRANCIS S. FISKE of N. H.,
Judge G. H. WILLIAMS of Iowa, Gov. WM. BEBB of Ohio,
M. A. CHANDLER of Maine, ANDREW W. LOOMIS of Penn.,
WM. T. EUSTIS of Mass., HAMILTON HOPPIN of R. I.,
JOHN H. TWEEDY of Wisconsin.

SECRETARIES:

SCHUYLER COLFAX of Indiana, PETER MCMARTIN of N. J.,
NELSON G. EDWARDS of Ill., WM. J. OTIS of Ohio,
AARON HOBART of Mass., FREDERICK S. LOVELL of Wis.,
DAVID A. NOBLE of Michigan, HENRY W. STARR of Iowa,
FRANCIS U. FENNO of N. Y., A. B. CHAMBERS of Missouri.

Charles King of New Jersey, moved to strike out the name of Edward Bates of Missouri, as the presiding officer, and insert the name of Thomas Corwin of Ohio.

Mr. Corwin immediately arose, and peremptorily and positively declined serving, under the circumstances.

Mr. King thereupon withdrew his motion.

The question recurring, upon concurring in the nominations of the Committee for permanent officers, it was decided in the affirmative, and the officers, as given above, were therefore elected to the offices designated in the Committee's report.

The President-elect, Edward Bates of Missouri, being conducted to the chair, addressed the Convention in· an appropriate speech.

RULES FOR THE CONVENTION.

The Committee then made a further report [through Robert C. Schenck of Ohio,] recommending the following rules of conduct, order of business, etc., to the Convention:

1st. *Resolved*, That the Convention shall be governed, in its deliberations and action, by the ordinary rules of parliamentary law—provided that no Delegate shall speak more than fifteen minutes at one time, on any question.

2d. *Resolved*, That a Committee of seven be appointed by the President of this Convention, to prepare and publish, as soon as convenient, an address, on behalf of this Convention, to the People of the United States.*

---

* This Address may be found in Wheeler's Hist. of Cong., Vol. II, p. 304.

3d. *Resolved*, That a Committee of two from each State and Territory represented in this Convention, be appointed by the President, to prepare and report such resolutions as they may recommend to be adopted by this Convention.

4th. *Resolved*, That an Executive Committee be appointed, of one member from each State and Territory represented in this Convention, to be selected by the respective Delegations, whose duty it shall be to prepare a memorial to Congress, embracing the views and purposes of this Convention, with proper statistics to sustain them; and to urge upon the attention of Congress such subjects of improvement as may be most urgent, proper, and expedient; that the said Committee shall appoint such sub-committees, for the collection of statistical information as they may deem expedient and necessary; that the said Executive Committee be, and it is hereby, directed, for more convenient and concentrated action, to appoint a sub-committee to attend the next session of Congress, to present the said memorial, and to promote its success; that the said Executive Committee be, and it is hereby, directed to call, at such time and place as it may consider most convenient, another Convention, to which the said Committee shall report its proceedings and progress; and, if *unsuccessful* in obtaining the aid of the Government to carry out the beneficent purposes of this Convention, to report the causes of its failure, in order that such future Convention may take such more efficient action in the premises, as may be deemed necessary to command success; and further, that such projects of improvement and such statistical information as may be presented to this Convention, be referred, without debate, to the said Executive Committee, for its deliberate consideration and action.

The question recurring, "Will the Convention concur in the report of the Committee, and adopt the resolutions introduced by them?"

J. Young Scammon of Illinois, moved to lay the above report on the table, and that they be printed.

A division of this motion being called for by Horace Greeley of New York, Mr. Scammon finally, after debate, withdrew his motion.

The first resolution finally passed.

The second resolution coming up, it was finally, on motion of S. Treat of Missouri, laid on the table.

The third resolution coming up in order, Joseph Stringham of Buffalo, New York, moved to lay it on the table, which motion was rejected.

Norman B. Judd of Illinois, moved to amend, by providing

that the Committee shall be designated by the Delegations of the States and Territories, instead of the presiding officer; which motion was, after debate, rejected.

The question recurring on the original resolution, it was, after further debate, adopted.

Before considering the fourth resolution, the Convention adjourned till to-morrow (Tuesday) morning, at 9 A.M.

LIST OF DELEGATES.

The following are the names of the Delegations from the different States represented, as handed in by the respective Delegations, to the Secretaries, according to the instructions of the Convention:

CONNECTICUT.
ELLINGTON.
John H. Brockway,
Sol. Pitkin.

NORWICH.
John A. Rockwell,
Joel W. White,
Gardner Green.

GRISWOLD.
Horatio Willes.

VERNON.
Norman O. Kellogg.

FLORIDA.
John G. Camp.

GEORGIA.
Hon. Thos. Butler King,
William B. Hodson.

INDIANA.
LAPORTE COUNTY.
Hon. Gustavus A. Rose,
John P. Early,
Sutton VanPelt,
Samuel E. Williams,
Hon. Chas. W. Henry,
Wm. D. Shumway,
Hon. Andrew L. Osborn,
Joseph Orr,
James Forrester,
A. H. Robertson,
David Garland Rose,
Jonathan Burr,
Gustavus A. Rose, jr.,
William Taylor,
William Rudolph Bowes,

Benjamin Rush,
Hon. Silvanus Evarts,
Dr. Daniel Meeker,
Franklin Buren,
Luther Mann,
E. M. Low,
Addison Ballard,
Capt. M. Miller,
James S. Stewart,
Lyman Blair,
Alden Patrick Bowes,
John Andrews,
Joshua S. McDowell,
William Hawkins,
John B. Fravel,
Hon. John M. Barclay,
G. T. Harding,
Jacob G. Sleight,
Charles W. Henry, jr.,
Capt. Ely,
George W. Haines,
George W. Allen,
Benajah Stanton,
Edward H. Noyes,
Truman H. Best,
John Millikan,
Franklin Thwing,
George Ames,
Samuel Organ,
Hon. Franklin W. Hunt,
Edward Vail,
Hon. Samuel Stewart,
Willys Peck,
J. Hunt,
B. Salsbury,
A. H. Markham,
Noah Francis,
Myron H. Orton,

Chauncey B. Blair,
Manlius Brown,
William Henry,
William B. Gustine,
Reynolds Couden,
Jacob S. Carter,
G. W. Kipp,
Temple Windle,
Henry Lusk,
A. Loomis,
Alva Mason,
Lazarus Whitehead,
Capt. Abner Bailey,
Benjamin P. Walker,
Thomas D. Lemon,
William J. Walker,
Hon. Wm. W. Higgins,
James Wendover,
Oscar A. Barker,
Stephen Holloway,
Nathan Holloway,
William Clark,
Elam Clark,
Thomas Jernegan,
G. H. Andrews,
Wm. H. H. Whitehead,
John Hayden,
M. Barber,
Howell Huntsman,
G. Pruntney,
George C. Havens,
I. Ford,
Judson Sawin,
George L. Andrew,
L. Bradley,
Samuel Harvey,
J. Vardeman,
E. Presston,

PROCEEDINGS—LIST OF DELEGATES. 53

Calita Preston,
J. Cooley,
J. Coplin,
Franklin D. Evarts,
Henry Willets,
Anson Wait,
John Walker,
James Lemon,
Marcellus Hawkins,
G. W. Haines,
J. J. Brown,
Conrad Everhart,
John Lemon,
Stephen Oaks,
Alex. H. Robinson,
Geo. B. Roberts,
William Cummins,
Rev. Francis P. Cummins,
Seth Brown.

ST. JOSEPH CO.

Hon. Samuel C. Sample,
Hon. Harris E. Hurlbut,
Hon. Thos. S. Stanfield,
Hon. William Miller,
Schuyler Colfax,
Henry Johnson,
Charles M. Heaton,
Augustine P. Richardson,
John W. White,
Benjamin F. Price,
William G. Norris,
Edmund P. Taylor,
John Listenberger,
Samuel M. Chord,
John T. Lindsey,
George S. Harris,
Matthias Stover,
Christopher W. Emerick,
Benjamin F. Miller,
Dr. Louis Humphreys,
Alonzo Wilson,
John Ryan,
Samuel P. Hart,
Alonzo Delano,
William Riggin,
Nelson Ferris,
Lot Vail,
Able A. Whitlock,
Oliver T. Niles,
Rolent T. Curtis,
Benjamin Wall,
William Ruckman,
Danforth Richmond,
James Davis,

Nathaniel Wilson,
William Wilmington,
Charles N. Ryan,
Dr. R. Pierce,
Thomas D. Vail,
John M. Terrill,
Dwight Deming,
J. P. Jones,
Dr. John A. Henricks,
Shelem Crockett,
Jonathan Crews.

ALLEN CO.

John Haigh, jr.,
James W. Cushman,
Wallace B. White.

CASS CO.

Jay Mix.

CARROLL CO.

W. H. Shaw.

PORTER CO.

William Cheney,
John Herr,
John S. Wallace,
John Dunning,
John R. Skinner,
John C. Ball,
Willys P. Ward,
Joseph Brown,
Ruel Starr,
Henry Buell,
Henry Eusch,
John Eusch,
Ellis Sergeants,
Thos. A. E. Campbell,
David White,
Nathaniel Campbell,
William Tainter.

MARSHALL CO.

A. G. Deavitt,
—— Hard,
—— Howe,
Hiram Griffin.

LAKE CO.

Solon Robinson,
John W. Dinwiddie,
A. F. Brown,
William Clark,
William B. Rockwell,
Timothy Rockwell,
David Turner,

Thomas Clark,
Henry D. Palmer,
Henry Wells,
William C. Ferrington,
David K. Pettibone,
C. McCord.

LAGRANGE CO.

John B. Howe,
John W. Demming,
T. J. Spaulding,
William Martin,
S. P. Williams,
Jonathan Woodruff,
Delavan Martin.

TIPPECANOE CO.

Samuel A. Huff,
James Demming,
T. T. Benbridge,
S. H. Hazard,
Zebulon Baird,
J. L. Reynolds,
J. H. Williams,
Hon. Daniel Mace.

ELKHART CO.

Nelson E. Marston,
Thomas G. Harris,
Erastus W. H. Ellis,
John Fitzpatrick,
A. N. Harscall,
John Cook, jr.,
Dr. M. M. Latta,
W. Earle,
H. H. Hall,
Sewall Thompson,
Calvin Martin,
John Simonton.

FOUNTAIN CO.

Dr. Fraley.

WAYNE CO.

Charles Suffims.

ILLINOIS.

BOONE CO.

Sidney Avery,
James L. Loop,
A. D. Bishop,
Henry Loop,
James Crosby,
W. F. Giddings,
Samuel Longcor,

54 CHICAGO RIVER-AND-HARBOR CONVENTION.

A. Persels,
S. Carpenter,
Simon Peter Doty.
Joel Walker,
R. B. Hurd,
Thomas Hart,
F. B. Hamlin,
S. S. Whiteman,
William Stewart,
Oliver Hale,
Daniel Howell,
W. Smith.

BUREAU CO.

Daniel Radcliff,
Cyrus Langworthy,
Robert E. Thompson,
Arthur Bryant,
Joel Doolittle,
Roland Moseley,
Cyrus Bryant,
Roland P. Moseley,
S. L. Bangs,
Selby Doolittle,
John Martin,
Dr. George R. Ames,
Dr. William Converse,
Christopher C. Tallett.

BOND CO.

J. W. Fitch,
S. Colcord,
P. G. Vauters,
J. D. Lansing.

COOK CO.

Matthias Lane Dunlap,
Homer Wilmarth,
John Hill,
D. Adams,
James Michie,
John B. Witt,
Wesley Polk,
Wilson McClintock,
Samuel Vial,
Henry Carrington,
Theodorus Doty,
J. Gates,
Joseph Filkins,
J. H. Martin,
A. Luce,
Wm. Hopps,
S. M. Salsbury,
Milo Winchell,

John Shrigley,
Silas W. Sherman,
—— Burlingame,
William H. Davis.

CITY OF CHICAGO.

Hon. James Curtiss,
Hon. Wm. B. Ogden,
George W. Dole,
John H. Kinzie,
Grant Goodrich,
Thomas Church,
Ebenezer Peck,
James H. Collins,
Anton Getzler,
Hon. Buckner S. Morris,
Hon. Alanson S. Sherman,
Charles McDonnell,
Charles Walker,
Hon. John P. Chapin,
Richard Lush Wilson,
Dr. Wm. Bradshaw Egan,
Hon. Wm. H. Brown,
James Carney,
Mark Skinner,
Daniel McElroy,
Justin Butterfield,
John M. Wilson,
John S. Wright,
Thomas Hoyne,
Asher Rossetter,
Hon. Benj. W. Raymond,
Hon. Jesse B. Thomas,
Hon. Isaac N. Arnold,
Norman B. Judd,
Samuel Lisle Smith,
Giles Spring,
Gurdon Salton. Hubbard,
Stephen F. Gale,
Hiram J. Winslow,
Joel C. Walter,
Theron Pardee,
Thomas Richmond,
James Peck,
James H. Rochester,
Edward H. Hadduck,
Capt. Robert C. Bristol,
Henry R. Payson,
Samuel N. Stebbins,
Cyrus Bentley,
Richard Jones Hamilton,
James H. Woodworth,
Hugh T. Dickey,
Dr. Daniel Brainard,

John Rodgers,
Judge Henry Brown,
Walter L. Newberry,
John J. Brown,
Dr. John Brinkerhoff,
Hon. Alexander Loyd,
William Jones,
Charles M. Gray,
Eli B. Williams,
Wm. L. Whiting,
Samuel J. Lowe,
Frederick Hagerman,
Cyrenius Beers,
Wm. B. Snowhook,
George W. Meeker,
Jonathan Young Scammon
Sidney Sawyer,
Wm. L. Church,
John Ryan,
Hon. John Wentworth,
Capt. John B. F. Russell,
Hon. Augustus Garrett,
Isaac Cook,
James A. McDougall,
Henry B. Clarke,
Mahlon D. Ogden,
Samuel Hoard,
Jacob Russell,
Walter S. Gurnee,
Obadiah Jackson,
Isaac H. Burch,
John B. Turner,
Elisha Winslow Tracy,
Geo. A. Gibbs,
Allen Robbins,
Hon. Francis C. Sherman,
James A. Smith,
Dr. Charles Volney Dyer.

CARROLL CO.

R. W. Roust,
Wm. Halderman,
John Rinewalt,
Semple M. Journey,
E. Chamberlin.

DEKALB CO.

J. Easterbrook,
Samuel H. Lay,
C. Potter,
G. I. Latham,
B. Easterbrook,
David Merritt,
John L. Arnold,

PROCEEDINGS—LIST OF DELEGATES. 55

Alex. R. Patton,
Thomas Geo. Beveridge,
Lyman Bacon,
L. Marion,
Richard Garrett,
Jerome B. Carpenter,
Edward Devine,
James Hall Beveridge,
William French,
Daniel N. Boyd,
Roswell Frye,
B. Harris.

DU PAGE CO.

James F. W. Wight,
Nathan Allen,
Selinus Milton Skinner,
John Granger,
Chas. Bingley Hosmer,
Alymer Keith,
Stephen J. Scott,
Michael Hines,
John J. Riddler,
John Thompson,
Thomas Andrews,
Asa Knapp,
Russell Whipple,
Daniel M. Green,
Charles R. Parmelee,
Walter Blanchard,
S. Davis,
A. Hills,
Rev. Francis A. Hoffman,
Samuel D. Pierce,
A. Dudley,
Julius M. Warren,
Wm. Smith,
W. C. Todd,
Capt. Hammond,
J. A. Smith,
E. Gilbert,
W. Jones,
John Stolp,
C. Hunt,
Nathan Loring,
Albin Lull,
H. C. Cobb,
P. R. Torode,
J. Tallmadge,
T. Hubbard,
M. Stacy,
J. Hackett,
Horace Brooks,
J. C. Hatch,

B. Hobson,
Wm. G. Strong,
Robert Nelson Murray,
C. N. Fox,
Allan McIntosh,
John J. Kimball,
W. Fitch,
D. Crane,
G. Roush,
Dr. David Hess,
John Sargent.

GREEN CO.

John Orr,
James D. Fry.

GRUNDY CO.

John Hooper,
Dr. A. F. Hand,
Richard Dunn,
Patrick Kelly,
George H. Kiersted,
Charles O. Hale,
Dr. Thomas M. Reed,
Thomas J. London,
A. G. Barber,
Wm. E. Armstrong,
Henry Norman,
Wm. P. Rogers,[U.S.N.]
L. W. Claypool,
John McNellis,
J. Claypool,
Henry Starr,
E. P. Seeley,
E. H. Little,
Dr. Huy Daniels,
Daniel W. Edgarton,
J. M. Craig,
Barton Holderman,
Leander Newport,
Perry A. Armstrong,
L. Wilkes,
H. Hyslop,
Philip Rose,
John M. Clover,
Isaac Hoyt,
James Cromer,
J. B. Moore,
James Kelly,
Salman Rutherford,
W. L. Perce,
P. Hynds,
Charles H. Gould,
Jet. Crotty,

Robert Peacock,
John G. Chambers,
J. M. Gurnsey,
H. McTagne,
M. P. Wilson,
M. D. Pendergrast,
Samuel Ayres,
Dr. J. Daggett,
J. W. Rutherford.

HANCOCK CO.

G. Edmonds, jr.

IROQUOIS CO.

W. Thomas,
C. Thomas,
N. Wilson,
John Young,
Isaac Williams.

JO DAVIESS CO.

Charles S. Hempstead,
Thomas C. Browne,
Thomas Drummond,
William Hempstead,
George M. Mitchell,
Terah B. Farnsworth,
James Carter,
Elihu B. Washburne,
E. S. Seymour,
Henry B. Truett,
Benjamin H. Campbell,
Charles R. Bennett,
John L. Slaymaker,
M. Haslitt,
William Bothwell,
W. Goodwin,
Lorenzo P. Sanger.

KENDALL CO.

J. Morgan,
W. W. Grant,
K. Makiney,
S. A. Roberts,
S. B. Hopkins,
John Robinson,
Horace Winchell,
D. B. Jewell,
S. Drow,
M. Shaw,
T. M. Mudgett,
L. C. Allen,
J. H. Hayden,
A. Wolcott,
W. A. Blane,

C. Dowd,
J. H. Hubbard,
Norman Dodge,
A. S. Reynolds,
A. B. Smith,
W. P. Boyd,
J. S. Petger,
L. B. Judson,
C. B. Chapin,
William Briggs,
D. Tole,
R. Walton,
D. Ashley, jr.,
J. A. McClellan,
J. Grimwood,
B. W. Barnes,
S. B. Craw,
L. E. McClellan,
D. I. Johnson,
G. H. Higley,
G. D. Richardson,
E. Morgan,
J. Gleason,
J. A. W. Buck,
L. D. Brady,
R. N. Matthews,
A. B. Ives,
S. A. Taubling,
E. Darnell,
G. W. Hadden,
James Scott,
S. Burris,
William Toobs,
Isaac Hatch,
B. A. Culver,
L. Bristol,
A. Ives,
J. Ryan,
F. B. Ives,
J. Luce,
G. Ryan,
W. Ives,
J. Evans,
C. Talman,
A. Looker,
J. S. Ives,
G. Stevenson,
A. D. Newton,
D. Neff,
D. M. Wisner,
F. Misner,
A. P. Black,
John Collins,
Garret Collins,

S. C. Collins,
C. Lacey,
A. Z. Taylor,
W. R. Cady,
Charles McEwen,
Henry McEwen,
Griffin Smith,
W. B. Field,
A. McClaskie,
L. Hills,
George Hollenbeck,
Thomas G. Wright,
W. Cowdry,
W. N. Davis,
D. J. Townsend.

KNOX CO.

R. B. Tripp,
Chauncey S. Colton,
A. B. Gardner.

KANE CO.

John F. Farnsworth,
Orville Everest,
Geo. H. Stevens,
Thomas Scott,
A. F. Stevens,
Horace Town,
John VanNortwick,
J. Massingham,
J. W. Churchill,
Thomas Spray,
D. Wheeler,
Wm. B. West,
J. Derby,
F. Baker,
N. B. Spaulding,
Rev. Flavel Bascom,
A. Rawson,
C. B. Gates,
E. W. Austin,
M. P. Houck,
L. H. Applebee,
S. C. Hapgood,
A. S. Bush,
Timothy C. Ellithorpe,
J. W. Hapgood,
J. M. Elithorpe,
A. White,
A. Edwards,
A. Yates,
J. Brown,
Nathan H. Dearborn,
Samuel S. Jones,

Charles A. Brooks,
Dr. I. S. P. Lord,
John Wilson,
Edward R. Allen,
A. Hayden,
Timothy Baker,
Daniel D. Waite,
Alex. H. Baird,
O. C. Baird,
George Ferson,
Robert Ferson,
James Ferson,
Ira Minard,
J. Danford,
John J. Chambers,
Dr. David Millington,
John More,
Frank H. Alexander,
Elisha Freeman,
E. Mead,
E. Wilcox,
Wm. C. Kimball,
N. Williams,
P. Sylla,
George W. Raymond,
Luther Dearborn,
George H. Merrill,
John Ranstead,
A. Walker,
I. Stone,
E. Ballance,
J. Kimball,
A. Hadlock,
A. Raymond,
R. L. Yarwood,
S. H. Hamilton,
J. Tefft,
W. H. Hubbard,
A. Hadlock,
E. Gifford,
J. W. Waldron,
J. Wilson,
J. H. Andrus,
J. C. Derby,
John Oatman, Sr.

LEE CO.

Silas Noble,
R. B. Loveland,
T. Murphy,
D. Frost,
—— Fender,
W. W. Welch,
Jacob Doan,

PROCEEDINGS—LIST OF DELEGATES. 57

W. Wright,
George A. Ingalls,
William W. Heaton,
W. Leaman,
A. L. Porter,
E. B. Baker,
T. Brown,
J. M. Johnson,
Veranius Ells,
John H. Page,
B. Stewart.

LA SALLE CO.

Madison E. Hollister,
John G. Nattinger,
George Mann,
Lucien B. Delano,
Jesse Dickey,
George H. West,
Isaac Abrahams,
C. H. Noble,
Harvey Leonard,
Churchill Coffing,
William Chumasero,
George W. Gilson,
Henry S. Bebee,
John C. Champlin,
Milton H. Swift,
Lorenzo Leland,
Arthur Lockwood,
Robert Rowe,
William Richardson,
Giles W. Jackson,
Levi Jennings,
S. Jennings,
John Armour,
William W. Lowe,
W. G. Webb,
Eri L. Waterman,
John Morris,
T. B. Elliott,
J. Pestland,
Richard Cody,
A. Johnston,
John B. Preston,
David L. Hough,
John S. Mitchell,
J. B. Rich,
Wm. Cogswell,
Joseph Avery,
Joseph Hall,
M. Newman,
Jeremiah Pembrook,
N. Springer,

Champlin R. Potter,
Rev. Charles V. Kelly,
Charles H. Sutphin,
N. Knickerbocker,
Z. Dickinson,
C. Dickinson,
Burton Ayres,
John Titus,
John D. Olmstead,
E. Neff,
John V. A. Hoes,
George B. Macey,
Marshall Havenhill.

LAKE CO.

James McKay,
Isaac Hopkinson,
Beecher Hitchcock,
Edward S. L. Bachelor,
Dr. Milton Bacon,
Dr. David Cory,
Daniel O. Dickinson,
W. Gilman,
O. T. Denney,
Edward O. Ely,
Mordecai J. Brown,
Ira Porter,
Robert Douglass,
Dr. Hezekiah Joslin,
Josiah Moulton,
Saul H. Flinn,
Hiram Butrick,
Augustus B. Cotes,
Samuel M. Dowst,
Dr. Robert W. Clarkson,
Lorenzo Hinkston,
Dr. Moses Evans,
Charles O. Walters,
Moses P. Hoyt,
John O'Connell,
John A. Tyrrell,
James Young Cory,
Wesley Munger,
Wm. Finn. Sheppard,
Jabez B. Porter,
David Ballentine,
Charles Richards Steele,
Elijah Middlebr'k Haines,
Elisha Peyre Ferry,
S. Howe,
Chris. Columbus Taylor,
John T. Clark,
Robert C. VanRensselear,
Nathaniel P. Dowst,

Wm. A. Boardman,
E. Winchester Hoyt,
DeWitt Spaulding,
Isaac R. Lyon,
Capt. Crawford,
Franklin Smith,
Francis Fenelon Munson,
Wm. C. Tiffany,
Volkert Peter VanRensselear,
Dr. David Kellogg,
Thomas Darling,
Dr. Jesse H. Foster,
Alva Trowbridge,
De La Fayette Clark,
James H. Trader,
Reuben D. Dodge,
Truman Hibbard,
Dr. Parley Dickinson,
Joseph Wood,
Thomas H. Payne,
Israel A. Jones,
Jacob T. Devoe,
David H. Sherman,
George Thompson,
Samuel S. King,
Alvan Truesdell,
Jehiel Compton,
Benjamin Welch,
James Lindsay,
Robert Carroll,
David Whitney,
Peter C. Schank,
Jeremiah Q. Morrill,
Isaac H. Smith,
Timothy B. Titcomb,
James Kapple,
Daniel Martin,
Levi Marble,
Elijah Huson,
Leonard Gage,
Jonathan Wood,
George Morill,
Isaac J. Smith,
Richard Huson,
George Ely.

MADISON CO.

Hon. Robert Smith,
Hon. Nathaniel Pope,
Hon. David J. Baker,
Simeon Ryder,
Benj. T. Long,
Hon. Wm. F. DeWolf,

4 *

Moses G. Atwood,
Nelson G. Edwards.

MARION CO.
Uriel Mills.

MORGAN CO.
R. B. Hatch.

MCHENRY CO.
Serrill P. Hyde,
Thomas Stephens,
C. H. Ames,
Lucian L. Crandle,
Anson Sperry,
Harry McIntyre,
John W. Dennison,
Wm. F. Combs,
Amos B. Coon,
Truman Safford,
Charles H. Williard,
Daniel Stewart,
Cornelius Lansing,
Thomas M. White,
Joel H. Johnson,
Wm. Sloan,
Ithream Taylor,
Elzaphan I. Smith,
Neill Donnelly,
Phineas W. Platt,
Derrick C. Bush,
Alvin Judd,
Joseph Green,
Ira C. Trowbridge,
John Brink,
Henry M. Wait,
John B. Parsons,
H. W. Hart,
Benjamin Douglass,
Henry Petre,
R. H. Mooney,
James T. Pierson,
Col. James M. Strode,
Beman Crandel,
Benjamin M. Peirson,
Major F. Erwin,
J. D. Ames,
James D. Kellog,
Christopher Walkup,
P. La Dow,
Jonathan Dyke,
John L. Douglass,
John F. Gray,
Alexander H. Nixon,
Robert B. Tuttle,

Avery A. Gates,
Anthony Overacker,
Abraham Reynolds,
C. Mease,
Joshua J. Barwick,
Chauncey Beckwith,
Starr Titus,
Sidney Condict,
Wm. Mead,
Albert Chamberlin,
Silas Griswold,
John Vasey,
David Baker,
Nathan H. Foster,
Rodolphus A. Hutchinson
Wm. H. Stewart,
Thaddius B. Wakeman,
Orson Diggins,
George W. Danna,
Frank Wedgewood,
Neri M. Capron,
Abraham Shaver,
Ira Nurse,
Bela H. Tyron,
Wm. A. McConnell,
Elias P. Sampson,
Wm. Stewart,
Darius P. Sampson,
Amos Cogswell,
Oliver H. P. Gougin,
Enos W. Smith,
Chas. H. Russell,
Fred. W. Smith,
S. Steele,
John E. Mann,
S. Perry,
Henry D. Huff,
Edwin A. Lay,
J. Brown,
Wm. Allen,
Martin L. Huffman,
Wm. Terry,
Asher M. Renwick,
Carlisle Hastings,
Edwin W. Hibbard,
B. Smith,
George T. Kasson,
Edwin Stringer,
C. Potter,
Wm. Sponable,
Andrew Purvis,
Edwin Terrill,
Dr. Ward Burley [Mason],
Wm. T. Potter,

Allen Sisson,
And'w Jackson Haywood,
Alonzo C. Diggins,
Daniel Blair,
A. Darley,
Peter McMahon,
John Fritz,
Henry T. Rice,
Eli Henderson,
Alexander Dawson,
Newell Colby,
Arad Sly,
Hosea B. Troop,
Stanton M. Thomas,
Wm. Gwing,
J. Potter,
Silas S. Pettit,
J. Hairn,
Capt. Silas Chatfield [1812]
Wm. L. Reynolds,
Spencer Flanders,
Thomas Carr,
George Harrison,
• Wm. Barnes,
R. Platt,
David Goff,
C. H. Burland,
Wm. C. Gunning,
J. G. Botter,
Truman Dutcher,
Nelson Diggins,
Hermon N. Owen,
A. R. Gray,
Martin Thrall,
Hiram Hazard,
Alfred Negus,
James M. Judd,
Lake W. Belcher,
Algernon C. Belcher,
Frederick W. Belcher,
Christopher C. Kelley,
Alonzo Platt,
George H. Griffing,
Robert W. Stewart,
John Donnelly,
David Kelley,
Charles E. Bromley,
Wesley Diggins,
Joseph Golder.

MONROE CO.
—— Kincannon.

PROCEEDINGS—LIST OF DELEGATES. 59

OGLE CO.

John Killebee,
James V. Gale,
S. S. Crowell,
Dauphin Brown,
Silas St. J. Mix,
David Lewis,
James Swan,
Albert F. Brown,
Henry Wheelock,
Alfred Helm,
Samuel Wood,
E. Payson Snow,
George Toney,
Phineas Chaney,
B. L. Beach,
Peter Wertz,
Clark Wait,
D. M. Coolbough,
John Ryder,
C. S. Marshall,
Augustus Ankney,
George Murphy,
Wm. G. David,
Wm. M. Bary,
W. A. House,
Charles C. Royce,
Lyman Morgan,
Willard P. Flagg,
Chester K. Williams,
Henry A. Mix,
B. Hiestand,
John Rice,
A. Q. Allen,
Henry Sharer,
Henry Haire,
James Johnston,
Clark Biggais,
Morgan Jewell,
Alex. Beire,
Benj. Langley,
Frederick Wagoner,
Isaac Rice,
Samuel Fouts,
Micler Seyster,
Riley Paddock,
John Etnyre.

PIKE CO.

Z. N. Garbutt,
H. T. Mudd,
Benj. D. Brown,
Jonathan Foye James,
S. Bamard,

John Webb,
Benj. Norris,
M. P. Mace.

PEORIA CO.

Charles Balliard,
Elihu N. Powell,
John H. Rankin,
Isaac Underhill,
G. W. Willard,
Capt. Thomas Baldwin,
Theodore Adams,
Isaac Hamblin.

ROCK-ISLAND CO.

J. W. Dwing,
P. Gregg.

RANDOLPH CO.

Cornelius S. Whitney.

SANGAMON CO.

Dr. E. H. Merryman,
Hon. Abraham Lincoln,
Fred. Doyle.

SCHUYLER CO.

Robert S. Blackwell,
Lewis D. Erwin,
Charles Farwell,
Francis E. Bryant.

STEPHENSON CO.

Martin P. Sweet,
Hon. Thomas J. Turner,
C. Waterman,
John H. Addams,
John K. Brewster,
Alfred Caldwell,
Frederick A. Strockey,
D. Kryder,
John Lerch,
John Miller,
J. A. Davis,
H. Davis,
L. Preston,
S. J. Giddings,
S. Scott,
F. Foley,
John Goddard,
D. A. Knowlton,
L. Grileard,
John A. Clark,
J. Replogle,
W. P. Belknap,

A. Dennis,
C. A. Sheets,
H. Tarbox.

TAZWELL CO.

Peter Menard, Jr.,
D. Briggs,
W. Cromwell,
W. S. Maus,
R. W. Briggs,
S. Rhodes,
Dr. Perkins,
W. Parker,
J. Chandler,
J. S. James,
G. W. Shair.

WHITESIDES CO.

N. G. Reynolds,
W. R. Cox,
D. B. Crook,
W. K. Whipple,
W. S. W. Wasson,
A. Crook,
Col. J. Holmes,
C. E. Fitch,
C. S. Deming,
W. W. Gilbert.

WINNEBAGO CO.

D. S. Haight,
Anson S. Miller,
S. G. Amor,
Thos. D. Robertson,
Wm. Hulin,
Spencer Post,
Chas. H. Spafford,
O. Jewett,
J. A. Wilson,
Jason Marsh,
Martin Crawford,
C. F. Miller,
Goodyear A. Sanford,
Wm. A. Dickerman,
R. R. Comstock,
Jesse Blinn,
J. B. Peterson,
Austin Colton,
S. Leach,
C. A. Huntington,
J. M. Wright,
J. B. Johnson,
Samuel Cunningham,
Horace Miller,

Cyrus Miller,
E. M. Miller,
W. P. Dennis,
H. Barross,
D. Corey,
M. H. Regan,
Dr. Carpenter.

WILL CO.

Isaac Scarritt,
John Miller,
Samuel Whallon,
T. E. Towner,
Amos C. Paxson,
Horace Boardman,
Robert Freeman,
Matthew C. Boughton,
Reuben W. Smith,
John Barber,
Leander Clifford,
Thomas G. Sprague,
Samuel Goodrich,
L. S. Buffum,
Luther Smith,
Robert Strong,
Hiram Warren,
Warren W. Boughton,
S. R. Rathbone,
Amasa S. Thomas,
Robert Clow,
Stephen Carpenter,
A. Williams,
M. Cavenor,
L. Warner,
A. B. Mead,
H. Williams,
John Lush Wilson,
Peter Stewart,
Hamilton D. Risley,
J. L. Young,
Franklin Mitchell,
Samuel G. Baldwin,
E. S. Strong,
H. M. Gilbert.
D. A. Watson,
J. Gutterson,
Henry Althouse,
Edmund Allen,
J. M. Johnson,
Jonathan Barnett,
V. Lamb,
Hiram Norton,
Nicholas Brown,
H. Hitchcock,

A. Davis,
Charles Wood,
J. W. Safford,
Norman Northrop,
Samuel Cushing,
Willard Wood,
Albert E. Bishop.
John E. Hewes,
L. Hewes,
Enoch Dodge,
A. P. Grung,
S. W. Cooper,
J. E. Phillips,
E. Grung,
Wm. R. Starr,
E. Cole,
David Haner,
—— Chapin,
H. Sprague,
H. E. C. Barrett,
John Kile,
Moses H. Cook,
S. Whipple,
H. A. Deen,
Joseph Campbell,
B. Boardman,
W. Hewes,
B. Brooks,
E. Baker,
W. Keeney,
Wm. Gooding,
L. Newton,
John L. Hanchet,
Joel Manning,
Geo. F. Greer,
John W. Padduck,
Gen. James B. Turney,
E. E. Bush,
Norman L. Hawley,
Edward B. Talcott,
Jacob Fry,
George W. Geddes,
Daniel Walley,
J. N. Brownell,
S. P. Cooper,
S. Baker,
J. B. Culver,
Thomas Shepperd,
Isaac Benham,
Hyram Shepperd,
John Shingle.

IOWA.

BLOOMINGTON.

B. S. Olds,
N. L. Street [Stout],
Adam Ogilvie,
Suel Foster,
J. A. Green,
H. Q. Jennison,
G. Olds.

WASHINGTON CO.

Norman Evertson.

BURLINGTON.

Henry W. Starr,
Judge Geo. H. Williams.

DAVENPORT.

Robert McIntosh,
George B. Sargent.

KENTUCKY.

VERSAILLES.

H. C. Blackburn,
T. H. Crawford.

MAINE.

F. B. Stockbridge,
M. A. Chandler.

MASSACHUSETTS.

BOSTON.

Wm. T. Eustis,
George Horatio Kuhn,
Samuel Phipps,
John Cleveland Proctor,
Benj. B. Mussey,
Chas. Wentworth Upham,
Wm. Whitwell Greenough,
Thos. Greaves Cary, Jr.,
Wm. Lawrence Green,
Philip J. Aubin,
Hon. Elisha Hunt Allen,
George A. Fiske,
J. E. Reed,
G. L. Drinkwater,
Geo. Girdlev Smith,
Aaron Hobart,
Anson Burlingame,
Ward Healey,
N. H. Hartwell,
Henry Loring, Jr.,
Joseph H. Buckingham,

PROCEEDINGS—LIST OF DELEGATES. 61

John L. Hunnewell.

FRAMINGHAM.
Benjamin Wheeler.

TEMPLETON.
Artemas Lee.

NORTHAMPTON.
Rev. Dr. Wm. Allen.

ABINGDON.
Joseph Hunt.

NEW BEDFORD.
Richard Williams.

WARE.
Eleazer Porter.

MICHIGAN.
ALLEGAN CO.
Henry H. Booth,
DeWitt C. Chapin,
Dr. Abram R. Calkins,
Wm. B. Kibby,
Dr. Ela Sawtell,
Stephen A. Morrison,
Chas. R. Wilkes,
Jabez Chadbourne,
James G. Carter,
A. S. Wells,
Otis R. Johnson,
A. B. Noyes,
Frederick Plummer,
John R. Kellogg,
Joseph Fisk.

BERRIEN CO.
A. C. Day,
F. A. White,
J. Cathcart,
W. Harrington,
J. Higby,
B. H. Bertrand,
J. G. Bond,
B. Wheeler,
F. Field,
J. H. Hoppin,
P. P. Maillard,
H. B. Hoffman,
A. Dolph,
Isaac Vandeventer,
J. Groves,
Henry Vanderhoof,

W. Harrison,
E. G. Adderly,
S. Webber,
H. W. Griswold,
George H. Hunter,
S. Waterman,
I. M. Stuart,
T. L. Stephens,
George Kemmel, Jr.,
Rufus W. Landon,
E. D. Wilson,
H. H. Barnes,
J. M. Platt,
J. B. Fitzgerald,
B. C. Hoyt,
Calvin Britain,
Jabez G. Sutherland,
Dr. Lucius Abbott,
John Witherell,
Dr. Tolman Wheeler,
S. C. McDowell,
S. A. Raymond,
H. Jones,
A. S. Andrews,
H. Cronkhite,
H. Compton,
A. P. Pinney,
Curtis Boughton,
A. S. Preston,
N. B. Milford,
W. Pearle,
W. Compton,
E. D. Wilson.

BRANCH CO.
Henry C. Gilbert,
Louis T. N. Wilson,
A. L. Porter,
D. R. Cooley,
S. Perkins,
D. S. Williams.

CASS CO.
John Clark.

CALHOUN CO.
Charles Dickey,
Charles T. Gorham,
Robert Cross,
C. B. Pratt,
P. Updike,
F. Bostwick,
H. Halsey,
H. Camp,

G. Vail,
W. C. Rowley,
S. S. Nichols,
W. M. Campbell,
Chester Buckley,
Elijah L. Stillson,
A. Noble,
Walter W. Woolnough,
H. Marsh,
G. G. Teers,
J. B. Mason,
J. L. Balcom,
F. S. Clark,
Marvin Hannahs,
J. Crowell,
C. Waldo,
L. Grant,
S. Fitch,
L. Campbell.

CHIPPEWA CO.
John N. Ingersoll,
E. G. Seymour,
A. P. Edwards,
J. B. Martell.

HILLSDALE CO.
A. P. Hogarth,
J. K. Kinman,
M. B. Couch,
S. W. Smith,
J. A. Laird,
H. Baxter,
Walter W. Murphy,
L. Russell,
J. W. King,
George C. Monroe.

JACKSON CO.
Orson W. Bennett,
L. W. Witherell,
Austin Blair,
Geo. Thompson Gridley,
F. A. McArthur.

KALAMAZOO CO.
Gen. Justus Burdick,
Mitchell Hinsdill,
Theodore P. Sheldon,
W. L. Booth,
Marsh Giddings,
P. P. Acker,
W. Price,
J. Fuller.

CHICAGO RIVER-AND-HARBOR CONVENTION.

KENT, IOWA, AND OTTAWA COS.

Rix Robinson,
Nathan H. White,
I. Brocket,
Wm. Clancey,
Warren P. Mills,
Robert M. Collins,
Frederick Hall,
B. T. Hall,
C. Elvert,
F. Sloan,
Chas. P. Babcock,
John W. Squire,
Daniel D. VanAllen,
Charles H. Taylor,
Wm. M. Ferry,
Hermon Terry,
Wm. B. Hill,
J. T. Davis,
Lucas Robinson,
A. S. Dane,
Geo. M. Mills,
Charles W. Taylor,
Amos Norton,
Henry Pennoyer,
Wm. Bemis,
Julius C. Abel,
Carlos Abel,
Dan Velsey,
J. Mortimer Smith,
I. E. Parker,
Dwight Rankin,
Hiram Rathbun,
James Davis,
Wm. H. Godfroy,
James M. Nelson,
Henry R. Williams,
Geo. C. Evans,
Alfred X. Cary,
Myron Harris,
Silas G. Harris,
George Roberts,
Benj. Smith,
James Dalton,
Peter Dalton,
E. Waite,
Amos Roberts,
John Ball,
John Colton,
W. Arnold,
Grosvenor Reed,
Louis S. Lovell,
George S. Isham,
Stephen Monroe,
Thomas W. White,
Capt. Henry Miller,
Capt. Warren,
W. Lasley,
John A. Brooks,
F. Hopkins,
Clark B. Albee,
M. M. Eastman,
A. I. Douglass,
Berrin Minahan,
Geo. C. Morton,
Charles Mears,
I. Baird,
Jacob W. Winsor,
Wm. G. Henry,
Wm. H. Withey,
Harry Eaton,
Boardman Noble,
Hiram Hinsdill,
Geo. L. Norton,
James M. Kidd,
G. W. Taylor,
William Carr,
S. T. Gleason,
O. Train,
Wm. H. Tanner.

MACOMB CO.

Richard Butler.

MONROE CO.

James Thornton,
John Burch,
W. V. Miller,
J. B. Mann,
W. A. Noble,
David A. Noble,
F. F. Fifield,
James Darrah,
F. B. VanBrunt,
D. S. Bacon,
John Darrow.

SAGINAW CO.

James Fraser,
Dan H. Fitzbugh,
Hiram L. Miller.

ST. JOSEPH CO.

L. Baxter,
G. Kellogg,
Joseph E. Johnson,
Joseph R. Williams,
E. Stephens,
Abraham C. Prutzman.

ST. CLAIR CO.

S. Morse,
H. N. Munson,
Rev. Oliver C. Thompson,
W. Cox,
Daniel B. Harrington,
M. S. Gillett,
J. M. Kelsey,
William L. Bancroft,
T. Luer.

VAN BUREN CO.

D. O. Dodge,
Isaac W. Willard,
S. Darling,
E. G. Cox.

WASHTENAW CO.

Wm. S. Maynard,
Volney Chapin,
G. Loomis,
C. Clark.
H. Becker,
C. Thayer,
Dwight Webb,
G. VanHusen,
J. Luddington,
Dorr Kellogg,
E. Becker,
E. C. Loomis.

WAYNE CO.

Gov. Henry P. Baldwin,
Zachariah Chandler,
Wm. Woodbridge,
John Biddle,
Alpheus S. Williams,
Ebenezer J. Penniman,
Henry Fralick,
Wm. N. Stevens,
Thomas P. May,
Julius A. Austin,
Asher S. Kellogg,
Isaac Featherly,
Oliver Newberry,
Richard Hawley,
R. C. Bradford,
J. N. Eldred,
Alexander H. Newbold,
Austin Wales,
P. A. Ladue,
Ezra C. Seaman,
J. W. Walker,
DeWitt C. Holbrook,

PROCEEDINGS—LIST OF DELEGATES.

Thos. C. Sheldon,
H. G. Miller,
Junius H. Hatch,
John L. Whiting.

MISSOURI.
ST. LOUIS.
Hon. Edward Bates,
Fletcher M. Haight,
Robert Simpson,
Wm. Simpson,
Charles Keemle,
Joseph M. Converse,
N. E. Janney,
D. B. Moorehouse,
H. S. Coxe,
J. Clemens, Jr.,
John G. Priest,
Thomas Allen,
Lewis V. Bogy,
Samuel Treat,
A. L. Paul,
G. B. Mann,
V. Stailey,
A. H. Guild,
A. B. Chambers,
Milton Knox,
E. R. Mason,
W. T. Essex,
James S. Robb,
J. Thockmorton,
N. J. Eaton,
J. Bredill,
Wells Colton,
J. G. Powers,
T. H. Warren,
T. Baldwin,
W. P. Fisher,
T. Yeatman,
Judson Allen,
John Segarson.

CAPE GIRARDEAU CO.
Gen. Nat. W. Watkins,
T. B. English,
E. W. Harris,
R. Guild,
R. Sturdivant,
A. Jackson,
Chas. A. Davis,
Joseph Wm. Russell.

MARION CO.
J. H. Kibbey.

BENTON CO.
N. C. Shepard.

GALLAWAY CO.
W. A. Bennett.

NEW HAMPSHIRE.
Francis S. Fiske,
J. T. White.

NEW JERSEY.
PASSAIC CO.
Roswell L. Colt.

ESSEX CO.
John Taylor,
Charles King.

MIDDLESEX CO.
Littleton Kirkpatrick.

HUDSON CO.
Peter McMartin.

MORRIS CO.
Freeman Wood,
Thomas L. King,
Joshua A. Black.

NEW YORK.
NEW-YORK CITY.
Jas. DePeyster Ogden,
David Dudley Field,
Philip Hone,
Horace Greeley,
John Peck,
James Brooks,
Edwin E. Burr,
N. B. Smith,
Julius Wadsworth,
Augustus Whitlock,
John R. Peters,
James O. Sheldon,
George M. Atwater,
Edward J. Faile,
Levi Beardsley,
Wm. Burger,
Amasa Wright,
James O. VanBergen,
Cyrus Backus,
R. J. Vandewater,
Horace Belsler,
M. A. Nixon,
Chas. P. Williams,

Elanson Frask,
Robert Olcott,
D. R. Bacon.

ALBANY.
John Canfield Spencer,
Thurlow Weed,
John Quintard Wilson,
Erastus Corning,
Edwin Croswell,
John Knower,
John L. Schoolcraft,
Thomas L. Green,
LeGrand Smith,
Wm. S. Gregory,
Lawson Anesly,
Wm. White,
Andrew White,
D. V. N. Radcliff,

SACKET'S HARBOR.
Leonard Dennison.

ORLEANS CO.
Henry R. Curtis,
Lyman H. Phillips,
Seth S. King,
Wm. Stead,
Eri Wood,
Roswell Clark,
E. D. Bacon,
F. Doty,
Paul B. Torry.

MONROE CO.
James K. Livingston,
Hamblin Stillwell,
Wm. Brewster,
Theodore B. Hamilton,
Isaac Butts,
Dr. Hartwell Carver,
Nathaniel Rochester,
Alexander Mann,
James H. Kelly,
S. R. Colvin,
Alex. Ely.

CHAUTAUQUA CO.
George W. Patterson,
Samuel A. Brown,
A. Purce,
A. H. Walker,
Henry A. Prendergast,
E. S. Garnsey,
John Davis,

Lorenzo Parsons,
H. Brigham,
James McCling.

ONTARIO CO.
Walter Hubbell.

NIAGARA CO.
Alfred B. Judd,
Luther Wilson,
Wm. G. McMaster,
Ira Gregory,
Jonathan Bell,
Amos S. Tyron,
Daniel Hall,
Freeman J. Fithian,
Charles Evans.

ONEIDA CO.
John H. Edmonds,
Wm. Osborn, Jr.,
Alex. Seward,
O. B. Mattison,
John E. Hinman,
John F. Seymour,
John Bryan,
E. F. Showmard,
John G. Crocker,
C. C. Bacon,
Henry Sherrill,
Harrold H. Pope,
Alva Mudge,
Wm. R. Osborn,
S. N. Dexter,
Delos DeWolf,
Heman Ferry,
Elakim Elmer,
James E. Sherrill,
J. C. Miker.

CATTARAUGUS CO.
Job Bigelow.

ST. LAWRENCE CO.
M. Ogden,
Wm. Bacon,
G. W. Shephard,
Samuel Dix,
Jos. H. Buckingham.

LIVINGSTON CO.
Gen. Micah Brooks,
Sidney Sweet,
George N. Williams,
Charles Shepard.

CHENANGO CO.
Ira Wilcox,
Walter M. Conkey,
James Clapp, Jr.

WASHINGTON CO.
John Hillibert,
Horatio G. Sherman,
Morgan Heath,
Moses Cowen.

WYOMING CO.
Isaac C. Bronson,
Samuel S. Blanchard,
Daniel S. Curtiss,
Calvin P. Bailey,
Wm. J. Chapin,
Peter Lawrence,
Lewis B. Parsons,
A. S. Green,
Walter Howard,
James L. Enos,
Josiah Hovey.

CAYUGA CO.
Darius L. Cole,
John T. Hunter.

SENECA CO.
Arad Joy,
Wm. A. Sackett,
Erastus Partridge.

ONONDAGA CO.
Lewis H. Redfield,
James Manning,
Patrick H. Agan,
Thomas G. Alvord,
Jesse McKinley,
J. F. Smith,
Samuel Larned,
James C. Griswold,
Wm. H. H. Smith,
J. L. Gage,
Jasper Smith,
Frederick Benson,
Moses Hinckley,
Theodore Sanford.

RENSSELAER CO.
Gen. George R. Davis,
Day O. Kellogg,
Daniel Gardner,
Bela Barber,
Wm. H. Warren,

James Sherry,
A. B. Elliot.

GENESEE CO.
Heman J. Redfield,
Trumbull Cary,
Wm. Server,
George W. Lay,
Heman Pomeroy,
Benjamin Pringle,
Samuel C. Holden.

[BUFFALO] ERIE CO.
Wm. A. Mosley,
Samuel Wilkeson,
James L. Barton,
Elbridge G. Spaulding,
Hon. Nathan K. Hall,
Bela D. Coe,
Wm. Mosley Hall,
Orlando Allen,
James O. Brayman,
Thomas M. Foote,
Cyrenius C. Bristol,
Elisha A. Maynard,
Wm. Ketchum,
Mahlon Kingman,
Thomas C. Love,
George C. White,
Frederick P. Stevens,
Peter Curtiss,
Wm. Hollister,
Horatio Shumway,
Thaddeus W. Patchin,
Joseph Stringham,
Henry Weisser,
Stephen G. Austin,
Isaac J. Hathaway,
George H. Bryant,
Sidney Shepard,
Ralph Farnsworth,
Hunting S. Chamberlain,
John Patterson,
Lorenzo K. Haddock,
John F. Porter,
James G. Brown,
Birdseye Wilcox,
Wm. Laverack,
Samuel Fursman,
John R. St. John,
George W. Clinton,
Henry Randall,
Capt. Gilman Appleby,
Daniel N. Barney,

PROCEEDINGS—LIST OF DELEGATES. 65

James Murray,
Benjamin Burdett,
Seth C. Hawley,
C. S. Chase,
Orrin P. Ramsdell,
Samuel M. Chamberlain,
Chas. R. Gold,
Daniel G. Marcy,
Amasa T. Kingman,
C. Litchfield,
Joseph Dart, Jr.,
Walter Cary.

OSWEGO.

Alvin Bronson,
Sylvester Doolittle,
George Fisher,
Patrick Smyth,
H. H. Coats,
J. B. Penfield,
Hiram Davis,
Amos Wright.

OHIO.
COLUMBUS.

Gov. Wm. Bebb,
A. S. Chew,
John Woods,
A. B. Buttles,
W. S. Sullivant,
D. Tallmadge,
Theo Tallmadge.

CINCINNATI.

R. Buchanan,
Hon. James Hall,
Hon. John C. Wright,
Wm. Green,
W. S. Johnson,
Darius Lapham,
Robert S. Dean,
L. A. Hena,
Stanley Mathews,
S. C. Parkhurst,
John F. Hunt,
Joseph Ross,
Maynard French.

HURON CO.

George S. Patterson,
John B. Wilbur,
D. G. Branch.

MILAN.

S. F. Taylor,
Clark Wagoner,
J. D. Smith.

NEWARK.

Wm. Stansbury, Jr.

OHIO CITY.

Reuben Lord,
Luke Risley,
E. L. Stephens,
Wm. W. Pratt,
Henry L. Whitman,
Wm. Hortnass,
A. D. Elliott,
J. H. Sims,
Lyman Crowe.

PERRYSBURG.

Elijah Huntington.

MAUMEE CITY.

Horatio Conant,
Charles Coatsworth
Pinckney Hunt.

TOLEDO.

J. W. Scott,
Charles O'Hara.

HAMILTON, BUTLER CO.

John Hittell,
Wm. H. Miller.

WARREN CO.

Gov. Jeremiah Warren,
Gov. Thomas Corwin,
A. H. Danbury,
John M. Milborn.

MORGAN CO.

James L. Gage.

LORRAINE.

Dr. Luther D. Griswold.

CONNEAUT.

J. Reed.

XENIA, GREEN CO.

Dr. Joshua Martin,
Wm. Mills,
R. McBartney,
J. W. Merrick,
Dr. W. Grimes,

H. P. Gallaway.

DAYTON.

H. G. Phillips,
Robert C. Schenck,
E. W. Davies,
John W. VanCleve,
Edward P. Smith,
R. R. Dickey,
Henry B. Perrine.

LAKE CO.

Hon. Aaron Wilcox,
Peleg P. Sanford,
Solomon S. Osborne,
*John H. Moseley,
Benjamin Adams,
J. H. Howe,
L. P. Converse,
Chas. A. Moseley,
Roland Moseley,
L. C. Howard,
Joseph S. Mount,
H. C. Gray.

CLEVELAND.

Josiah A. Harris,
Samuel Williamson,
Wm. F. Allen,
S. Sage Coe,
Joseph W. Gray,
Irad Kelley,
Samuel Holliday,
Samuel O. Mathews,
David L. Wood,
Wm. H. Hayward,
J. Walworth,
Wm. E. Lawrence,
Wm. L. Standart,
H. Geer,
George Kelley,
Wm. Gowan,.
H. Smith,
I. N. Fitch,
James Barnett,
H. Palmer,
Wm. H. Potts,
Wm. W. Pickersgill,
George M. Atwater,
Martin B. Scott,
Wm. J. Otis,
Albert G. Lawrence,
E. Tracy,
E. G. White,

F. W. Morse,
H. A. Sheldon.

SANDUSKY CITY.

E. Cook,
John C. Camp,
Rice Harper,
Abner W. Porter,
Wm. Townsend,
Isaac A. Mills.

PENNSYLVANIA.

PHILADELPHIA.

Hon. Joseph R. Ingersoll,
A. G. Ralston,
Elliott Cresson,
C. E. Spangler,
J. H. Harkness,
Charles E. Davis,
J. A. Davis,
Hugh Campbell.

PITTSBURG.

Hon. Andrew W. Loomis,
Henry Sterling,
C. O. Loomis,
W. J. Totten,
Nicholas Voeghtly,
Joseph R. Henderson,
T. J. Bigham.

ERIE.

Hon. John B. Johnson,
J. C. Marshall,
Murray Whallon,
E. Mehaffey,
W. W. Dobbins,
B. F. Sloan,
Wm. Nicholson,
J. W. Witmore,
Joseph M. Sterrett.

CRAWFORD CO.

J. Stuart Riddle,
Gilbert D. V. Shattuck.

CHESTER CO.

Isaac A. Pennybacker.

RHODE ISLAND.

PROVIDENCE.

Edward Seagrave,
Hamilton Hoppin,
John F. Chapin.

SOUTH CAROLINA.

CHARLESTON.

Dr. Thos. L. Halsey Cross.

WISCONSIN.

RACINE CO.

Philo White,
Dr. Bushnell B. Cary,
Horace T. Sanders,
Matthew B. Mead,
Thomas Jackson,
Marshall M. Strong,
Rufus S. King,
Chas. S. Wright,
Nelson Pendleton,
Levi Blake,
Capt. Gilbert Knapp,
Capt. Seth Johnson,
Henry Smith Durand,
George S. Wright,
Dr. Elias Smith,
John Ramsdell,
Seneca Raymond,
Dr. Edwin Everett,
Wm. B. Rogers,
James O. Titus,
Philander Judson,
Richard E. Ely,
Hiland S. Hulburd,
George W. Taggart,
Ira A. Rice,
Silas C. Chapman,
Joseph Bishop,
Edwin Gould,
Sidney S. Dickinson,
Dr. Orville W. Blanchard,
James H. Hall,
M. Folsom,
James E. Lockwood,
Dr. Samuel W. Wilson,
Sam'l Carey Tuckerman,
Edward F. Sexton,
Harry Griswold,
James Puffer,
Jeremiah Hagerman,
J. Scudder,
Wm. H. Waterman,
Reuben N. Norton,
Horace N. Chapman,
James A. Griswold,
Edward Bliss,
Consider Heath,
John Dexter,

J. C. Dowse,
Tyler Caldwell,
Henry Courtenay,
Morris Smith,
R. W. Benham,
Cyrus Udell,
Francis Paddock,
George W. Jackson,
David McDonald,
Elisha Raymond, Jr.,
Robert Cather,
John Dickson,
James N. Killip,
Clark W. Spafford,
Henry F. Cox,
Ira Hurlbut,
Lucas Bradley,
Edwin A. Robey,
Daniel Slauson,
Nelson Slater,
Albert H. Blake,
Lucius S. Blake,
Henry Sherman,
Wm. Thos. Richmond,
Salmon F. Heath,
Henry Bryan,
Joseph S. Grandy,
Nicholas D. Fratt,
Marcus Weed,
C. I. Hutchinson,
Charles Durkee,
Hiram Tuttle,
Geo. Kimball,
Samuel Hale,
Daniel Hugunin,
Michael Frank,
Chauncey Davis,
Oscar F. Dana,
Vinal Danels,
David Blish,
John H. Nichols,
Richard B. Winsor,
Quartes K. Lee,
Joseph V. Quarles,
David Crosset,
Henry B. Hinsdale,
Epaphro Seymour,
Theodore Newell,
Sereno Fisk,
Volney French,
W. Ward Wheeler,
Sylvender Baldwin,
H. H. Titcomb,
E. Sprague Elkins,

PROCEEDINGS—LIST OF DELEGATES. 67

E. Treadwell,
Seth Doane,
Wm. Bone,
Wallace Mygatt,
John Noble,
David W. Holbrook,
James M. Stryker,
Dr. John Parker,
Richard G. Barrows,
Wm. Henry Smith,
L. B. Richardson,
George W. Harris,
Dr. H. E. Hall,
John D. Kingsland,
Frederick S. Lovell,
John V. Ayer,
George S. Willis,
Samuel Kepigne,
Nathan Hawley,
Alfred W. Doolittle,
Michael Holmes,
John B. Gillson,
Alvin B. Tobey,
A. P. Cronin,
Hon. Peter D. Hugunin,
David Walker, Jr.,
B. W. Farnam,
John S. Bloom,
Alexander H. Peters,
Isaac George,
A. P. Allen,
Wm. B. Slocum,
Charles Latham Sholes,
Thomas D. Bond,
A. Morgan,
P. Ebenezer Pomeroy,
L. Chapin,
Walter Prosser,
Joseph H. Hackley,
Harvey Durkee,
Reason Bell,
Sam'l Franklin Comstock,
Geo. W. Brandt,
Russel Smith,
Samuel Holmes,
George W. Boardman,
George N. Cobb,
Wm. E. Waite,
Wm. H. Fifield,
L. Newberry,
L. B. Kinney,
G. L. Rider,
Charles C. Sholes.

MILWAUKEE CO.
Wm. Duane Wilson,
Hans Crocker,
John H. Tweedy,
Thomas L. Ogden,
Dr. Benj. McVickar,
Alanson Sweet,
John B. Smith,
Lester H. Cotton,
Robert H. Strong,
Dr. Erastus B. Wolcott,
John Anderson,
Dr. Jas. P. Greves,
Daniel Wells, Jr.,
Herman L. Page,
Leonard J. Farwell,
John King, Jr.,
Haven Powers,
John S. Fillmore,
John E. Cameron,
Henry Miller,
Wm. Brown, Jr.
Dr. John B. Dousman,
Dr. George W. Mygatt,
Henry M. McConnell,
Jacob P. Rapelje,
Lewis J. Higby,
Alonzo F. Cady,
John Webb,
Anson Eldred,
Chas. E. Jenkens,
Tertelleus D. Butler,
Increase Allen Lapham,
Benjamin Church,
John G. Barr,
Dr. Thos. J. Noyes,
Emanuel M. Shoyer,
Louis Franchere,
Lewis Ludington,
Harrison Ludington,
Charles Ludington,
John F. Rague,
John Hustis,
Jas. B. Crass,
Alexander Mitchell,
Moses Kneeland,
Gideon P. Hewitt,
Henry C. Heide,
Wm. W. Brown,
John W. Medbury,
Nathaniel S. Donaldson,
George D. Dousman,
Dr. Charles Wandesly,

David Merrill,
Uriah H. Persons,
Allen W. Hatch,
Benj. H. Edgerton,
Morgan L. Burdick,
Wm. A. Hawkins,
John White,
Cicero Comstock,
Ambrose Ely,
George T. Fowler,
Richard Hoppin, Jr.,
Levi Blossom, Jr.,
Abel Hawley,
Dr. Edwin S. Marsh,
James Kneeland,
Orlando Alexander,
John T. Bradford,
Henry K. White,
Alonzo Blossom,
Eli C. Kellogg,
Edward D. Holton,
John S. Pardee,
Charles H. Hurd,
Clark Brookins,
S. M. Dorfield,
George E. H. Day,
Sylvester Pettibone,
Wm. Brown,
Henry Sivyer,
Charles Mears,
Cyrus D. Davis,
Levi Hubbell,
Sidney L. Rood,
Charles Jones,
Charles Crane,
Gen. Rufus King,
Wm. M. Cunningham,
Daniel W. Bayles,
Chas. F. Ilsley,
Jonathan Myers.
Thomas H. Williams,
Thomas Smith, Jr.,
Andrew N. Dixon,
Ezra Lowell,
Frank B. Putnam,
Peter G. Jones,
Edwin Palmer,
James Christie,
Archibald P. Allen,
Horatio N. Wells,
Alexander Matherson,
Francis Randall,
Wm. Bonnell.

JEFFERSON CO.
Ira Miltimore,
Lyman E. Boomer,
T. J. Carmichael,
Eli Petay,
D. Foster,
Alonzo S. Horton,
Robert Barry.

SHEBOYGAN CO.
Henry K. Conklin,
B. F. Lee,
E. Gilman,
W. Wampter,
W. Smith,
H. Camp,
H. L. Newberry,
J. B. Cole,
S. B. Ormsbee,
Samuel Daniels,
Wm. P. Gorsline,
Elihu S. Thorp,
D. Burhans,
J. Maynard,
E. H. Howard,
A. V. Fryer.

WAUKESHA CO.
Wm. Blake,
John Howell,
C. Dansmer,
R. W. Wright,
W. D. Baker,
J. L. Benne,

A. Steeling,
T. Stockson,
J. Polham,
O. Haseltine.

WALWORTH CO.
A. A. Hemmenway,
E. Elderkin,
Sewall Smith,
N. H. Harwood,
E. H. Ball,
F. Y. Howe,
Henry Whitney,
Wm. Boardman,
E. Eastbrook,
A. Hastings,
Wm. Berry,
Augustus Smith,
Charles Hibbard,
J. C. Mills,
C. Bellows,
Wm. R. Beld,
W. A. Blanchard,
F. K. Pheonix,
C. H. Sturdesant,
M. Taggart,
D. I. Broadway.

WASHINGTON CO.
Wooster Harrison,
Solon Johnson,
Wm. H. Baylies,
Thomas W. Smith,
G. W. Foster.

WINNEBAGO CO.
J. D. Doty.

FOND-DU-LAC CO.
N. P. Talmadge.

SAUK CO.
James Maxwell.

ROCK CO.
John M. Keep,
Edward D. Murray,
L. P. Haney,
Lucius Geo. Fisher,
Hazen Cheeney,
D. Fargo,
Jesse Moore,
George F. Winch.

COLUMBIA CO.
Henry Merrill,
Joseph Kerr.

LA FAYETTE CO.
Wm. S. Hamilton,
Samuel Young.

DODGE CO.
Charles H. Larrabee,
Wm. M. Larrabee,
L. H. Jackson.

GRANT CO.
Wm. B. Biddlecomb.

SECOND DAY, TUESDAY, JULY 6TH, 1847.

At 9 A.M. the Convention met pursuant to adjournment, Hon. Edward Bates of Missouri, president, presiding.

The minutes of yesterday's proceedings being read, were amended, and as amended, accepted.

The Delegates from Rhode Island and Kentucky reported that their reports were ordered on file.

The President announced the following as the Committee on Resolutions, appointed under the resolution of yesterday:

Connecticut—N. O. KELLOGG and JOEL W. WHITE,
Florida—JOHN G. CAMP,
Georgia—THOS. BUTLER KING and WILLIAM B. HODSON,
Illinois—JESSE B. THOMAS and DAVID J. BAKER,
Indiana—DANIEL MACE and ANDREW LAWRENCE OSBORN,

Iowa—GEORGE H. WILLIAMS and N. L. STOUT,
Kentucky—H. C. BLACKBURN and T. H. CRAWFORD,
Maine—M. A. CHANDLER and F. B. STOCKBRIDGE,
Massachusetts—GEORGE H. KUHN and ARTEMAS LEE,
Michigan—WM. WOODBRIDGE and CALVIN BRITAIN,
Missouri—JOHN D. COOK and FLETCHER M. HAIGHT,
New Jersey—ROSWELL L. COLT and CHARLES KING,
New York—JOHN C. SPENCER and ALVIN BRONSON,
Ohio—JOHN C. WRIGHT and JOSEPH W. GRAY,
Pennsylvania—T. J. BIGHAM and J. C. MARSHALL,
Rhode Island—EDWARD SEAGRAVE and HAMILTON HOPPIN,
Wisconsin—N. P. TALMADGE and J. D. KINGSLAND.

Anson Burlingame of Massachusetts, resigned as a member of the Committee on Resolutions, whereupon the chair substituted the name of Artemas Lee.

Daniel Gardner of New York, presented resolutions which were referred.

Thomas Allen of Missouri, moved that all resolutions and reports presented to the Convention be referred to the Committee on Resolutions. Carried.

Resolutions were presented by Robert S. Blackwell of Illinois, which were referred to the Committee on Resolutions.

A Resolution was presented by John R. St. John of New York, which was referred to the aforesaid Committee.

Resolutions, three in number, presented by Wm. Mosley Hall of New York, were referred as above.

A letter from Capt. I. T. Cleveland of Howard County, Mo., giving statistics of the commerce of the Missouri River, was referred to the aforesaid Committee.

Thomas Allen of Missouri, in behalf of the Missouri Delegation presented the following letter from Hon. Thomas H. Benton, which was read:

ST. LOUIS, *June 20th, 1847.*

To Messrs. Wayman, Crow, Edward Walsh, James E. Yeatman, and others, a Committee, etc.:

GENTLEMEN:—In my brief note addressed to you on my return from Jefferson, I expressed the gratification I should have felt in going with the St. Louis delegation to the Chicago Convention, and made known the reason which would prevent me from having that pleasure.

The lake-and-river navigation of the great West, to promote which the Convention is called, very early had a share of my attention, and I never had a doubt of the constitutionality or expediency of bringing that navigation within the circle of internal improvement by the federal government, when the object to be improved should be one of general and national importance.

The junction of the two great systems of water which occupy so much of our country—the Northern lakes on the one hand, and the Mississsippi River and its tributaries on the other—appeared to me to be an object of that character, and Chicago the proper point for effecting the union; and near thirty years ago I wrote and published articles in a St. Louis paper in favor of that object, indicated, and almost accomplished by Nature herself, and wanting but little from man to complete it. Articles in the *St. Louis Enquirer*, of April, 1819, express the opinions which I then entertained, and the '*report*' of that period, published in the same paper, to the Secretary of War, by Messrs. Graham & Philips, in favor of that canal (and which '*report*' I wrote), was probably the first formal communication, upon authentic data, in favor of the Chicago Canal. These gentlemen, with Mr. John C. Sullivan, of Missouri, having been appointed by the Secretary of War to run a line from the south end of Lake Michigan to the Mississippi, I proposed to them to examine the ground between Chicago and the head waters of the Illinois River, with a view to the construction of a canal by the federal government. They did so, and, on their return to St. Louis, submitted all their observations to me, and hence the publications in the newspapers, and the report of the Secretary of War. I mention this to show that my opinions on this subject are of long standing, and that the nationality of the Chicago Canal, and, of course, the harbor at its mouth, are by no means new conceptions with me. But I must confess I did not foresee then what I have since seen—the Falls of Niagara surmounted by a ship-canal, and a schooner clearing from Chicago for Liverpool.

The river navigation of the great West is the most wonderful on the globe, and, since the application of steam power to the propulsion of vessels, possesses the essential qualities of open navigation. Speed, distance, cheapness, magnitude of cargoes, are all there, and without the perils of the sea from storms and enemies. The steamboat is the ship of the river, and finds in the Mississippi and its tributaries the amplest theatre for the diffusion of its use and the display of its power. Wonderful river! Connected with seas by the head and by the mouth—stretching its arms toward the Atlantic and the Pacific—lying in a valley which is a valley from the Gulf of Mexico to Hudson's Bay—drawing its first waters, not from rugged mountains, but from the plateau of the lakes in the centre of the continent, and in communication with the sources of the St. Lawrence and the streams which take their course north to Hudson's Bay—draining the largest extent of richest land—collecting the products of every clime, even the frigid, to bear the whole to market in the sunny South, and there to meet the products of the entire world. Such is the Mississippi! And who can calculate the aggregate of its advantages, and the magnitude of its future commercial results?

Many years ago, the late Governor Clark and myself undertook to calculate the extent of the boatable waters in the Valley of the Mississippi: we made it about fifty thousand miles, of which thirty thousand were computed to unite above St. Louis, and twenty thousand below. Of course we counted all the infant streams on which a flat, a keel, or a batteau could be floated, and justly, for every tributary of the humblest boatable character helps to swell, not only the volume of the central waters, but of the commerce upon them. Of this immense extent of river navigation, all combined into one system of waters, St. Louis is the centre, and the *entrepôt* of its trade; presenting even now, in its infancy, an astonishing and almost incredible amount of commerce, destined to increase forever. It is considered an inland town. Counting by time and money, the only true commercial measure of distances, St. Louis is nearer to the sea than New Orleans was before the steam tow-boat abridged the distance between that city and the mouth of the Mississippi. St. Louis is a seaport as well as an inland city, and is a port of delivery by law, and has collected $50,000 of duties on foreign imports during the current year, and with a liberal custom would become a great *entrepôt* of foreign as well as domestic commerce. With the attributes and characteristics of a seaport, she is entitled to the benefits of one as fully and as clearly as New York or New Orleans.

About twenty years ago, I moved in the Senate and obtained an appropriation for a survey of the Rapids of the Upper Mississippi: it was probably the first appropriation ever obtained for the improvement of the upper part of the river. About twenty-five years ago, I moved, and succeeded in the motion, to include the Missouri River in a bill for the improvement of Western rivers: it was the first time that river had been so included. Thus, on the important items of the Chicago Canal, the Rapids of the Upper Mississippi, and the Missouri River, I was among the first to propose to include them within the circle of internal improvements by the federal government. I have always been a friend of that system, but not of its abuses; and here lies the difficulty, and the danger, and the stumbling-block to its success. Objects of general and national importance can alone claim the attention of the federal government, and in favor of such objects I believe all the departments of the government are united. Confined to them, and the Constitution can reach them and the treasury sustain them. Extended to local or sectional objects, and neither the Constitution nor the treasurer could uphold them, National objects of improvement are few in number, definite in character, and manageable by the treasury; local and sectional objects are innumerable, and indefinite, and ruinous to the treasury. Near twenty years ago the treasury was threatened with a demand for two hundred millions of dollars for objects of internal improvement, then applied for, and many of them of no national importance. The enormity of the sum balked the system; and so it must be again, if the proper discrimination is not kept up between local and national subjects. It is for Congress to make that discrimination; the President can not: he must reject or approve the bill as a whole. Here, then, is the point at which the friends of the system in Congress must exert all their care and vigilance. No arbitrary rule can be given for the admission or exclusion of proper objects; but really national objects admit of no dispute, and, confined to them, I apprehend but little danger of losing a bill, either from executive vetoes or for want of votes in Congress.

Very respectfully, gentlemen, your friend and fellow-citizen,
THOMAS H. BENTON.

On motion of Daniel Gardner of New York, the foregoing letter was referred to the Committee on Resolutions.

Thomas Allen of Missouri, in behalf of the Missouri Delegation presented a report on the commerce and navigation of the Valley of the Mississippi; and also that appertaining to the city of St. Louis, considered with reference to the improvement by the General Government, of the Mississippi River and its tributaries; being "A Report, prepared by authority of the Delegates from the city of St. Louis, for the use of the Chicago Convention of the 5th of July, 1847," which was referred to the same Committee.

The President called on Henry W. Starr of Iowa, one of the secretaries, to read the other letters received from invited guests. The following letters were then read:

LETTER FROM SILAS WRIGHT.

CANTON, *31st May, 1847.*

GENTLEMEN:—Your Circular inviting me to attend a "North-Western River-and-Harbor Convention," to be assembled in Chicago, on the first Monday of July next, was duly received, forwarded by Mr. Whiting, of your Committee. My attention had been previously called to the same subject by the invitation of a friend, at your City, to attend the Convention, who generously tendered me quarters in his family during its sitting. I was forced, from the state of private business, to inform him that I could not make the journey at the time named, and the period which has elapsed since I declined his invitation has only tended to confirm the conclusion pronounced to him. Were it possible for me to attend the proposed Convention without an unreasonable sacrifice, I should most gladly do so, as my location gives me a strong feeling in reference to the prosperity and safety of the commerce of the lakes. The subject of the improvement of the lake harbors is one which my service in Congress has rendered somewhat familiar to me in a legislative aspect, while my personal travel upon the two lower lakes has made the necessity for these improvements manifest to my senses. I am aware that questions of constitutional power have been raised in reference to appropriations of money by Congress for the improvement of lake harbors, and I am well convinced that honest men have sincerely entertained strong scruples upon this point, but all my observation and experience have induced me to believe that these scruples, where the individual admits the power to improve the Atlantic harbors, arises from the want of an acquaintance with the lakes and the commerce upon them, and an inability to believe the facts in relation to that commerce, when truly stated. It is not easy for one familiar with the lakes and the lake commerce, to realize the degree of incredulity, as to the magnitude and importance of both, which is found in the minds of honest and well-informed men, residing in remote portions of the Union, and having no acquaintance with either, while I do not recollect an instance of a member of Congress who has traveled the lakes and observed the commerce upon them within the last ten years requiring any further evidence or argument to induce him to admit the constitutional power and the propriety of appropriations for the lake harbors as much as for those of the Atlantic coast. I have long been of the opinion, therefore, that to impress the minds of the people of all portions of the Union with a realizing sense of the facts as they are in relation to those inland seas, and their already vast and increasing commerce, would be all that is required to secure such appropriations as the state of the national treasury will from time to time permit, for the improvement of the lake harbors: I mean the improvement of such harbors as the body of the lake commerce requires for its convenience and safety, as contradistinguished from the numerous applications for these improvements which the various competing local interests upon the shores of the lake may prompt, and I make this distinction because my own observation has shown that application for harbor improvements at the public expense are made and passed within distances of a very few miles, and at locations where, from the natural position of the lake coast, a good harbor at either point would secure to the commerce of the lakes all the convenience and safety of duplicate improvement. Much of the difficulty of obtaining appropriations grows out of these conflicting applications; and the sternness with which all are pressed, as necessary to the lake commerce, impairs the confidence of strangers to the local claims and interests in the importance of all.

It is the duty of those who urge these improvements, for the great objects for which alone they should be made at the expense of the Nation, viz., the convenience and safety of the lake commerce, to be honest with Congress, and to urge appropriations only at points where these considerations demand them. The river improvements constitute a much more difficult subject, and the connection of them with the lake harbors has often, to my knowledge, fatally prejudiced the former. There are applications for improvements of rivers about which, as a matter of principle and constitutional power, I have no more doubt than about the harbors upon the lakes or the Atlantic coast, and there are those which, in my judgment, come neither within the principle nor the constitutional power; but draw a line between the two classes of cases I can not. I have witnessed numerous attempts to do this, but none of them have appeared to my mind to be very sound or very practical. The facts and circumstances are so very variant between the various applications, that I doubt whether any general rule can be laid down which will be found just and practical; and I think the course most likely to secure a satisfactory result, with the least danger of a violation of principle, would be for Congress to act separately and independently upon each application. There has appeared to me to be one broad distinction between these cases, which has not always been regarded, but which I think always should be. It is between the applications to protect and secure the safety of commerce upon rivers, where it exists and is regularly carried on in defiance of the obstructions sought to be removed, and in the face of the dangers they place in its way, and those applications which ask for improvement of rivers, that commerce may be extended upon them where it is not. The one class appear to me to ask Congress to regulate and protect commerce upon rivers where commerce in fact exists, and the other to create it upon rivers where it does not exist. This distinction, if carefully observed, might aid in determining some applications of both classes, but is not a sufficient dividing line for practical legislation, if it is for the sentiment of the principle upon which all such applications should rest. I use the term "commerce" in this definition, as I do in this letter, in its constitutional sense and scope.

I must ask your pardon, gentlemen, for troubling you with so long and hasty a communication in reply to your note. It is not made for any public use, but to express to you very imperfectly some of my views upon the interesting subjects you bring to my notice which I shall not have the pleasure of communicating in person, and to satisfy you that I am not indifferent to your request.

Be pleased to accept my thanks for your polite invitation, and believe me your very respectful and obedient servant,

SILAS WRIGHT.

To Messrs. N. B. Judd and others, Committee, etc.

LETTER FROM HENRY CLAY.

ASHLAND, *May 24th, 1847.*

DEAR SIR:—I received your letter, accompanied by the circular of the Committee, requesting my attendance at the North-Western River-and-Harbor Convention, proposed to be held at Chicago, on the first Monday in July next. Cordially concurring in what is announced to be the object of the Convention, I should be happy to assist in the accomplishment of it, if it were in my power; but I regret that I can not conveniently attend the Convention.

Wishing that its deliberations may be conducted in a spirit of harmony, and that they may lead to good practical results, I am, with great respect, your obedient servant,   HENRY CLAY.

E. W. TRACY, Esq.

LETTER FROM MARTIN VAN BUREN.

LINDENWALD, *May 21st, 1847.*

MY DEAR SIR:—I thank you kindly for the obliging terms in which you have been pleased to communicate to me the invitation of the Committee to attend the North-Western River-and-Harbor Convention, and beg you to be assured that you do me but justice in assuming that I am by no means indifferent to its objects. Having visited most parts of your interesting country, and witnessed, with admiration and high hopes, its peculiar capacities for improvement, I can not but wish success to all constitutional efforts that have that direction. Regretting that it will not be in my power to comply with your request, I beg you to make my acknowledgements to the Committee for this proof of their respect.

I am, very respectfully and truly yours,   M. VAN BUREN.
E. W. TRACY, Esq.

LETTER FROM LEWIS CASS.

DETROIT, *May 17th, 1847.*

DEAR SIR:—I am much obliged to you for your kind attention in transmitting me an invitation to attend the Convention on internal improvements which will meet in Chicago in July. Circumstances, however, will put it out of my power to be present at that time.

I am, dear sir, respectfully yours,   LEWIS CASS.

LETTER FROM THOMAS P. CURTISS.

BOSTON, *May 17, 1847.*

W. L. WHITING, ESQ., Chicago.

Dear Sir:—I have received the invitation to attend a Convention in your City on the 5th of July. Nothing of a like character could interest me more than this, and I wish it could be within my power to be present. My engagements with the City of Boston as one of the Commissioners, to introduce water from the country, compels close attendance until it is finished.

Here in Boston we are in the habit of observing whatever of public improvement is contemplated in every, the most distant region of our country, and none with more interest than that which involves the safety and facility of internal intercourse, whether it be towards our own New England or by the more roundabout way of the Rivers—ALL tends to the general good of ALL. Wishing you great success,

I am, dear Sir, yours,
THOMAS B. CURTISS.

LETTER FROM JOSEPH GRINNELL.

NEW BEDFORD, *19th June, 1847.*

My Dear Sir:—I thank you and the Committee for your polite invitation to attend the Convention, to be held in Chicago on the 5th of next month. If I can leave home, I shall be with you, to do whatever may be in my power to press upon the country the vital importance of improving, in every way possible, our Harbors and Rivers, and in all ways to facilitate and cheapen transportation. You are authorized to pledge my vote on all occasions for these purposes, when they are combined in one bill, so that all parts of the country are fairly dealt by.

With great respect, your obedient servant,

JOSEPH GRINNELL.

W. L. WHITING, Esq., Chicago.

LETTER FROM BRADFORD R. WOOD.

ALBANY, N. Y., *22d June, 1847.*

Gentlemen:—I regret that neither in compliance with the invitation of the Committee, nor as one of the delegates from this City, shall I be able to attend the River-and-Harbor Convention about to assemble in your City, on the 5th of July next. The course pursued by myself on the River-and-Harbor Bill in the 29th Congress, is the best assurance I can give that I shall not look with indifference on the proceedings of that Convention. That no appropriation was made by the last Congress, for the improvement of the Harbors of the Lakes, is, you are aware, no fault of mine. Nor can I forbear the reflection, that while war (however originating) is waged, ostensibly to obtain indemnification and the payment of a doubtful debt, practically, I fear, to extend slave territory, at the cost of hundreds of millions of money, and thousands of lives, unless it shall soon terminate, no appropriations, however small, could be obtained, to save from destruction on our Lakes, property worth far more than all that Mexico ever justly owed, to say nothing of hundreds of lives sacrificed every year, for want of safe and accessible harbors.

I remain, very truly, yours, etc.,

BRADFORD R. WOOD.

To Messrs. JOHN WENTWORTH, WM. B. OGDEN, and others, Committee, etc.

LETTER FROM ALPHEUS FELCH.

ANN ARBOR, Michigan, *June 28th, 1847.*

Dear Sir:—Your favor inclosing an invitation of the Committee of Correspondence, to attend the River-and-Harbor Convention about to be held at Chicago, came duly to hand. Business engagements, which can not be postponed, will put it out of my power to be present with you on that occasion. The interest which Michigan has in the safe and convenient navigation of the

Great Lakes, and the improvement of the Harbors, without which it can never be attained, will insure the coöperation of this State and its representatives in support of all judicious appropriations for that purpose.

With my acknowledgments to your Committee for the kind attention which prompted their polite invitation, and with sentiments of respect,

I am, my dear Sir, your ob't servant,
ALPHEUS FELCH.

W. L. WHITING, Esq., Chicago.

LETTER FROM GEORGE P. BARKER.

BUFFALO, *May 31st, 1847.*

To GEORGE W. MEEKER, Esq.

Dear Sir:—I am honored with the receipt of your favor, inclosing an invitation of a Committee of Correspondence, to attend a North-Western River-and-Harbor Convention, to be held at your City on the first Monday in July next. I would gratefully acknowledge the honor conferred by this invitation, and sensibly appreciate the very flattering manner in which you have been pleased to communicate it. Ever since the subject of this Convention was agitated, I have felt a deep interest in its success, and strongly desirous that it should be in numbers and spirit all that its great, and as yet unmeasured, objects demand; and I have hitherto promised myself much pleasure in visiting this very interesting portion of the West, and in meeting, on such an occasion, so many of those whose sagacious enterprise have so astonishingly developed her mighty resources, and upon whose present efforts its future destiny is so much dependent; but I fear I shall be compelled to forego the gratification of these anticipations.

My health has been such for the last year that I have been advised by medical counsel that an immediate visit to salt water is indispensable; should their determination be followed, it will of course be out of my power to be at the Convention. In such an event, however, I shall have the consolation of knowing that there will be many there who better understand the great interests involved in the objects of the Convention, although I would hardly concede that there would be any one more determined to sustain them.

With respect for the Committee, whose invitation you did me the honor to send, and for yourself personally,

I have the honor to be your ob'd't
GEO. P. BARKER.

Letter from Washington Hunt.

Lockport, N. Y., *June 26, 1847.*

Gentlemen—I had the honor to receive your letter, dated 1st May, inviting me to attend the North-Western River-and-Harbor Convention, which is about to assemble at Chicago.

I had hopes to be able to avail myself of your friendly invitation, but private engagements compel me most reluctantly to relinquish that intention. Whilst I am deprived of the satisfaction of participating personally in the deliberations of the Convention, you will permit me to assure you that I shall regard its proceedings and results of the day with the deepest interest. The rapid growth and expansion of our Western Commerce make it important that the country will, for any length of time, submit to that unfortunate course of policy which has caused the Government for some years to disregard its powers and deny its obligations to this regard.

Whether considered with reference to the federal revenues, the increase of our foreign trade, or the prosperity of the country at large, the safe, easy, and unobstructed navigation of our Lakes and Rivers is an object of national concern, as important and legitimate as the regulation of our commerce on the ocean.

It is to be hoped that the entire subject may be presented to the public, on the present occasion, enforced by an array of facts and arguments which shall effectually silence partisan clamor, and expose the absurdity and barrenness of these narrow abstractions which would constrain the government of the United States to close its eyes to the actual progress and destiny of the country.

I have been gratified to observe that "all distinctions of party" are banished in this great popular movement.

The protection of the Lake-and-River Commerce is one of those practical questions, of pervading interest and general concern, which ought never to have been forced into the arena of party struggles. It is too large a subject to be reduced to a party affair, and exposed to the chances of political fluctuation. It requires a strong, united, and emphatic expression of public sentiment to separate the subject from its unnatural connection with party politics. That separation will, I am persuaded, be among the first and most valuable results of the Convention. Nothing is wanted but an unequivocal demonstration of the popular will to elevate the question above the reach of partisan combinations, thus disarming, at once and forever, that political hostility which has proved so fatal to the cause of public improvements. Let us have a final divorce of our great navigating interest from all mere party test-words and theories. The time has come when public men and aspirants for popular national honors must cease to sport with those grand national objects which you now seek to advance. In considering the general policy of improvements in the navigation of our Great Lakes and Rivers, I hope the Convention will not fail to turn its attention to the importance of opening a communication, suitable for large vessels, between Lake Michigan and the Mississippi; and another around the Falls of Niagara, connecting Lakes Erie and Ontario by means of a ship-canal. These two links, added to the great chain which Nature has furnished, will open a complete line of ship navigation from the St. Lawrence to the Gulf of Mexico—watering in its course the soil of fifteen States of our confederacy, and securing a direct channel for foreign commerce to every inland State, as well as to the States whose are watered by the Atlantic or the Gulf.

I am, gentlemen, with great respect,

Your obedient servant,

WASHINGTON HUNT.

A communication was received from the city of Detroit, transmitted by the Common Council of that City, which in accordance with the preceding resolution, was referred to the Committee on Resolutions, without reading.

On motion of Daniel Gardner of New York, it was resolved that all the letters read or received be entered upon the record and printed.

On motion of Hon. John Wentworth of Illinois, *Resolved*, That if there be any letters addressed to the Committee, the Secretary shall obtain them, to be read to the Convention and entered upon the minutes.

The unfinished business was then taken up. The Fourth Resolution presented by the Committee on Rules, and spread at length on the record of yesterday's proceedings, was taken up and read.

On motion of H. J. Redfield of New York, the said resolution was laid on the table.

On motion of Mr. Carver of Illinois, it was *Resolved*, That when any Delegate rises to address the Chair, he shall announce his name.

On motion of the same gentleman, it was *Resolved*, That States who had not reported yesterday should have the privilege of appointing a vice-president of this Convention.

Andrew Stewart of Pennsyvania, and David Dudley Field of New York, being severally called upon, addressed the Convention on the subjects connected with the objects of this Convention.

On motion of Jason Marsh of Illinois, it was

Resolved, That the Delegates to this Convention are pained at the expression of ill-feeling evinced this morning during the time that David Dudley Field of New York, occupied (by invitation) the stand; and in future pledge themselves to regard the rights of all members of the Convention, who confine themselves to the rules prescribed and passed by this Convention.

S. Treat of Missouri, offered the following resolution:

Resolved, That no proposition or remarks, not directly connected with recognized River-and-Harbor improvements of a national character shall be entertained by this Convention.

On motion of Wm. Mosley Hall of New York, the said resolution was laid on the table.

Abraham Lincoln of Illinois, being called upon addressed the Convention briefly.

RESOLUTIONS OF THE CONVENTION.

John C. Wright of Ohio, from the Committee on Resolutions, presented the following for the consideration of the Convention, which were read by Charles King of New Jersey:

The Convention submit to their fellow-citizens and to the Federal Government the following propositions as expressing their own sentiments and those of their constituents:

1st. That the Constitution of the United States was framed by practical men, for practical purposes, declared in its preamble, "To provide for the common defence, to promote the general welfare, and to secure the blessings of liberty;" and was mainly designed to create a government whose functions should and would be adequate to the protection of the common interests of all the States, or of two or more of them, which could not be maintained by the action of the separated States. That, in strict accordance with this object, the revenues derived from commerce were surrendered to the general government, with the express understanding that they should be applied to the promotion of those common interests.

2d. That among these common interests and objects were, 1st, foreign commerce, to the regulation of which the powers of the States severally were confessedly inadequate; and, 2d, internal trade and navigation, wherever the concurrence of two or more States was necessary to its preservation, or where the expense of its maintenance should be equitably borne by two or more States, and where, of course, those States must necessarily have a voice in its regulation; and hence resulted the constitutional grant of power to Congress, "to regulate commerce with foreign nations and among the States."

3d. That, being thus possessed of both the means and of the power which were denied to the States respectively, Congress became obligated, by every consideration of good faith and common justice, to cherish and increase both the kinds of commerce thus committed to its care, by expanding and extending the means of conducting them, and of affording them all those facilities and all that protection which the States individually would have afforded had the revenue and authority been left to them.

4th. That this obligation has ever been recognized from the foundation of the government, and has been fulfilled, partially, by erecting light-houses, building piers for harbors, breakwaters and sea-walls, removing obstructions in rivers, and providing other facilities for the commerce carried on from the ports of the Atlantic coast; and the same obligations have been fulfilled, to a much less extent, in providing similar facilities for "commerce among the States," and that the principle has been most emphatically acknowledged to embrace the Western Lakes and Rivers, by appropriations for numerous light-houses upon them, which appropriations have never been questioned in Congress as wanting constitutional authority.

5th. That thus, by a series of acts which have received the sanction of the people of the United States, and of every department of the Federal Government, under all administrations, the common understanding of the intent and objects of the framers of the Constitution, in granting to Congress the power to regulate commerce, has been manifested and has been confirmed by the people, *and this understanding has become as much a part of that instrument as any one of its most explicit provisions.*

6th. That the power "to regulate commerce with foreign nations, and among the States, and with the Indian tribes," is on its face so palpably applicable in its whole extent to each of the subjects enumerated, equally and in the same manner, as to render any attempts to make it more explicit idle and futile; and that those who admit the rightful application of the power to foreign commerce in facilitating and protecting its operations, by improving harbors and clearing out navigable rivers, can not consistently deny that it equally authorizes similar facilities to "commerce among the States."

7th. That "foreign commerce" is dependent upon internal trade for the distribution of its freights, and for the means of paying for them, so that whatever improves the one advances the other, and they are so inseparable that they should be regarded as one. That an export from the American shore to a British port in Canada is as much foreign commerce as if it had been directly to Liverpool; and that an exportation to Liverpool neither gains nor loses any of the characteristics of foreign commerce by the directness or circuity of the route, whether it passes through a custom-house on the British side of the St. Lawrence, or descends through that river and its connecting canals to the ocean, or whether it passes along the artificial communications and natural streams of any of the States to the Atlantic.

8th. That the general government, by extending its jurisdiction over lakes and navigable rivers, subjecting them to the same laws which prevail on the ocean, and on its bays and ports, not only for purposes of revenue, but to give security to life and property, by the regulation of steamboats, has precluded itself from denying that jurisdiction for any other legitimate regulation of commerce. If it has power to control and restrain, it must have the same power to protect, assist, and facilitate; and if it denies the jurisdiction in the one mode of action, it should renounce it in the other.

9th. That, in consequence of the peculiar dangers of the navigation of the Lakes, arising from the want of harbors for shelter, and of the Western Rivers from snags and other obstructions, there are no parts of the United States more emphatically demanding the prompt and continued care of the Government to diminish those dangers, and to protect the life and property exposed to them; and that any one who can regard provisions for those purposes as sectional or local, and not national, must be wanting in information of the extent of the commerce carried on upon those lakes and rivers, and of the amount of teeming population occupied or interested in that navigation.

10th. That, having regard to the relative population or to the extent of commerce, the appropriations heretofore made for the interior rivers and lakes, and the streams connecting them with the ocean, have not been in a just and fair proportion to those made for the benefit of the Atlantic coast; and that the time has arrived when this injustice should be corrected, in the only mode in which it can be done, by the united, determined, and persevering efforts of those whose rights have been overlooked.

11th. That, independent of this right to protection of "commerce among the States," the right of "common defence," guaranteed by the Constitution, entitles those citizens inhabiting the country bordering upon the interior lakes and rivers to such safe and convenient harbors as may afford shelter to a navy, whenever it shall be rendered necessary by hostilities with our neighbors;

and that the constructions of such harbors can not safely be delayed to the time which will demand their immediate use.

12th. That the argument most commonly urged against appropriations to protect "commerce among the States," and to defend the inhabitants of the frontiers, that they invite sectional combinations to insure success to many unworthy objects, is founded on a practical distrust of the Republican principles of our Government, and of the capacity of the people to select competent and honest representatives. That it may be urged with equal force against legislation upon any other subject, involving various and extensive interests. That a just appreciation of the rights and interests of all our fellow-citizens, in every quarter of the Union, disclaiming selfish and local purposes, will lead intelligent representatives to such a distribution of the means in the treasury, upon a system of moderation and ultimate equality, as will in time meet the most urgent wants of all, and prevent those jealousies and suspicions which threaten the most serious danger to our confederacy.

13th. That we are utterly incapable of perceiving the difference between a harbor for shelter and a harbor for commerce, and suppose that a mole or pier which will afford safe anchorage and protection to a vessel against a storm, must necessarily improve such harbor, and adapt it to commercial purposes.

14th. That the imposts on foreign goods and the public lands being the common heritage of all our citizens, so long as these resources continue, the imposition of any special burden on any portion of the people, to obtain the means of accomplishing objects equally within the duty and the competency of the General Government, would be unjust and oppressive.

15th. That we disavow all and every attempt to connect the cause of internal trade and "commerce among the States" with the fortunes of any political party, but that we mean to place that cause upon such immutable principles of truth, justice, and constitutional duty as shall command the respect of all parties, and the deference of all candidates for public favor.

John C. Wright of Ohio, in presenting the report of the Committee and moving its adoption, made some brief remarks, informing the Convention that the Committee had been unanimous in recommending the propositions presented by him in their behalf.

John C. Spencer and Daniel Gardner of New York, addressed the Convention in support of the propositions.

David Dudley Field of New York, objected to adopting the propositions as a whole; and thereupon, on motion of Jesse B.

Thomas of Illinois, it was resolved that the vote be taken on them separately.

The first, second, third, and fourth propositions were adopted unanimously.

The fifth proposition coming up, David Dudley Field of New York, moved to strike out all after the word "people," which amendment was rejected, and thereupon the propositions were adopted as reported by the Committee.

The sixth, seventh, eighth, ninth, tenth, eleventh, twelfth, and thirteenth propositions were then severally and unanimously adopted.

The fourteenth proposition coming up in its order. It was suggested by Mr. Stimson of New York, and moved by John C. Spencer of New York, to strike out "imports on foreign goods being taken mainly from the pockets of the consumers," and insert the following, "revenue derived from imports on foreign goods, belongs to the people," which motion was agreed to and the proposition as amended was adopted.

The fifteenth and last proposition was then taken up and unanimously adopted.

John C. Wright of Ohio, from the Committee on Resolutions, submitted the following resolution:

Resolved, That for the purpose of making known to Congress the principles and views of this Convention, and the important facts connected with the subject of its deliberations, a committee of two from each State and Territory be appointed by the President to transmit the proceedings of this Convention to the President of the United States, and to both Houses of Congress, and to communicate to them such information as the committee may be able to collect, to guide intelligent and just legislation. And that such committee be requested to collect accurate information of the nature and extent of the trade and commerce of the Lakes and navigable Rivers, and the amount of the losses of lives, property, and vessels by storm, for the want of adequate harbors, or in consequence of obstructions in the navigable Rivers of the United States and the condition of our harbors. And that such committee be authorized to appoint such sub-committee as may be deemed necessary to carry out the objects of this resolution.

The question being taken on the resolution, it was unanimously adopted.

H. J. Redfield of New York, submitted the following resolution, and moved its adoption:

Resolved, That it is inexpedient to embark in any system of

Internal Improvement without a previous amendment of the Constitution, explaining and defining the precise powers of the Federal Government over it, assuming the right to appropriate money to aid in the construction of National works, to be warranted by the contemporaneous and continued exposition of the Constitution, its insufficiency for the successful prosecution of them must be admitted by all candid minds.

Which, on motion of Thomas C. Love of New York, was laid on the table.

Thomas Butler King of Georgia, being called upon, addressed the Convention, and then on motion the Convention adjourned till to-morrow morning, at 9 o'clock.

THIRD DAY, WEDNESDAY, JULY 7TH, 1847.

At 9 A. M. the Convention met pursuant to adjournment, Hon. Edward Bates of Missouri, President.

The session was opened with prayer by the Rev. Wm. Allen of Massachusetts, at the request of the President.

On motion, the reading of the minutes of yesterday's proceedings was dispensed with.

Robert S. Blackwell of Illinois, moved for adoption a resolution, which, after modification by request of members present, read as follows:

Resolved, That the members of the General River-and-Harbor Committee, appointed at the meeting held in the city of New York in September last, residing in Chicago, be, and they are hereby, authorized and requested to contract for, and superintend the publication and distribution in pamphlet form, and of the number of copies they may see fit to have printed.

The resolution was adopted.

Wm. Green of Ohio, moved a reconsideration of the last vote. Carried.

John C. Spencer of New York, moved in lieu of Mr. Blackwell's resolution the following:

Resolved, That the proceedings of this Convention, after being duly authenticated by the officers thereof, be published in pamphlet form, by a Committee of three residing in Chicago, to be appointed by the President, and be circulated freely throughout the Union. And that the expense of such publication and all expenses incurred by the Committee appointed to transmit the said proceedings to Congress in the transaction of their duties, be defrayed by contributions from the different places which have sent delegates to this body, to be collected in such mode and in such proportions as the said Committee shall direct.

The said modification was adopted.

The President appointed as the Committee under this resolution, S. Lisle Smith, George W. Dole, and Wm. B. Ogden.

The following letter from Daniel Webster was then read, received with 3 cheers, and ordered to be spread upon the minutes:

MARSHFIELD, *June 26, 1847.*

GENTLEMEN:—I am quite obliged to you for your very kind and respectful letter, addressed to me at Nashville, inviting me to attend the Chicago Convention. If my health had allowed me to continue the journey, which I was then prosecuting, it would have brought me into the North-West in time to have been with you the 1st of July; but being compelled, by illness, to abandon the purpose of getting over the mountains, it was, of course, not in my power to attend the Convention.

You speak, gentlemen, in terms of too much commendation, I fear, of my efforts in the cause of Internal and Western Improvement. I can only say that these efforts have been earnest, long-continued, and made from the single desire of promoting the great interests of the country. Of the power of the Government to make appropriations for erecting harbors and clearing rivers, I never entertained a particle of doubt. This power, in my judgment, is not partial, limited, obscure, applicable to some uses and not applicable to others, to some States and not to others, to some rivers and not to others, as seems to have been the opinion of gentlemen connected with the Memphis Convention. For one, I reject all such far-fetched and unnatural distinctions. In my opinion, the authority of the Government, in this respect, rests directly on the grant of the Commercial power to Congress; and this has been so understood from the beginning, by the wisest and best men who have been concerned in the administration of the Government; and is consequently general, and limited only by the importance of each particular subject, and the discretion of Congress.

I hope the Convention may do much good, by enforcing the necessity of exercising these just powers of the Government. There are no new inventions, nor new constructions, or qualifications of the Constitutional power to be resorted to; there is no new political path to be struck out. It is simply for the people to say, whether prejudice, party prepossessions, and party opposition shall at length give way to fair reasoning, to precedent and experience, to the judgment of the great men who have gone be-

fore us, and to those momentous considerations of public interest, which now so imperatively call on Congress to do its duty.
I am, Gentlemen, with much regard,
Your obliged friend and fellow-citizen,
DAN. WEBSTER.

To Messrs. S. LISLE SMITH, JUSTIN BUTTERFIELD, I. H. BURCH, and others.

Wells Colton of Missouri, moved that the several reports and other documents presented to the Convention, be printed with the proceedings thereof, but at the suggestion of Jesse B. Thomas of Illinois, modified the motion, so that such reports and documents be referred to the Executive Committee. Thus modified, the motion was adopted.

Wm. Mosley Hall of New York, offered three resolutions relating to the subject of "a Railroad from the States to the Pacific," which, after being read, were, on motion of Gov. Wm. Bebb of Ohio, laid on the table by a unanimous vote. [See page 91.]

The President announced the following named gentlemen as composing the Executive Committee, authorized to make known to Congress the principles and views of the Convention, etc., under the last resolution reported by the Committee on Resolutions:

Abbott Lawrence, Boston, John Mills Springfield,	Massachusetts.
John C. Spencer, Albany, Samuel B. Ruggles, New York,	New York.
James T. Morehead, Covington, James Guthrie, Louisville,	Kentucky.
Jacob G. Sleight, Michigan City, Zebulon Baird, Lafayette,	Indiana.
Thomas Allen, St. Louis, Joseph M. Converse, St. Louis,	Missouri.
Alexander Duncan, Providence, Zachariah Allen, Providence,	Rhode Island.
George C. Stone, Bloomington, Wm. B. Ewing, Burlington,	Iowa.
James Hall, Cincinnati, Joseph L. Weatherly, Cleveland,	Ohio.
Thomas W. Williams, New London, Philip Ripley, Hartford,	Connecticut.
T. J. Bigham, Pittsburg, John B. Johnson, Erie,	Pennsylvania.

PROCEEDINGS—EXECUTIVE COMMITTEE.

Rufus King, Milwaukee, Cyrus Woodman, Mineral Point,	Wisconsin.
Thomas Butler King, Savannah, Wm. B. Hodson, Savannah,	Georgia.
John G. Camp,	Florida.
Joseph R. Williams, Constantine, David A. Noble, Monroe,	Michigan.
Charles Jarvis, Surry, George Evans, Gardiner,	Maine.
David J. Baker, Alton, Jesse B. Thomas, Chicago,	Illinois.
Charles King, Jersey City, Littleton Kirkpatrick,	New Jersey.
James Wilson, Keene, John Page,	New Hampshire.

John R. St. John of New York, moved a reconsideration of the resolution authorizing an Executive Committee: which motion was, on motion of Isaac Butts of New York, laid on the table.

Judge Henry Brown of Illinois, offered a series of resolutions, relating to the free navigation of the River St. Lawrence, and the state of the Erie Canal, which, on motion of John C. Spencer of New York, were laid on the table.

Gen. N. W. Watkins of Missouri, offered the following resolution:

Resolved, That the thanks of the Convention be presented to the citizens of Chicago, for the hospitality and kindness extended to the members during their sojourn in this City.

Which was unanimously adopted.

On motion of Hon. Thomas Corwin of Ohio, it was unanimously

Resolved, That the thanks of this Convention are due, and are most cordially tendered, to the Hon. Edward Bates for the able, dignified, and courteous manner in which he has discharged the duties of President of this Convention.

On motion of Solon Robinson of Indiana, it was

Resolved, That the original record and papers of this Convention be placed in the hands of the Mayor of Chicago, after the close of the Convention, to be preserved among the archives of the City.

A motion having been made to adjourn the Convention *sine die*, the President (Mr. Bates) rose, and, before putting the question, addressed the Convention in a speech which was frequently interrupted by vehement applause, and greeted at the close with nine enthusiastic cheers.

The question on the motion to adjourn being then put, was carried, and thereupon the President pronounced the Convention adjourned without day.

EDWARD BATES, *President.*

JOHN H. BROCKWAY,	N. W. WATKINS,
JOHN G. CAMP,	ERASTUS CORNING,
THOMAS BUTLER KING,	LITTLETON KIRKPATRICK,
ERASTUS H. W. ELLIS,	WILLIAM BEBB,
CHARLES S. HEMPSTEAD,	A. W. LOOMIS,
G. H. WILLIAMS,	HAMILTON HOPPIN,
M. A. CHANDLER,	JOHN H. TWEEDY,
WILLIAM T. EUSTIS,	FRANCIS S. FISKE,
WM. WOODBRIDGE,	*Vice-Presidents.*
A. B. CHAMBERS,	PETER MCMARTIN,
SCHUYLER COLFAX,	WILLIAM J. OTIS,
NELSON G. EDWARDS,	FREDERICK S. LOVELL,
AARON HOBART,	HENRY W. STARR,
DAVID A. NOBLE,	*Secretaries.*
FRANCIS UPTON FENNO,	

COMMITTEE OF THE WHOLE.

Immediately after the adjournment of the Convention, it was, on motion of Solon Robinson of Indiana,

Resolved, That Horace Greeley of New York, be requested to take the Chair and that this Convention now be resolved into a Committee of the Whole.

Short addresses were made by Gov. Wm. Bebb of Ohio, Hon. Andrew W. Loomis of Pittsburg, Penn., Gen. Levi Hubbell of Milwaukee, Wis., Samuel Lisle Smith of Chicago, Ill., Anson Burlingame and Hon. Elisha H. Allen of Boston, Mass., and Horace Greeley of New York, on general matters connected with the cause which brought them together.

Wm. Mosley Hall of Buffalo, N.Y., was then called upon and arose to respond, but gave way for the dinner-hour adjournment. (1 P. M.). Adjourned to 3 o'clock.

AFTERNOON SESSION, 3 P. M.

On reassembling, Mr. Hall took the floor, and after alluding to the rapid increase of population and wealth of the West, and the objects of the Convention—(of which he was originator)—occupied the earnest attention of the audience for upwards of an hour in advocating the construction of a "National Railroad to the Pacific," in accordance with the plan of Geo. Wilkes of New York, and in opposition to the private schemes of speculators. He was frequently interrupted by the acclamations of the vast audience. On concluding, the re-reading of his Resolutions, presented to the Convention, was called for, and, after being read, were submitted and adopted by a unanimous vote. And then, at 5 P. M., the meeting adjourned without day.

A Railroad from the States to the Pacific.

RESOLUTIONS OF WM. MOSELY HALL.

RESOLVED, That we believe a Railroad from the States to the Pacific to be practicable, and ultimately calculated to be of immense benefit to the United States and its citizens; that with these convictions, we recommend an early survey of the entire line by the general government, and that its final construction and control be confided to sworn Commissioners, selected by the State Legislatures, or elected by the people of the various States, whose equitable distribution of the benefits and patronage of the work among the citizens and laborers of the whole country may prevent it from becoming a political engine or a speculating monster.

RESOLVED, That we further recommend that the said Railroad may commence at some point on the line of the Missouri River, and from thence run westward to the Pacific, over territories under the jurisdiction of the general government; and that one of the earliest measures in connection with the said work be to guard the lands, along the said line of the proposed route, from falling into the hands of speculators, to the future exclusion of the superior rights of the workmen on the road.

RESOLVED, That the said Railroad, when finished, be open to all the world; and that its revenues be kept down at the lowest rates adequate to the current expenses of attendance and repairs. In this connection, we heartily recommend the National Project of George Wilkes, of New York (embracing and enforcing the above views), to the favorable consideration and report of the Committees of Congress, to whose preliminary examination it now stands referred; and subsequently, to the favorable action of the two branches of the National Legislature, to whom the reports of those committees must be made.

SPEECH OF WM. MOSLEY HALL OF NEW YORK.

Mr. President:—In urging these resolutions upon the favorable attention of this Convention, I am actuated by a sincere belief that their affirmative decision will insure results of more importance and greater of advantage to the country than will perhaps attend the decision of any other question that may come within the deliberations of this body.

Though comparatively a new idea, the subject of a Railroad to the Pacific has already been extensively agitated throughout this country; and, indeed, so wide an impression has it already made, that I doubt if there be a gentleman within the sound of my voice who has not given the proposal a share of his attention. As, however, the notice conferred upon it by many may not have extended to an examination of its complete practicability, or to a due calculation of its great national advantages, it may be well to consider both.

The great benefits the proposed work will confer upon the country at large, and particularly upon that portion of it in the name of which we now assemble, are susceptible of easy demonstration. We have but to take a glance at the map of the world to appreciate in a moment the remarkable advantages of our geographical position among nations; and to perceive, at the same time, that this great work will place it in our power to enhance that position into one, not only of commercial preëminence, but of absolute maritime command. Stretching perpendicularly almost from pole to pole, our favored continent lies midway between the two great Oceans. On the east, Africa and civilized Europe confront it with their three hundred millions of inhabitants, while its western coast looks out upon Asia and the Polynesian groups, which, together, are said to teem with six hundred millions more. For ages, it was supposed that these two faces of the Old World were confronted with each other on the opposite shores of one vast ocean, without the intervention of any hemisphere between, and nearly fifty-five centuries elapsed ere man became bold enough in science, and sufficiently reliant upon the conformation of the earth, to plunge into the unknown abyss and to seek to unite them by stretching the white thread of his rudder upon the ocean billow in a direct westward line. That line was at length commenced, however, in the fifteenth century of the present era; but we have seen the Pioneer of Destiny, when half-way to his aim, strand his first hopes in the still brighter future of the discovery of the New World. Though defeated in his attempt to pursue a direct course to India by the interposing barrier of this continent, Columbus still cherished the hope to find some central avenue which would let him through into the Pacific at an advantage over the old routes; and when he died, the great commercial nations took up the enterprise which he had left undone. The efforts of all, however, resulted only in the repeated proof of their futility, and till this day the long-sought-for western route still ends where it was left by the great Genoese in 1492.

These repeated explorations, and the tremendous expenditures which they involved, were made, nevertheless, upon the basis of rational calculations. A substantial experience had proved that whichever nation should forestall the world, in possession of the shortest route to the riches of the East, would win the diadem of commerce and wield the sceptre of the seas. Hence, the great struggle of contending powers for the last four centuries, and the proposal of the most sanguine even to cleave the continent itself to accomplish the design. Indeed, of latter years, though Britain, with commendable enterprise, still despatches her exploring squadrons to the North Pole in the hope of attaining the object even through the Frigid Zone, it has generally been conceded that the direct "westward passage" could only be accomplished by the separation of the Isthmus in the Gulf of Mexico. While, however, this opinion was strengthening itself upon the successsve reports of every new expedition, a mighty reformer came upon the field—a reformer, destined not only to overthrow all theories of physical resistance, but to grapple with the great globe itself, to crush the mountains with a conqueror's step, and make the rugged wilderness more humble to its purpose than the cringing sea. Men paused in their ordinary speculations to wonder at the terrific progress of this young Titan of the latter day. They saw him pluck out the forests, tear up and fling aside the seated hills, and with the rejoicing sons of progress in his train, make way into the body of the continent with the step of a bridegroom going to his chamber, or a prince to occupy his throne. It was then that the grand thought burst simultaneously upon several minds that this mighty agent, who had already made one-half of the continent subject to his power, could also pierce, with equal ease, the other half, and consummate in favor of the new people, for whom he had already done so much, the brilliant hope which had so long possessed the imagination of mankind. The fancied advantages of the Isthmus were forgotten or despised, and the most reluctant were ready to concede that, if the railcar could sail upon the surface of the land with more speed, more safety, and less cost than the ship could navigate the ocean, there was no further need to seek for straits or permeating gulfs to enhance the peril and delay, or to limit our advantages by a tedious deviation to some narrow point.

I have said, Mr. President, that the idea of applying steam and the railway as the agents to complete the Asiatic route which they had already half perfected across the body of the continent, burst simultaneously upon severa minds; and I repeat the assertion, with direct reference to those who have sought to usurp the thought for other purposes than those of a legitimate pride or a justifiable ambition.

The truth is, Mr. President, the man does not live who can come upon this floor and claim the original conception of a Railroad to the Pacific. The thought was the natural and inevitable sequence to the progress of steam; and though by no means general at first, was for a long time as common to the silent speculations of the intelligent as was the idea of applying the new agent to the ocean. The fact is, sir, that, previous to the years 1842-3, all was vague speculation on this subject. We had neither population nor ascertained ports upon the western ocean; and the man who could, under such circumstances, have gravely urged the government to undertake a railroad across two thousand miles of *terra incognita*, filled, as it was thought, with "Antres vast and deserts idle," would have been treated as a visionary; or, if he had talked of undertaking it by himself, he would have incurred the danger of a straight-jacket.

The practicability of a grade for a railroad over the broad and gentle surface which intervenes between the Missouri River and the great South Pass, and the almost equal facility of its continuation beyond that point in angular diversions either north or south to the Pacific, appears to be too well established.to require that I should detain the Convention by the recapitulation of of evidence upon that subject. The high authority of the surveys of Col. John C. Fremont,[*] and the abundant superaddition of testimony of several intelligent private travelers, many of whom are known to members of this Convention, would seem to render such a task, at this time, a work of supercrogation. It may be well, nevertheless, for the purpose of freshening our thoughts upon this important branch of the subject, to take a brief glance at the general topography of the region under consideration.

[*] Fremont's report, which was the first satisfactory demonstration of the facility of the Pass and the route, is dated "Washington, March 1, 1843."

From the Missouri River the traveling distance is estimated at two thousand miles. This immense stretch is divided into two vast sections of nearly equal width, the one commencing at the Missouri River sloping upward to the South Pass, and the section beyond it declining downward to the sea. The highest point in the line is at the Pass, in the centre, which is 5,490 feet above the level of the starting point upon the Missouri, leaving but an average of six feet to the mile to overcome. The greater part of this ascent varies but from 2 1-2 to 9 feet to the mile; two hundred miles has but an ascent of from 16 to 17 feet to the mile; while but a single piece of eighteen miles has a rise of 42 feet to the mile. It will be seen, therefore, that the whole of this first vast section sweeps so gradually to the Pass, that the traveler upon its surface can not distinguish between the true and apparent level; and the culmination at the Pass itself is so imperceptible from the gradual flow and intermixture of the plain, that even the practiced eye of an engineer could not detect it without the assistance of his instruments. The slope westward from the dividing point descends in much the same gradation to the western ocean, but, though it is more capricious in its variations, its feasibility for a railway grade is equally testified to, and, indeed, has been familiarly demonstrated by the fact that it is regularly traveled by the emigrants with their loaded teams. To say that such a route as this is not feasible for a railway grade, is to deny the simplest capacities of science; and to assume that because the road is unparalleled in continuous extent, it is too gigantic for human enterprise, is to insult the spirit of the age.

This, sir, is the road to India! This is the great "western passage" for which contending nations have struggled for centuries, and I am the less inclined to marvel while gazing with awe upon the mighty revolutions it foreshadows, that there have been those who have confounded its stupendous promise with the simplicity of its character, and condemned it as too grand for hope.

This, sir, is the road to India! for it will be perceived, by the time it has stretched to its Pacific outlet, fraternal lines from every branch of the Atlantic slope will converge together to give it an iron grasp of welcome on the banks of the Missouri, which, branches starting thence on equal terms to nearly equal distances, both east and south, will whistle their portions of its Asiatic freight in radiating lines to every part of our vast semicircular border—from Eastport to the Crescent City. Thus, then, do we settle the great problem which has so long puzzled the subtlest genius and most daring energies of man. Starting from the ports of China, we sail across the placid western ocean in twenty days. Embarking next upon the bosom of the land, we double our speed and glide across the vast width of the continent in six days more, and, with ten days left to fill the race, roll out our Indian treasures on the shores of Europe. There will be no more crossings of the equator—no more tedious and perilous weatherings of the Capes. The whole human family, thirty-nine fortieths of whom lie north of the equator, will pursue a direct intercourse with each other around this civilizing belt, and the navies of the world, recalled with commerce to the common line, will have little else to do than drowsily look on at the happy bustle which condemns them to worthlessness and to decay. On the Atlantic, the smallest powers, protected by the general equality, will enter into generous competition with the greatest, while on the Pacific we shall reign alone and be the common carrier for all. From our new cities on the western coast will launch the ships with which no nation will be able to compete by sending rival bottoms round the Capes, while in the centre of a row of bustling ports will sit one giant mart—the mistress of the West—the modern Tyre.

Internally, the benefits of the road will be commensurate with its exterior and national advantages. The dull silence of the wilderness will give place to the sharp buzz of population; towns and thrifty villages will spring up all along its line, and the adjacent wastes, challenged to production by the increased demand, will wave with wheat and corn. The West will then be relieved from its dependence on the Atlantic slope. Its grains will go direct to immense markets of its own, while its pork, its lard and butter, unable heretofore to make two crossings of the torrid zone, will proceed without fear of harm to their destination in the temperate latitudes, without approaching the equator.

It may seem strange, Mr. President, that with this brilliant destiny before us—a destiny which extends its promise alike to every portion of the Republic—there should be those who agitate the almost obsolete idea of the Isthmus route. I can hardly bring myself to believe, however, that a project so unwise and so at variance with our true interests can be seriously entertained; but if it be, I think I may venture to advise its ostensible proposers to abandon it at once. The close-calculating, straight-ahead spirit of our people will never be content to circumnavigate half the continent by a perilous route, when they may go safely straight across it; nor will they consent to the expenditure of some fifty millions in a foreign country and for foreign benefit, when the same amount may be spent among our own people, and secure an avenue within our own control. I have said fifty millions, Mr. President, for it will be seen that to the small, good-looking estimate for the Mexican canal, must be added the advantages we shall be obliged to resign in the treaty with Mexico, to secure from a nation so jealous in regard to territory a right of way which they will be so reluctant to concede.

"But if we should conquer and possess the route?" some gentleman may say in reply. Well, Mr. President, if we should conquer on until we come to South America, I would still lock up the entire line of coast from permeation, and thus insure the course of trade to the direct and consistent parallel of 42°. Why need we deviate an inch to follow the ocean, when the land will serve us better? Why wish to pitch and toss upon the billows, at the rate of ten miles the hour, when we can more safely sail at the rate of thirty and forty and fifty upon the land? Why put to sea on the Atlantic, to strain almost side by side with Great Britain for the same point, and there wait with her and with the whole crowd of commercial customers, our turn to be admitted through?

It has been said, however, that the West will not be forced to the Atlantic coast, but will send its commerce down the Mississippi, and push it through into the Pacific by the Isthmus route. Well, so it may; but if it does, it must send it through sweltering heats and torrid latitudes, and who shall say that the returns of Asiatic stores will get back and ascend the Mississippi with the same facility? Who shall say that the West will then carry for any but herself? The Northern railroad will roll the golden stream of commerce by their doors, but the Mexican canal will confer this advantage upon others, and while it does so, will not only deprive the West of its promise of the carrying-trade, but open a passage in the continent to slip through foreign bottoms to compete with western ships upon the western ocean.*

---

* It may be said that they will not be able to compete with us in this way; but it must be borne in mind, that when this road is opened, the shortness of the canal-passage around the world will increase the carrying capacity of the commercial marine trebly beyond its wants. What before took from four or five months to accomplish, will then require but thirty-six days; consequently, one-third the number of ships can do it. Europe would therefore send her idle bottoms into the Pacific, at the mere cost of navigating them.

Why, sir, this is the rival passage; insignificant, it is true, if the railroad be built, but calculated to postpone the railroad and its advantages indefinitely, and to oblige the United States to maintain, in common with the other powers, tremendous fleets on the pestilential coasts of the Gulf to preserve the integrity of the Grand Canal. Reflect, sir, for a moment, and tell me if, in time of war, we could always hope to remain masters of this passage, or at any rate if we could remain so without cost. This, sir, alone would be enough for me to reject the Isthmus project. We have had enough of war. The world is sick of armies and navies—their pompous shows, their fripperies of rank, their despotic inequalities—and the masses of all nations wish to grasp each other by the hand. It is the interest of a republic, as well as its duty, to aid these aims and foster this fraternal spirit. The railroad will do the whole. It will promote an intercourse that will be its own protection, and the possession of the ponderous gates of commerce which we shall hold on either ocean will enable us, by the mere lifting of our finger, to command peace throughout the world! Peace, or the exclusion of the brawler from the highway of the nations!

This, sir, I conceive to be our proper destiny, and these are a few of the reasons why I claim the route which our Government can control and which will insure to the nation the largest portion of advantage.

With these remarks I shall leave this portion of the subject, but it is not proper that I should conclude it without stating my entire disbelief of the rumor that the strange project of a Mexican canal can be seriously contemplated by our Government. If such a rumor emanates from the Government at all, I am rather inclined to regard it as a cabinet feeler, the whole object of which is to test the public mind as to how far it will answer to "enlarge the boundaries of freedom" in a southerly direction. Indeed, I am disposed to ascribe it to any thing, rather than believe that an administration, which is so extremely sensitive on the constitutionality of National Improvement, should risk burning its fingers by dipping its hands into the treasury of the State, to build a foreign improvement, by foreign hands, in a foreign country, for foreign benefit.

Having satisfactorily ascertained, Mr. President, the perfect practicability of a direct and speedy commercial highway from ocean to ocean across the broad longitudes of this continent, and having also satisfied ourselves of the advantages it will confer upon the country, it now remains for us to ascertain in what manner it may best be done.

There are two methods which have been proposed for the construction and control of this work. One of these propositions is that the road be constructed and owned by private persons for private benefit, and the other that it be built and held by the Government for the benefit of the whole people. The national proposition, which I have taken as the basis of these resolutions, is the proposal of George Wilkes of New-York City; and the proposition that it shall be chartered into a private monopoly on the one hand, and made the subject of a monster contract on the other, are the respective schemes of Dr. Hartwell Carver of Western New York, and Mr. Asa Whitney of Connecticut. I mention them in this connection, that we may examine them in order.

Mr. Carver claims to be the very first man who ever dreamed of a railroad across the Rocky Mountains, and under this impression has suddenly woke up and hurried on the heels of Mr. Wilkes and Mr. Whitney, to demand that the Government should hold its hands from touching the work in its own behalf, and to insist that the rewards and privileges, which Mr. Whitney angles for, belong to him, the petitioner, by a prior right of thought. Actuated by this spirit, he asks Congress to give him "and his associates" an *exclusive* and *perpetual* charter to run a railroad from Lake Michigan to the

South Pass, with branches from that point, through California to San Francisco, and through Oregon to the mouth of the Columbia. He asks, also, a like exclusive charter for an electric telegraph over the same route. He further asks Congress to give him, in fee simple, a belt of land for the track over 3000 miles long; and as an incident to this portion of his demand, he requires stone from the public quarries, timber from the public forests, and iron and lead and other metals from the public mines. He proposes to avail himself of the public mines to the greatest extent, by establishing monster foundries, at various portions of the route, for the manufacture of the rail and other metal works required for the road, and of course for the supply of the populations that would grow up alongside and beyond it. These are the moderate requirements of Dr. Carver's petition, so far as the details of the road are concerned, having finished which, the Doctor winds up by asking the Government to sell to him "and his associates" eight millions of acres of the public lands, at the government price of $1,25 the acre. These 8,000,000 of acres are to be selected by the Doctor, at pleasure, out of any public lands within thirty miles of the line, but instead of paying *money* for them, like any other purchaser, he offers only "scrip," or stock of the road as it becomes finished, remarking, with a really amusing complacency, that this scrip, issued by himself "and his associates," will be "really better than cash down, as no one can tell how much above par it may be when the road shall have been in operation *a few years.*" Unfortunately for Dr. Carver, there happens to be a complete absence in the Constitution of the United States of any provision authorizing the Government to become a party to a stock-jobbing speculation, by taking fluctuating scrip in payment for the People's property. I will not stop at present, Mr. President, to examine all the odious features of Dr. Carver's scheme, as they will come sufficiently in view under the examination of the congenial project of Mr. Whitney; but I may as well add that he denounces both Whitney's and the Government plan, and with much spirit declares that if Congress refuses to grant him his requests he will appeal to the People—"the *common* people," as he calls them—to come out and sustain him.

Mr. Whitney proposes to build the road on a *contract*, the provisions of which will be found to be still more exorbitant than those of Dr. Carver's *charter*. *He* is not satisfied with asking land enough for the track, but asks the Government to grant him a strip of the public domain stretching from the lower point of Lake Michigan in Illinois for 2400 miles to the Pacific Ocean, and for such deficiences as may exist in this strip, by reason of lands already sold out of it, he asks an equivalent in an equal portion of unsold lands in other places, so that he shall be sure to have, at any rate, the full amount of 92,160,000 acres. On this capital of the public domain, with the forests and the quarries and the mines thrown in, he agrees to go to work and build a road, selling the land to produce the means, but retaining for himself and his heirs all that remains unsold after its completion. He offers then, in relation to the subsequent management and control of the work, if Government will allow him to charge one-half per cent per ton a mile for freight for long distances (and his own price for short ones); 20 cents the bushel for Indian corn; $1,25 the barrel for flour, and half the usual railroad price for passage, during the first twenty years after its completion; to carry, in consideration thereof, the public mails, troops, and munitions of war, free of charge; and also to *allow* Congress, after that date, to make an alteration in the tolls.

Strange to say, these enormous and unparalleled demands were favorably reported on by a committee of the Senate, who, on the 31st of July, 1846, brought in a bill of six sections of the most remarkable character, each of which may be said to evince the influences under which it was gotten up, by the fact that it helps to give Mr. Whitney much more than he asks. It is true the second section pretends to provide that the work shall belong to the Government as fast as it is done, but the mockery of the phrase is shown by a "provided always," which winds it up, and which conditions, that if Mr. Whitney "and his associates" shall at any time before or after the completion of the road pay, or secure to be paid, *sixteen* cents the acre for the granted land, then and in that case "the lands, the road, the machinery *and all*, shall belong to him and his associates, and their successors forever." The plain English of this manœuvre seems to be, that the title to the vast domain was thought better in the way of purchase than as a naked grant, and in this view there could be but little objection for a wealthy company to pay, or agree to pay, at their own convenience, *sixteen* cents the acre, for what would cost all other purchasers from five dollars to five hundred dollars the acre, cash down. The same section accepts of the proposal to carry the Government stores free of freight, but in its magnanimity it exacts no conditions from Mr. Whitney in relation to his other customers, but allows him "and his associates" to tax the internal trade and foreign commerce of the nation according to their conscience and their pleasure. The third section of the bill empowers him to enter into contracts with States and companies *to help him build the road*. This is an important provision, for it enables him to supply himself with convict labor from the States and to contract with land companies to furnish him with troops of bonded serfs. The fourth section is devoted to glossing over the grant, and restricts him from receiving the immense windfall except in installments of five miles (by sixty) at a time, for every ten miles of rail laid down, the proceeds of the remaining fives along the railroad being held as a fund, *subject to his order*, when required by him to build the road along the unproductive portion of the route beyond the Missouri. This imposing condition only applies to the rich lands this side of the Missouri, however, and so far from being a restriction, is only a guarantee in his favor, for it merely obliges him to be prudent in throwing his good lands into market, and, after leading him in a shower of gold to the banks of the Missouri, enables him to draw and appropriate all the glittering savings which the friendly restriction had garnered against waste or misappropriation. He may then either put these millions in his pocket and leave the work for Government to finish, or, if he be a man of really comprehensive ambition, he can go on and lay out the bulk of his previous gains to secure a still more monstrous harvest in the future. The fifth section, like the second, lets Mr. Whitney off more easily than he asks in his petition, for, instead of the Commissioners to assist him in selling the lands and signing the titles, which he there so plausibly expresses himself willing to submit to, it only provides for *one* Commissioner, whose salary is to be paid by Mr. Whitney himself, whose indefinite duty it is to *see that every thing goes right*, and to report to Congress once a session—the existence of his office, be it borne in mind, depending entirely upon his reporting *that every thing does go right*. The sixth section performs the last service for Mr. Whitney "and his associates" by removing the objection which mechanics and laborers might have to enter his employ, by the provision that if he fail in his enterprise and leave them in the wilderness without employ, they shall be entitled to preëmption rights to the land, and be subject to pay the United States only the minimum price for the acres. These are the preëmption rights for his laborers of which Mr. Whitney has made such an ostentatious display, but which, as they only accrue in case of his breach of contract, and their discharge, can hardly be considered as tempting to the laborer, or magnanimous on the part of Mr. Whitney. The bill then winds up without requiring any guarantees from Mr. Whitney "and his associates," or establishing any penalties against them for the non-performance of their contract.

These, Mr. President, are the true features of the monster speculating project which Mr. Whitney has for the last year been misrepresenting to the country as a plan in which *he asks for nothing for himself*. In reply to this, sir, I would merely remark, that if to receive a sweep of territory larger than the domain of eight sovereign States, with a railroad in its centre and an ocean front of sixty miles, comprising Oregon City, the mouth of the Columbia, and five or six smaller harbors; if to possess the contracting powers and patronage of an emperor, and to hold the commerce of the world at the mercy of his tariff or tolls, be in Mr. Whitney's estimation *nothing*, I think it highly necessary that Congress, and the People, and this Convention, if he should appear before it, should ascertain, before they confer any favor or power upon him, what may be his idea of the mean circumference of *something*.

I will not denounce this scheme as infamous, Mr. President, but I do denounce it as exorbitant, as sordid, and as dangerous in the extreme; more monstrous as a monopoly, if carried out, than even the British East-India Company, and liable to place our foreign commerce, our domestic trade, and our common interests at the mercy of the secret legislation and the secret political influences of a set of foreign stockholders, whose votes and whose views would be very likely to be predominant in a private corporation of this character. I denounce it as false in its pretensions, if not fraudulent in its motives, and, instead of being calculated to enlarge the capacities of the West, as directly tending to blast its fields with withering land speculations, and to inflame the mind of the whole Nation with a delirium for stock, equal to the fatal intoxication of the South-Sea bubble or the famous Mississippi scheme, which in the beginning of the last century prostrated France and Gt. Britain in financial ruin.

It is no argument for me, sir, nor for this Convention, that these individuals and their plans have been treated in some quarters with public favor, or that they have made great personal efforts to be successful in their aims. Their anxieties and their endeavors must rank with those which men institute to benefit themselves, and the expression of bodies who have not hesitated to declare them both original projectors, without inquiry into the matter at all, only go to show that men who could be so easily deceived as to points of fact, are still more likely to have been misled upon matters of judgment. These results of management and these gimcracks of expression do not weigh with me, sir. I stand here a free man, on the basis of my own mind, and I am determined not to have my individual opinions forestalled or trodden out, by the moccasin-footed approaches of any insidious and deceptive speculations whatever.

Happily, sir, in every unjust exercise of the human thought, there live inherent weaknesses which if seen in time are fatal to the calculations of the subtlest schemers. Such in this case are the undue aims of the monster private projects, and such particularly is the fatal obstacle which the Indian title offers to them both. The land asked for by Dr. Carver and by Mr. Whitney does not belong to the United States in fee, though it claims a particular jurisdiction over it. It is the property of independent nations known as the Indian tribes, whose right to the soil is perfect, and who can not be dispossessed except by treaty or by conquest. Now, though the United States might be disposed to grant to Mr. Whitney or Dr. Carver such public lands as are its own, it can not undertake to give them what belongs to its neighbors. It must first possess before it can dispose, and a very simple knowledge of the constitutional powers of the Government will inform us that it has no right to pledge the exercise of the sovereign attributes known as the war-and-treaty-making powers for a private object and as the incident of a private charter.

The Indian who is driven from his hunting-ground must be located upon other and equally spacious fields of chase. The Great Father must not drive his red children from the graves of their ancestors and the forests which have supplied them and their little ones with food, without a compensation. If he takes from them 92,000,000 of acres for the railroad he must give them the same amount of territory somewhere else. He must likewise give them a liberal consideration to consent to the exchange; he must defray all the expenses arising out of the transmigration and he must send his captains and his men of war to supervise the exodus. I am conjuring no imaginary obstacles, Mr. President, neither am I drawing upon any vague and illusory ideas of philanthropy. I am pointing to a condition of things which the United States have always recognized as just, and as necessary upon the assumption for actual use of Indian territory, and I again insist that the Government has no right to drive out these nations to consumate a charter to a corporation, or to enter into an immense and expensive diplomatic operations with the tribes, to make good a special grant to an individual for individual purposes.

The Government may, however, enter into these arrangements in its own behalf; but though this may not be considered in itself a sufficient reason that it should do so, it places it superior to objections which will prove insurmountable to all other parties, at least for a long period of years.

The idea that Government has not the constitutional capacity to authorize and to build this road over its own territories, is a fallacy which has perhaps but few sustainers except among those interested in the private schemes; but the hostile quibble is shot with very little force, by those, who in another breath and to conceal the heinousness of their own designs, ostentatiously stipulate that "*the road, the machinery and all,*" shall belong to the Government in case they fail to perform some of their gingerbread conditions. Now, Mr. President, if the Government can seize and possess the road, and finish and control it, in case it is first plundered and deceived, it surely can do so without incurring the danger of such mishaps; and I think it will appear equally plain that if the Government has the capacity to furnish to others all the means for its construction, it is perfectly capable of retaining and disbursing them itself in behalf of the Nation.

It is hardly necessary, Mr. President, that I should undertake to vindicate to this Convention the power of Congress to appropriate funds and to undertake a national improvement of this kind, but as constitutional incapacity has been charged, it may be well to show that the enterprise under consideration stands aloof from the scope of any and all of the objections which have been conjured up from time to time against a liberal exercise of the inherent powers of the Government, in the way of expenditure for national objects. It is not liable to the opposition preferred against improvements within the boundaries and between the several States, for it lies beyond the States, on the vast prairie ocean, and in the language of our resolutions, only runs accross the territories under the sole jurisdiction of the General Government. Neither can it be objected that it is sectional in its character, as its advantages would plainly be general and common to the whole Nation.

It has but two exact precedents in the way of expenditure that I now bear in mind, and these are the purchase of Louisiana from France, and Florida from Spain. These countries were paid for out of the national treasury under the clauses of the Constitution which empower Congress "to make regulations of commerce" and to "adopt measures for the general welfare and provide for the common defence." Neither were within the States, but their acquisition was plainly so valuable to all alike, that the Nation willingly consented to the liberal construction of the clauses which sanctioned their purchase from the common fund. The purchase of Louisiana particularly, gave the greatest satisfaction, because its acquisition was necessary to secure a national outlet for the productions of the great valley of the Mississippi, and in this view it is the exact parallel to the National Railroad to the Pacific. The rule that authorized the expenditure in the first case, doubly justifies a similar outlay in the present one, for while the acquisition of Louisiana only secured an avenue to a single section of our broad dominions, the National Railroad will open a new highway to the whole country and the whole world. It comes, therefore, more completely within the commerce clause than even Louisiana; and as a military road for the transportation of troops to Oregon and California, or munitions for the arsenals and fleets that must guard the integrity of our interests in the western ocean, it presents stronger claims upon the provision for "the general welfare and common defence," than both Louisiana and Florida together. But in addition to these *general* constitutional authorizations, Mr. President, we find a special warrant for the work in the clause which empowers Congress "to establish post-offices and post-roads." Under this provision there has recently been authorized by the General Government a monthly mail by steamers through the Gulf, and overland, across the Isthmus to Oregon and California; and who shall say that a government which has a right to lay out routes upon the ocean under the post-road clause, has not an equal right to build a railroad across the land, for the better accomplishment of the same purposes.

Thus fall the hypercritical objections to the constitutionality of the national plan; and the further quibble that Government has no right to engage in such a scheme of revenue or speculation, also finds the ground, by the condition of our third resolution which requires that its revenues be kept down to the measure of its current expenses, in the way of attendance and repairs.

The truth is, Mr. President, the national plan comprehended in these resolutions, is the only constitutional, as it is the only safe and feasible project of the three that are now before Congress; and the only thing which takes the color of an objection to it at all, is the expense it may occasion to the Government at the present time. This objection, however, will be found upon examination to be much less formidable than might be supposed, and when compared with Mr. Whitney's enormous demands upon the national fund, will appear absolutely trifling. According to the estimate of Colonel Abert, the accurate head of the Topographical Bureau at Washington, this road may be built for $20,000 per mile, or twenty per cent less than the average cost of the other railroads of the country, in consequence of its superior facility of grade. This estimate applied to the 1950 miles lying west of the Missouri, makes an aggregate of $38,600,000 for the whole work; whereas, if Mr. Whitney build it on his proposed terms it will cost us in the first place 92,000,000 acres for him, as much more in compensation to the Indians whom he dispossesses, and heavy outlays in cash down to induce the bargain and to secure the peacable transmigration of the tribes. I leave the difference of these two vastly different projects to the intelligence of this Convention; and I also leave it to their intelligence to say, whether a sum, which in the language of the plan of Mr. Wilkes, "is but little more than half larger than that cheerfully incurred by the single city of New York for her Croton aqueduct, shall be an obstacle to a work, which will render all the nations of the earth our commercial tributaries."

Though $38,600,000, Mr. President, is the deliberate estimate of an official inquirer of known scientific accuracy—made with direct reference to the whole character of the route, and in view of all the usual contingencies, we will place the cost at the liberal maximum of $50,000,000. This sum, expended at the rate of ten millions per year for five years, will be the entire cost of the work, and the period named will, probably, be the entire time required to complete it. When, therefore, we compare these calculations with their consequent results, and take into consideration at the same time that the highest sum named is less than has been cheerfully incurred by the country for a single year of war, I think the opposition on the ground of expense may be withdrawn.

The plan upon which it is proposed by Mr. Wilkes that the Government shall construct and control this road, has been ably developed by him in a printed memorial of considerable length, but as its points and characteristics are briefly and comprehensively given in a letter addressed by him to the chairman of a committee of Congress to which numerous petitions in its favor from various parts of the country were referred, I will save the time of the Convention by introducing a copy of that paper. I do this the more willingly as it develops the honorable ground upon which its projector stands, and I beg the Convention to mark the contrast between its pretentions and its sentiments, and the claims and the aims of Dr. Carver and Mr. Whitney:

" NEW YORK, *9th January, 1847.*

"*Dear Sir*,—In taking the liberty of addressing you on the subject of my Memorial for a National Railroad to the Pacific, now before the Committee of which you are chairman, I trust I may be excused by the engrossing interest which the subject holds in my attention. I have been deprived of this privilege for some time by a severe illness, but I now take the first opportunity to add a few words upon one or two points before any final action be taken in the premises.

"It may not be improper at the outset, for me to say to a committee whose attention I am about to request, that I do not appear before them as the advocate of any personal interest, or as the claimant of any special credit. I merely claim, as may perhaps many others, the separate inception of the idea of a Railroad to the Pacific, independent of any other mind, and to have dwelt upon it with enthusiasm as a means of national greatness, long before Mr. Whitney broached his private scheme. Beyond that I claim nothing, save the possession of a sincere desire to see the grand design so carried out as may result most largely to the happiness of our own country, and to that of the whole world. It is with these views that I have assiduously devoted myself to the advocacy of the National Project for the last three years, and it is to these motives that I must trust for an apology for this intrusion upon your committee.

"The main points of my proposal you will find to be: 1st, That the road be built and owned by the Government. 2d, That its construction and control be confided to sworn Commissioners, to be appointed by the State Legislatures or elected by The People of the various States. 3d, That it start from the line of the Missouri River, in the vicinity of the parallel which strikes the South Pass, and thence run westwardly over territories under the jurisdiction of the General Government. 4th, That its revenues be confined strictly to the measure of its expenses of attendance and repairs, and that it be open to foreigners and their merchandise on the same terms as to our own citizens, —the latter result to be secured by regulations of debenture, returning all customs charges on such merchandise on its reshipment. Lastly, that it be built out of the public treasury without any allotment of the public lands for sale for that purpose. This latter consideration I regard as of the utmost importance, and is one of those on which I desired to express myself more fully than I had space to do toward the close of my memorial.

"I believe that any measure that would subject the public lands to the reach and appropriation of speculators, or indeed that would dispose of them to the hands of any but *actual settlers*, would be highly unpopular, and would excite a wide and determined opposition throughout the country. I think therefore that the most just as well as the most satisfactory disposal of these lands, would be to insert a provision in the Bill recommending the road (if such should be the decision of the Committee), securing to each laborer or mechanic who shall have worked upon it for one year, *one hundred acres of land, along or contiguous to the line.* This regulation, instead of making a few rich men richer, would make prosperous landholders of the most deserving poor, and while it conferred a priceless population on the West, would perform the highest achievement of Republican philanthropy, by elevating labor to its true importance in the social scale."

These, Mr. President, are the views which I have introduced into these resolutions, and this is the sublime project, which, whenever developed in contrast with the private schemes, has won the selection of all unbiassed minds. I have, therefore, but little doubt that every member within this arena will make a like recognition of its generous superiority, and decide in favor of a plan capable of conferring the benefits of the "westward passage" upon the country, without depressing labor or plundering the people of the soil; and capable of guaranteeing the civil and financial integrity of the work, by national guardians elected from every State, whose various politics and equal claims to local favor, will secure the work from an invidious distribution of its patronage, or from concentrated political action.

In soliciting for this question the just expression of this Convention, I desire them to bear in mind that upon the weight of their decision may depend the choice of Congress, first between two lines of policy: one of which will confer the commerce of the world upon its proper latitude, and confide the mastery of the oceans and the new avenue to our sole control; and the other of which will divert it to a remote and torrid region for the advantage and the rivalry of others, and the conversion of the surface of the Gulf, into the common battle field of all the navies of the earth. I desire them to bear also in mind that upon their expression likewise may depend the selection of two plans, one of which will fall upon the West and her rising hopes like a withering curse; blighting her whole domain with ruinous land speculations; enmeshing and enslaving every acre with financial ties; cursing her social state with monster monopolies and degraded labor; and rendering the prosperity and personal independence of every man whose foot shall fall west of the Great Lakes, at the mercy of a company, the enormous wealth and gigantic influence of which will stand without a precedent in the history of the world.

The national plan, on the other hand, will guarantee the soil from sudden and wholesale purchase, and preserve it for the homestead of the settler; it will recognize its honorable workers as men and not as serfs; and it will pay them in honest coin and in unshackled land instead of round jackets, shoes, and "orders" upon huge corporation groceries. It will not establish monopolizing foundries to crush out the hopes of individual enterprise, nor will it condemn the land to waste through the continual transfers of infesting land-companies; but it will draw in upon the rich and yielding soil, thousands and tens of thousands of enterprising emigrants whose unfettered competitions will challenge its generous bosom to production, make solitude vocal with the songs of contented labor, and confer upon the rising West a class of free, intelligent, and substantial husbandmen, who will be the chief pride and the chief dependence of the country.

These, Mr. President, are the sublime and patriotic views in favor of which I now ask this Convention to decide; and the opposite and narrow aims to be found in the private schemes, are the blighting evils of which I conjure them in the name of their country, in the name of the West, and by all things sacred to a patriot and lover of his kind, to beware!

PITTSFORD, MONROE CO., N. Y.,
June 23d, 1871.

MY DEAR SIR:—Your kind and good letter of the 17th inst. came duly to hand, and was read with much pleasure I do assure you. My old and long-cherished friend, Dr. Haight,* and your Hon. self, and my humble self makes a *trio* of three of nature's noblemen, which, as Kit Carson told me many years since, "makes a full team, and a horse to let."

I have known the Doctor from a boy, and his father before him.

There are two kinds of noblemen, as I have classed the human family, blooded noblemen and nature's noblemen, and of these two classes I always gave the preference to nature's noblemen, for they were certain while the others were uncertain.

But, sir, after all, 'tis from high life high characters are drawn—*drawn*, and a saint in silk is twice a saint in *lawn*. I can say truly and in presence of my God, that I have always meant to be honest, and give every man his due, and therefore spoke the truth to Dr. Haight in reference to you as helping in the Pacific Railroad, which, as you very truly say, is really one of the most sublime and grandest national improvements of the age. Hurrah for our side and nature's noblemen.

Did I tell you that the Hon. W. H. Seward wrote me two letters before he left on his last long tour, inviting me to accompany him? I met him at San Francisco the last time I was in California. He had been out to Alaska, thence to Oregon, and came up from Portland to San Francisco, and I called on him several times, and he called on me at the Cosmopolitan Hotel after he got better—he was quite sick and feeble when he first arrived.

I have been much pleased at the flattering reception Seward has, and is still receiving, wherever he goes.

Did I tell you that the Prince of Wales drank my health last summer at the close of an address he delivered at the dedication of a college in England? He said, "I will close by drinking the health of my particular friend, Dr. Hartwell Carver." When he was in Montreal, I was at Saratoga Springs, and I went over and staid a week, and he became much attached to me. I have written his mother three letters and have had one from her which I would not take ten thousand dollars for. I attended her birthday in London in 1832. I am now only 83 years old.

Give my kind regards to Dr. Haight, and tell him to write me. You must write often and much. I am old, and can not write readily or often.

Sir, I am most truly yours,
HARTWELL CARVER.

For WM. MOSLEY HALL, Stamford, Conn.

---

* Nathaniel D. Haight, M.D., since deceased; and when he died, Stamford lost an honored citizen, and the poor an inestimable friend.—W. M. Hall.

APPENDIX.

The following letter from the Hon. John M. Botts, was addressed to the Committee of Correspondence, but was not read to the Convention. It was, after the adjournment of the Convention, published by the newspapers in connection with the proceedings:—

RICHMOND, *June 12, 1847*.

My Dear Sir:—Your letter of the 12th May, accompanying an invitation from the Committee on Correspondence, "to attend a North-Western Harbor-and-River Convention, to be held in Chicago, on the first Monday in July next," was duly received, and its not being answered at an earlier day, arose from the earnest hope I had indulged (notwithstanding the distance from home) that I should have been able to accept the invitation, and to have been with you on that interesting occasion in person, as I shall be in feeling and in principle. I am sorry, however, to say that just now it seems to be altogether impracticable.

Nevertheless, at a future day and upon a different theatre, I hope to have it in my power to render you more efficient aid than I could in your proposed Convention. For the subject of these *National Improvements* I have no morbid sensibilities, I labor under no Constitutional difficulties, and I indulge no metaphysical abstractions; for, in my judgment, we should have bestowed very unmerited eulogy upon the wisdom of the illustrious dead, the framers and builders of that godlike instrument to which our Government owes its existence, if they had *neglected* to confer upon the Representatives of all the interests, of all the people in the land, the power to protect the property and lives of those same people, by removing obstructions to navigation, constructing Harbors, and erecting Light-Houses, as well within our own territory as beyond it—as well upon the River-and-Lake navigation as upon the High Seas—as well upon the Mississippi as upon the Lakes—and as well upon the shores of Lake Michigan as upon the Atlantic coast, provided the "*commerce among the several States,*" in the language of the Constitution, should render it necessary and expedient—that they did not neglect, but fully provided for the exercise of this indispensable power, is clear to my mind, and how much more it would have become an enlightened and civilized Government, and how much more our individual and national property would have been advanced by the expenditure of the untold millions in the accomplishment of such works, than for the indiscriminate and wholesale slaughter of a defenceless and unoffending race of semi-barbarians, whose chief cause at last (as will be found) consisted in owning territory that "*must be acquired*" under the guise of "*Indemnity*," is a question that time will determine, and that the people of all classes, and of all parties, will have an opportunity of understanding and appreciating before we get through with, and recover from, the effects of this horrible and most unnecessary and iniquitous war.

Yet it is pretended that He who can make war, after two bloody battles have been fought, communicate its existence to Congress, and thereby himself escape the responsibility; who can, through his subordinates, annex territory and dismember empires, and establish civil governments, succor in citizens by the wholesale, require them to take an oath of allegiance to the United States, try them by a drum-head court-martial, and hang them up in six hours as rebels or traitors, make laws for, and collect customs in Mexico, when by the Constitution it is declared that "*Congress shall have power to make rules concerning captures on land or water,*" when all this can be done with impunity by the one-man power, the people are to be cheated out of their rights and dearest interests, under the shallow pretence that *that* same one man can not find constitutional warrant for affixing his signature, either to a bill passed by the representatives of the people for the payment of what they recognized as a just debt due from the Government, or for another, making appropriations for their own means, for the general improvement and interests of the country, and for the protection and preservation of American life and property; if our Constitution were fairly susceptible of such a reading, what odium would it bring upon its authors, and who would be satisfied to live under it another day?

Without undertaking to decide what does, or what does not constitute an "*Inland Sea,*" as the term is not to be found in the Constitution, nor yet in the celebrated resolutions of '98 and '99 —which are of more importance with some of our distinguished statesmen, I have no hesitation in expressing it as the firm conviction of my mind, that the navigation of the Northern and Western Lakes and Rivers is entitled to the fostering care of Government, and that the interests of that region of country imperatively demand it; and I sincerely hope the day is not distant when it will be obtained.

I should despise myself if I were capable of occupying a position in public life with views so narrow and contracted, as not to see and be willing to administer to the wants of every section of our ever-to-be-cherished Union, with as free and liberal a hand as I would to that where my own more immediate interests were concerned—No! *sections* of the country have no influence over my mind in giving construction to *sections* of the Constitution.

As this letter is designed as an answer to the Committee as well as yourself, you will be pleased to hand it over to them and oblige
Very truly yours,
JOHN M. BOTTS.
S. LISLE SMITH, Esq., and through him to the Committee.

The following letter, from Hon. Daniel Webster, was received by the Committee of Correspondence on the day after the adjournment of the Convention :—

MARSHFIELD, *June 26, 1847.*

GENTLEMEN:—I had the honor to receive, some weeks ago, an invitation signed by you, as a Committee of Correspondence, to attend a "North-Western River-and-Harbor Convention," to be assembled at Chicago, on the first Monday in July, without regard to distinctions of party. If circumstances had allowed me to fulfill my purpose of being in the Western country at this season of the year, I should have complied with that invitation. But events occurred to defeat that purpose.

Understanding that I should not be able to be present, several gentlemen, elected to the Convention, have expressed a wish that I should, nevertheless, communicate my sentiments upon the important objects which have called them together. A willingness to comply with that wish, as well as a desire to treat with just respect the invitation received from you, induces me to address to you this letter.

The improvement of North-Western rivers and harbors has become an interesting subject, not only from the augumented business and population of that part of the country, but also from recent legislative and political occurrences. I do not understand, however, that the North-Western harbor and river improvements are to be the exclusive objects, of that description, which shall engage the attention of the Convention. I take it for granted that those who propose the Convention regard such improvements, all over the Union, as standing on the same ground of constitutional authority, and the same principles of public policy. Although the necessity of making and improving harbors, and for the clearing out of rivers, may be felt to be most pressing at the present moment on the North-Western frontiers, and the greatest disappointment felt in that quarter at the recent and repeated failures of measures adopted by both houses of Congress to provide for such necessity, yet it hardly needs be remarked that the West and the South-West, and the South, the North, and the East, are all deeply interested in the fate of such measures. The question is general, not local. It affects every part of the country, and every State in the Union. Any proceedings, therefore, of conventions, or other public bodies, called to deliberate on such subjects, and to express opinions either on points of constitutional law or public policy, must, to meet my concurrence, be as broad and comprehensive as the questions themselves. They must be such as are fit to be adopted by the government for the good of the whole country, and the equal advancement of the interests of all its parts; and I have entire confidence that no more limited or restricted construction of constitutional power, and no narrower or more local view of public policy, will receive the sanction of the Convention now about to assemble.

Gentlemen, it is an easy task to communicate to the Convention my opinions upon the subjects which are to engage its attention. I have only to refer to my public conduct, to the measures which I have supported, and to my public speeches in and out of Congress for the last twenty years. Full extracts from these speeches I shall now proceed to transcribe. Although this may not be the most interesting or attractive mode of presenting my opinions to the Convention, it will, at least, be attended with one advantage: it will show that my opinions, whatever they are, are not of recent adoption. They have not been recently espoused by me in consequence of any new degree of favor or popularity attaching to the cause of internal improvement. On the contrary, they have been steadily maintained for a long course of years, not only against able and ingenious argument on the opposite side, but also against the most powerful party influences, and the most vehement denunciations of their alleged tendencies toward consolidation.

Nineteen years ago, that is to say, in June, 1828, it pleased the citizens of Boston to give me a public dinner. On that occasion I made a speech containing the extracts which I now transcribe from a printed volume:

"Another subject, now becoming exceedingly interesting, was in various forms presented to Congress at the last session, and in regard to which, I believe, there is substantially a general union of opinion among the members from this commonwealth. I mean what is commonly called internal improvement. The great and growing importance of this subject may, I hope, justify a few remarks relative to it on the present occasion.

"It was evident to all persons of much observation at the close of the late war, that the condition and prospects of the United States had become essentially changed in regard to sundry great interests of the country. Almost from the commencement of the government down near to the beginning of that war, the United States had occupied a position of singular and extraordinary advantage. They had been at peace, while the powers of Europe had been at war. The harvest of neutrality had been to them rich and ample, and they had reaped it with skill and diligence. Their agriculture and commerce had both felt sensibly the benefit arising from the existing state of the world. Bread was raised by our farmers for those whose hands were otherwise employed than in the cultivation of the field, and the seas were navigated by our sailors for account of such as, being belligerents, could not safely navigate them for themselves. These opportunities for useful employment were all seized and enjoyed by the enterprise of the country, and a high degree of prosperity was the natural result.

"But with general peace a new state of things arose. The European states at once turned their own attention to the pursuits proper for their new situation, and sought to extend their own agricultural, manufacturing, and commercial interests. It was evident that thenceforward, instead of enjoying the advantages peculiar to neutrality in times of war, a general competition would spring up, and nothing was to be expected without a struggle. Other nations would now raise their own bread, and, as far as possible, transport their own commodities, and the export-trade and the carrying-trade of this country were therefore certain to receive new and powerful competition, if not sudden and violent checks. It seemed reasonable, therefore, in this state of things, to turn our thoughts inward to explore the hitherto unexplored resources of our own country, to find out, if we could, new diversifications of industry, new subjects for the application of labor at home. It was fit to consider how far home productions could properly be made to furnish activity to home supply; and, since the country stretched over so many parallels of latitude and longitude, abounding, of course, in the natural productions proper to each, it was of the highest importance to inquire what means existed of establishing free and cheap intercourse between those parts, thereby bringing the raw material abounding in one under

The Indian who is driven from his hunting-ground must be located upon other and equally spacious fields of chase. The Great Father must not drive his red children from the graves of their ancestors and the forests which have supplied them and their little ones with food, without a compensation. If he takes from them 92,000,000 of acres for the railroad he must give them the same amount of territory somewhere else. He must likewise give them a liberal consideration to consent to the exchange; he must defray all the expenses arising out of the transmigration and he must send his captains and his men of war to supervise the exodus. I am conjuring no imaginary obstacles, Mr. President, neither am I drawing upon any vague and illusory ideas of philanthropy. I am pointing to a condition of things which the United States have always recognized as just, and as necessary upon the assumption for actual use of Indian territory, and I again insist that the Government has no right to drive out these nations to consumate a charter to a corporation, or to enter into an immense and expensive diplomatic operations with the tribes, to make good a special grant to an individual for individual purposes.

The Government may, however, enter into these arrangements in its own behalf; but though this may not be considered in itself a sufficient reason that it should do so, it places it superior to objections which will prove insurmountable to all other parties, at least for a long period of years.

The idea that Government has not the constitutional capacity to authorize and to build this road over its own territories, is a fallacy which has perhaps but few sustainers except among those interested in the private schemes; but the hostile quibble is shot with very little force, by those, who in another breath and to conceal the heinousness of their own designs, ostentatiously stipulate that "*the road, the machinery and all,*" shall belong to the Government in case they fail to perform some of their gingerbread conditions. Now, Mr. President, if the Government can seize and possess the road, and finish and control it, in case it is first plundered and deceived, it surely can do so without incurring the danger of such mishaps; and I think it will appear equally plain that if the Government has the capacity to furnish to others all the means for its construction, it is perfectly capable of retaining and disbursing them itself in behalf of the Nation.

It is hardly necessary, Mr. President, that I should undertake to vindicate to this Convention the power of Congress to appropriate funds and to undertake a national improvement of this kind, but as constitutional incapacity has been charged, it may be well to show that the enterprise under consideration stands aloof from the scope of any and all of the objections which have been conjured up from time to time against a liberal exercise of the inherent powers of the Government, in the way of expenditure for national objects. It is not liable to the opposition preferred against improvements within the boundaries and between the several States, for it lies beyond the States, on the vast prairie ocean, and in the language of our resolutions, only runs accross the territories under the sole jurisdiction of the General Government. Neither can it be objected that it is sectional in its character, as its advantages would plainly be general and common to the whole Nation.

It has but two exact precedents in the way of expenditure that I now bear in mind, and these are the purchase of Louisiana from France, and Florida from Spain. These countries were paid for out of the national treasury under the clauses of the Constitution which empower Congress "to make regulations of commerce" and to "adopt measures for the general welfare and provide for the common defence." Neither were within the States, but their acquisition was plainly so valuable to all alike, that the Nation willingly consented to the liberal construction of the clauses which sanctioned their purchase from the common fund. The purchase of Louisiana particularly, gave the greatest satisfaction, because its acquisition was necessary to secure a national outlet for the productions of the great valley of the Mississippi, and in this view it is the exact parallel to the National Railroad to the Pacific. The rule that authorized the expenditure in the first case, doubly justifies a similar outlay in the present one, for while the acquisition of Louisiana only secured an avenue to a single section of our broad dominions, the National Railroad will open a new highway to the whole country and the whole world. It comes, therefore, more completely within the commerce clause than even Louisiana; and as a military road for the transportation of troops to Oregon and California, or munitions for the arsenals and fleets that must guard the integrity of our interests in the western ocean, it presents stronger claims upon the provision for "the general welfare and common defence," than both Louisiana and Florida together. But in addition to these *general* constitutional authorizations, Mr. President, we find a special warrant for the work in the clause which empowers Congress "to establish post-offices and post-roads." Under this provision there has recently been authorized by the General Government a monthly mail by steamers through the Gulf, and overland, across the Isthmus to Oregon and California; and who shall say that a government which has a right to lay out routes upon the ocean under the post-road clause, has not an equal right to build a railroad across the land, for the better accomplishment of the same purposes.

Thus fall the hypercritical objections to the constitutionality of the national plan; and the further quibble that Government has no right to engage in such a scheme of revenue or speculation, also finds the ground, by the condition of our third resolution which requires that its revenues be kept down to the measure of its current expenses, in the way of attendance and repairs.

The truth is, Mr. President, the national plan comprehended in these resolutions, is the only constitutional, as it is the only safe and feasible project of the three that are now before Congress; and the only thing which takes the color of an objection to it at all, is the expense it may occasion to the Government at the present time. This objection, however, will be found upon examination to be much less formidable than might be supposed, and when compared with Mr. Whitney's enormous demands upon the national fund, will appear absolutely trifling. According to the estimate of Colonel Abert, the accurate head of the Topographical Bureau at Washington, this road may be built for $20,000 per mile, or twenty per cent less than the average cost of the other railroads of the country, in consequence of its superior facility of grade. This estimate applied to the 1950 miles lying west of the Missouri, makes an aggregate of $38,600,000 for the whole work; whereas, if Mr. Whitney build it on his proposed terms it will cost us in the first place 92,000,000 acres for him, as much more in compensation to the Indians whom he dispossesses, and heavy outlays in cash down to induce the bargain and to secure the peaceable transmigration of the tribes. I leave the difference of these two vastly different projects to the intelligence of this Convention; and I also leave it to their intelligence to say, whether a sum, which in the language of the plan of Mr. Wilkes, "is but little more than half larger than that cheerfully incurred by the single city of New York for her Croton aqueduct, shall be an obstacle to a work, which will render all the nations of the earth our commercial tributaries."

Though $38,600,000, Mr. President, is the deliberate estimate of an official inquirer of known scientific accuracy—made with direct reference to the whole character of the route, and in view of all the usual contingencies, we will place the cost at the liberal maximum of $50,000,000. This sum, expended at the rate of ten millions per year for five years, will be the entire cost of the work, and the period named will, probably, be the entire time required to complete

Gentlemen, five years after the expression of these opinions, that is to say, in July, 1833, I had occasion to repeat them in substance in an address to the citizens of Pittsburg. Extracts from that address, taken from a printed volume, I take the liberty to insert:

"Gentlemen, your worthy mayor has alluded to the subject of internal improvements. Having no doubt of the power of the general government over various objects comprised in that denomination, I confess that I have felt great pleasure in forwarding them, to the extent of my ability, by means of reasonable government aid. It has seemed strange to me, that, in the progress of human knowledge and human virtue (for I have no doubt that both are making progress), the objects of government should so long have been principally confined to external affairs, and to the enactment of the general laws, without considering how much may be done by the government, which can not be done without it, for the improvement of the condition of the people. There are many objects, of great value to man, which can not be attained by unconnected individuals, but must be attained, if attained at all, by association. For many of them, government seems the most natural and the most efficient association. Voluntary association has done much, but it can not do all. To the great honor and advantage of your own State, she has been forward in applying the agency of government to great objects of internal utility. But even States can not do everything. There are some things which belong to all the States, and if done at all, must be done by all the States. At the conclusion of the last war, it appeared to me that the time had come for the government to turn its attention inward; to survey the condition of the country, and particularly the vast Western country; to take a comprehensive view of the whole; and to adopt a liberal system of internal improvements. There are objects not naturally within the sphere of any one State, which yet seemed of great importance, as calculated to unite the different parts of the country to a better and shorter way between the producer and the consumer, to be also of the highest advantage to government itself, in any emergency. It is true, gentlemen, that the local theatre for such improvement is not mainly in the East. The East is old, pretty fully peopled, and small. The West is new, vast, and thinly peopled. Our rivers can be measured, yours can not. We are bounded, you are boundless. The West was, therefore, most deeply interested in this system, though certainly not alone interested even in such works as had a Western locality. To clear her rivers was to clear them for the commerce of the whole country; to construct harbors, and clear entrances to existing harbors, whether on the Gulf of Mexico or on the lakes, was for the advantage of that whole commerce. And if this were not so, he is but a poor public man whose patriotism is governed by the cardinal points; who is for or against a proposed measure according to its indication by compass, or as it may happen to tend further from, or come nearer to, his own immediate connections. And look at the West! Look at those rivers—look at the lakes—look especially at Lake Erie, and see what a moderate expenditure has done for the safety of human life and the preservation of property in the navigation of the lake, and done, let me add, in the face of a fixed and ardent opposition!"

Gentlemen, I pass over what I have said on other occasions in support of measures for river-and-harbor improvements, and in defence of the grounds of right and policy, on which I suppose such measures to rest, and I come to certain recent and most interesting occurrences.

It is well known, gentlemen, that a bill for the improvement of harbors and the navigation of rivers passed both Houses in July, 1846. This bill was disapproved by the President, and his veto message, as it is called, was sent to Congress on the third day of August.

This message, the first of its kind transmitted to Congress by the present President of the United States, may well be supposed to have been drawn up, not only with care, but also upon consultation with his usual advisers, the heads of departments, whose concurrence and support it no doubt received; at least it is not known that any dissent was expressed in the cabinet, or by any of its members; and its doctrines were supported by a majority of the President's friends in the House of Representatives, when the bill was again put to the vote there, according to the forms of the Constitution. It was lost, of course, by the want of concurrence of the votes of two-thirds of the members.

This veto message, as it is the most recent, may also be regarded as the most authentic exposition of the principles and opinions of those leading politicians who are opposed to grants of money for improving harbors and rivers, and for works of similar character.

The message is in everybody's hands, and has, of course, been universally read. It is not my present purpose to comment on it, except so far as to show in what light its doctrines and its character struck me, and how widely it differed from my own opinions.

Three or four months after the defeat of the Harbor Bill by

the veto message, on the 2d day of December, 1846, I made a speech to a meeting of merchants and other citizens of Philadelphia. On that occasion, so interesting a matter as the loss of this bill could not but attract attention. From my printed speech, delivered before that assemblage, I transcribe the following extracts:

"Let us contemplate for a moment the Mississippi. This noble and extraordinary stream, with seven or eight millions of people on its banks, and on the waters falling into it, absolutely calls for harbors, for clearing out rivers, for the removal of *snags*, and other obstacles to safe navigation. Who is to do this? Will any one of the States do it? Can all the States do it? Is it the duty appropriate of any State, or any number of States? No, no, we know it is not. We know that unless this government be placed in the hands of men who feel that it is their constitutional authority and duty to make these improvements, they never will be made, and the waters of the Mississippi will roll over *snags*, and *snags*, and *snags* for a century to come.

"These improvements must come from the government of the United States, or, in the nature of things, they can not come at all; and I say that every steamboat that is lost by one of these *snags*—every life that is sacrificed—goes to make up a great account against this government. Why, what a world is there! What rivers, and what cities on their banks! Cincinnati, New Orleans, St. Louis, Louisville, Natchez, and others that spring up while we are talking of them, or, indeed, before we begin to speak of them—commercial marts, great places for exchange of commodities along these rivers, which are so many inland seas, as it were! And what! the general government no authority over them —no power of improvement? Why, that will be thought the most incredible thing, hereafter, that ever was heard of. It will not be believed that it ever had entered the head of any administration that these were not objects deserving the care and attention of the government. I think, therefore, that the Harbor-Bill, negatived by the President, raises a vital question. This question was put in Congress, it has been put since, it was put at the polls. I put it now to be the question, whether these internal improvements of the lakes and rivers shall be made or shall not be made; and those who say they shall not be made are right to adhere to Mr. Polk, and those who say they shall be made, and must be made, and they will have them made, why, then, they have the work in their own hands, and they, being a majority of the people, will do it. I do not know that we of the East and North have any especial interest in this, but I tell you that we of the East think that we have an especial interest in it. I have thought so, at least, ever since I have been in Congress, and I believe all my associates from Massachusetts have also thought so. We think we have an interest—an especial interest—in manifesting a spirit of liberality in regard to all expenses for improvements of those parts of the country watered by the Mississippi and the lakes. We think it belongs both to our interest and our reputation to sustain improvements on the Western waters."

Now, let us not be carried away by a vague notion that the Constitution of the United States has no power to make internal improvements, and therefore does not authorize expenditures on a harbor. We are speaking of things, not by any general name, not by classification or classes, we are speaking of things by phrases descriptive of the things themselves. We call a harbor a harbor. If the President of the United States says that is a matter of internal improvement, why then I say that the name can not alter the thing the thing is a harbor. And does not every one of these harbors touch navigable waters? Is not every one of them on the shore of the sea, bay, gulf, or navigable river? and are not the navigable waters of the ocean, the gulf, and bays, and rivers, are they not all for commercial purposes, out of the jurisdiction of the States, and in the jurisdiction of the United States?

How can it be said that these are within the particular jurisdiction of the States? Wherever the money is so expended, it is expended within the jurisdiction of the United States, and for the purposes conceded to it by the Constitution, that is to say, the regulation and protection of commerce.

But now let us go to the origin of this power. Let us appeal from the opinions of the President of the United States to the written text of the Constitution, and let us see what that is. The power of the government of the United States in this respect is expressed in the Constitution in a very few words. It says that *Congress shall have power to regulate commerce with foreign nations, and among the several States, and with the Indian tribes!*

The whole force is concentrated in that word, "regulate." Well, Mr. Polk himself admits that the word regulate, as applied to facilities for foreign trade, does extend to the making of beacons, piers, and light-houses; but his whole message attempts to run a distinction between foreign trade and trade between the States.

But the power over each is given in the same clause of the Constitution, in the very same words, and is exactly of equal length and breadth with the other. If one is denied, both are denied; if one is conceded, both must be conceded. It is impossible to separate them by any argument or logical process worthy of the statesman's mind. It is wholly arbitrary, I say, without the least foundation, to say that Congress may make provision for a harbor accommodation for foreign commerce, and not for domestic trade. Is the latter not as important as the former? Is not the breakwater at the mouth of the Delaware Bay as important for the trade of Philadelphia with New Orleans as with Liverpool? and so everywhere else? Is not our coasting-trade one of the largest branches of our maritime interest, and can we yet do nothing for that?

It is strange that any man should entertain the idea that such a distinction could be drawn. I have before me a long list of acts of Congress, of a good deal of importance, as I think, tending to show that the President is mistaken when he speaks of the acquiescence and approbation of the people in opinions adverse to Harbor improvements. The opinion both of Congress and the people seems quite the other way.

Gentlemen, I now propose to quit this question. In the free discussions that have taken place on it, in and out of Congress, the argument is exhausted. The question is, Whether we are convinced, and whether we are to stand up to our convictions? The question is, Whether the great West, so important a part of the country, bearing its share of all the common burdens, is to be struck out of all participation in the benefits which are bestowed upon other portions of the Union? I think not. The question is put already. I expect to hear an answer to it from the North, North-West, and the South. But, then, I do not rely upon conventions at Memphis, at St. Louis; I do not rely on resolutions. I rely on the disposition of the people to understand what their constitutional rights are, and then to take care that those constitutional rights shall be fairly protected, by being intrusted to proper hands.

But, before I entirely leave this part of the subject, I must say a word upon an important report made to the Senate at the last session, by a committee to whom the resolutions passed by the Memphis Convention were referred. A distinguished Senator from South Carolina (Mr. Calhoun) was chairman of the Committee, and framed that elaborate report. So far as he admits any thing done by Congress to have been rightfully done, and admits any degree of authority in Congress to do what has not yet been done, I concur with him. The rest I reject, for I do not think the distinctions taken by that eminent man are sound. I regret that it is my misfortune to differ with him.

The report proposes, I may state in brief, that where a river divides two States, or only two States are concerned, these two States must make the necessary improvements themselves. I do not agree with that; I do not suppose that it is any matter of consequence whether the necessary improvements are connected with two States, or four, or only one.

It is not a question of location—it is a question of public importance. Look, for instance, at that portion of the North River which runs between two shores, both of which belong to New York. There, I suppose, the power of Congress over Governor Marcy's overslaugh farm, as it is called, is as perfect as it is to make a similar improvement further down, where the river divides the States of New York and New Jersey. The distinction attempted, as it strikes me, is a distinction without a difference.

Well, having thus alluded, in the most respectful manner, to the report of the Committee of the Senate, and not having time to discuss its propositions at any considerable length, I will now, by way of conclusion, give you my opinion on all this question of the power of making harbors. In my opinion, Congress has the power to make harbors on the rivers and the lakes, to the full extent to which it has ever proposed to exercise such power.

That, whether these proposed harbors be judged useful for foreign commerce, or only for commerce among the States themselves, the principle is the same, and the constitutional power given in the same clause and in the same words.

That Congress has power to clear out obstructions from all rivers suited to the purposes of commerce, foreign or domestic, and to improve their navigation and utility by appropriations from the treasury of the United States.

That, whether a river divides two States or more than two, or runs through two States or more than two, or is wholly confined to one State, is immaterial, provided its importance to commerce, foreign or domestic, be admitted.

For instance, the North River is a navigable, tide-water river for many miles, while running entirely within the territory of the State of New York. Yet I suppose the removing of obstructions in this part of the river is as fully within the power of Congress as the removing of obstructions in the other parts of the river, where it divides New York from New Jersey.

I think it wholly immaterial whether a proposed improvement in a river for commercial purposes be above or below an actual existing port of entry.

If, instead of clearing out the rocks, and in that manner improving the channel of a river, it is found better to make a canal around falls which are in it, I have no doubt whatever of the power of Congress to construct such a canal. I think, for instance, that Congress has power to purchase the Louisville Canal around the Falls of the Ohio, and that it ought to exercise that power now, if the work can be purchased at a reasonable price; and that the canal should then be free to all who have occasion to use it, reserving such tolls only as should be sufficient to keep the works in repair.

It seems to me that these propositions all flow from the nature of our government, and its equal power over trade with foreign nations and among the States, and from the fact resulting from these powers, that the commerce of the United States is a unit.

I have no conception of any such thing as seems to be thought possible by the report of the Committee of the Senate, that is, an external commerce existing between the two States, carried on by the laws and regulations of their own, whether such laws and regulations were adopted with or without the consent of Congress.

I do not understand how there can be a Pennsylvania vessel, built, manned, and equipped under Pennsylvania laws, trading as such Pennsylvania vessel with New York or Maryland, or having any rights or privileges not conferred by acts of Congress; and, consequently, that the idea is unfounded which supposes that when only two States are interested in the navigation of a river, or its waters touch only the shores of two States, the improvement of such river is excluded from the power of Congress, and must be left to the care of the two States themselves, under an agreement which they may enter into, with the consent of Congress, for that purpose.

In my opinion, the provision of the Constitution which forbids a State from entering into any alliance, compact, or agreement with another State, without consent of Congress, can draw after it no such conclusion as that, with the consent of Congress, two States ought to be bound to improve the navigation of a river which separates their territories; and that, therefore, the power of Congress to make such improvements is taken away. A river flowing between two States, and two States only, may be highly important to the commerce of the whole Union. It is sufficient to say that the whole argument is founded on the notion that the Constitution prohibits *more* than two States from entering into agreements, even *with* the consent of Congress.

This is manifestly untenable. The Constitution extends as fully to agreements between three, four, or five States, as between two only; and the consent of Congress makes an agreement between five as valid as between two. If, therefore, two States can improve rivers with the consent of Congress, so can five or more, and if it be a sufficient reason for denying the power of Congress to improve a river in a particular case, that two States can themselves do it, having first obtained the consent of Congress, is an equally valid reason in the case where five or ten States are concerned. They, too, may do the same thing with the consent of Congress. The distinction, therefore, between what may be done by Congress where only two States are concerned with a river, and what may be done in cases where more than two are so connected, entirely vanishes. I hold the whole doctrine of the report of the committee on this point to be unsound. I am also of the opinion that there is no difference between the power to construct a pier and the power to construct a harbor. I think that a single pier of itself affords a degree of shelter and protection from winds and seas; that two parallel piers make a harbor; and that, if one pier may be rightfully constructed, it is no extravagant stretch of constitutional power to construct another. In fine, I am of opinion that Congress does constitutionally possess the power of establishing light-houses, buoys, beacons, piers, breakwaters, and harbors on the ocean, the Gulf, the lakes, and the navigable rivers; that it does constitutionally possess the power of improving the great rivers of the country, clearing out their channels by deepening them or removing obstructions, in order to render navigation upon them more safe for life and property; and that, for the same reason, Congress may construct canals around falls in rivers, in all necessary cases.

All this authority, in my opinion, flows from the power over commerce, foreign and domestic, conferred on Congress by the Constitution; and if auxiliary considerations or corroborative argument be required, they are found in two facts, *viz.:* 1st. That improvements such as have been mentioned, whether on the ocean or the Gulf, on the lakes or the rivers, are improvements which, from their nature, are such as no single State, nor any number of States, can make, or ought to be called on to make. All idea of States undertaking such improvements is, in my opinion, preposterous. And, in the second place, as all the revenues derived from commerce accrue to the general government, and none of it to the States, the charge of improving the means of commerce and commercial intercourse, by such works as have been mentioned, properly devolves on the treasury of that government, and on that treasury alone.

I shall not trouble you, gentlemen, with any farther reference to opinions expressed by me on the subject of Harbor-and-River Improvements.

Every successive year, and, I may say, every successive month, strengthens and confirms these opinions, and I feel now, as I have always felt, that in the end they must prevail, and that end, I think, approaches. At the last session of Congress, a Harbor bill, similar in principle to that of the preceding session, passed both Houses of Congress, but it passed within the last ten days of the session; the President saw fit to retain it, as he had the power of doing, without approving or returning it, and, of course, it did not become a law. I suppose there is no doubt that the repeated loss of this great measure, by the refusal of the executive government to co-operate in it, has been the immediate cause of the calling of the Convention at Chicago. I wish all possible success and favorable results to the deliberations of that Convention. It may, I trust it will, do much good. It may hasten the triumph of a cause which is most assuredly destined to triumph. A great majority of the people are satisfied that the power to make these improvements does exist in the government of the United States, and that it is the bounden duty of the government to exercise that power. The will of the people is ascertained, it can not be doubted, and it will prevail. Not to mention other cases, I ask if any one imagines that an enlightened community will long consent that the shipping and commercial accommodations of the City of Buffalo shall be pent up in the narrow dimensions of Buffalo Creek? or does any one suppose that any government, or any administration, can receive any support and confidence, which refuses all Harbor Improvements to the City in which the Convention is now to assemble? Chicago, a commercial place of recent origin, is already a large city. It is the seaport of Illinois. It is now accessible by vessels from the Atlantic Ocean. It is also on a great line of internal communication from Boston and New York to New Orleans; shall it have no convenient harbor? Shall it be able to afford no safe refuge for property and life from the storms which vex the lake?

You have been pleased, gentlemen, to call a Convention without regard to the distinctions of party. I am glad of it. I am glad to find that it is believed that persons belonging to a party which heretofore, as a party, has strenuously opposed Harbor Improvements, are now ready to join in measures for their support. I have no doubt that this is true. I have no doubt, especially, that among the younger part of our fellow-citizens, who have not been, in times past, hopelessly committed on these subjects, a just and unprejudiced opinion is fast making its way. The truth is, that of the two great parties which have divided the country, one has been for Internal Improvements, and one against them; but in this latter party individuals have been found, principally, I believe, from the Western and North-Western States, who have voted for such improvements, and thereby created a majority in their favor in the House of Representatives, against the general voice of their party, and against the wishes and vetoes of the executive government. Broad and deep as has been the division of parties, yet these individuals have felt constrained, by a sense of duty and a clear conviction of what the public good requires, to reject the force of party ties, and vote with their opponents. This conduct is patriotic and honorable, and, I hope, will be imitated by others. Indeed, I should rejoice to see that which has so long been a party question become a national question, and a question which shall have but one side to it. I should rejoice to see no difference of opinion on a topic of such vital and general interest. This, however, I may perhaps not see; but I shall see, I am sure, the cause of Internal Improvement triumph by decided majorities. I shall see the Lake Harbors improved, and new ones constructed;. I shall see the noble rivers of the West cleared of their obstructions; I shall see the great internal interests of the country protected and advanced by a wise, liberal, and constitutional exercise of the powers of the government.

In laying this communication before the Convention, I pray you, gentlemen, to tender to its members my personal regards, and I pray you also to accept for yourselves my respects and good wishes. DANIEL WEBSTER.

To Messrs. N. B. Judd, E. W. Tracy, Thomas Hoyne, Wm. B. Ogden, S. J. Lowe, G. W. Meeker, and W. L. Whiting, Committee.

The remarks of Mr. Spencer of New York, on the introduction of the report of the Committee on Resolutions, contain the only formal exposition of the views of the Committee which were presented to the Convention, and are necessary to a full understanding of some of the propositions submitted. With the advice of numerous Delegates, the Committee on the publication of the proceedings have concluded to insert those remarks in the Appendix, believing they would thereby render an acceptable service to those interested in the subject, and would not depart from the spirit of the resolution appointing them.

They are informed by Mr. S. that in preparing them for the press, he has adhered as closely as his memory would permit to the chain of argument presented to the Convention; but that he has amplified with such illustrations as he thought would be useful, and which he was prevented from presenting to the Convention by the state of his health and by his unwillingness to detain the Delegates.

Remarks of John C. Spencer.

John C. Spencer of New York, rose after the reading of the report of the Committee on Resolutions, and addressed the Convention substantially as follows:

After thanking the members of the Convention for the cordial and flattering welcome they had given him, Mr. Spencer said he would not abuse their kindness by protracted remarks beyond what the occasion seemed to require. Some of the propositions reported required explanations, while others contained assertions, the proof of which should be exhibited before they were sanctioned by this meeting, and the general result of the whole series should be stated and illustrated. This duty he would now undertake.

He would assume that every one who heard him was acquainted with the language of the Constitution of the United States; instead of quoting it, he should, in most instances, merely refer to the clause bearing upon the matter under consideration. The question which he should first examine related to the constitutional power of Congress to appropriate the common funds of the people of this Union to the improvement of the navigation of the lakes and navigable rivers of the interior, so as to facilitate the existing commerce among the States, and to open new avenues and channels for that commerce.

A stranger, unacquainted with the disputes which have arisen, would be struck with surprise at the existence of a doubt whether any human government could be so badly constituted as to be incapable of applying the means at its disposal to the protection and maintenance of any essential interests of the community for whose benefit it was instituted. The exchange among themselves of the products of a people inhabiting different climes, cultivating different soils, and employed in occupations of almost infinite variety, would naturally be supposed to be the very first object of any government established by such a people. That exchange being dependent wholly upon the facilities of transportation, the end to be attained can be effected only by creating or improving such facilities. To suppose a government framed deliberately by a people in such manner as to deprive it of a power possessed by every other government on the face of the earth—a power to enable its citizens to reach a market with the products of their industry, and to return with the exchanges of other portions of their country and of foreign lands—would be imputing a degree of fatuity to our ancestors—to the strong heads and full and brave hearts that carried us through our revolutionary struggle, which no descendant of theirs ought to be willing to acknowledge; and yet this is our precise condition in relation to internal trade, unless the power referred to is vested in the federal government. I speak now of that internal trade which is described in the Constitution as "commerce among the States," and which requires for its regulation the concurrence of two or more States The prohibition in that instrument, that "no State shall enter into any treaty, alliance, or confederation" (section 10, article 1), would apparently interpose an insuperable obstacle to any preliminary treaty to secure the necessary concurrence. There is an apparent conflict between this and another prohibition of the same instrument, that "no State shall, without the consent of Congress, enter into any agreement or compact with another State" (same article, section 2, sub.). This last clause, however, can not be supposed to have intended that any States could, by compact, even with the assent of Congress, exercise jurisdiction over subjects already expressly vested exclusively in that body. Thus it can not be that two or more States could by compact regulate commerce with foreign nations; and especially for the reasons which will subsequently appear, the framers of the Constitution could not have been willing to throw such an apple of discord as to allow them to regulate commerce among the States; a power which was carefully withheld for most powerful reasons. It doubtless refers to those agreements which execute themselves, and do not look to future coöperation, which would be an alliance. Questions of boundary, or relating to common fisheries, or other common property, might with propriety be amicably settled by the States interested. But still the assent of Congress was required as a check upon any attempt to "form an alliance or confederation." As any agreement to regulate commerce among themselves would necessarily require an alliance for their common protection, such an agreement would fall within the absolute prohibition of the Constitution. And if it fell within the other clause, which it does not, still the independent power of the State is effectually denied by requiring the permission of Congress. But the views already presented, it is presumed, sufficiently show that it is impossible there could be even a contingent concurrent power over a subject that from its nature required exclusive control by the general government. We may safely conclude, therefore, that all power over foreign commerce, or commerce among the States, is absolutely prohibited to the States.

Since, then, it has been shown that the power in question ought to be possessed by some one of the two governments under which we live, and that it is not vested in the state governments, we are furnished at the threshold of the inquiry with the fair presumption that it does exist in the federal government. An investigation of the history of the debates in the Convention that formed the Constitution affords the most satisfactory evidence that the power was intended to be given to that government in the broadest amplitude declared by the propositions under discussion. Whoever reads those debates will find that the power to lay and collect imposts, given to Congress, and the denial of that power to the States, except for special purposes (and even then to pay the proceeds to the national treasury), were considered in connection with the power to regulate commerce, and that the limitations of the latter were intended to correspond exactly with the former; in other words, that by the clause to regulate commerce it was intended to give to Congress an authority commensurate with the means, and to impose a duty in the application of those means correspondent with the objects which it was supposed the several States would seek to promote if they retained them.

The ground on which it was proposed to vest in Congress the exclusive power to levy imposts were, 1st. To secure a uniform rule by which foreign trade would be governed; 2d. To prevent conflicts among the States; 3d. To obviate the danger of the Atlantic States taxing the Western and interior States, by imposing duties on goods passing through them, in order to promote their own interests at the expense of their neighbors; and it was particularly mentioned that there was danger of the Atlantic States opposing the improvement of the navigation of the Mississippi. This last view was pressed particularly by Gouverneur Morris, a delegate from New York. Mr. Clymer, from Pennsylvania, objected to the grant of all the revenues derived from imposts to the federal government, because he thought "the encouragement of the Western country was suicide on the part of the old States." This discussion, and particularly the last remark, indicate, with the clearness and force of concentrated sunbeams from heaven, the objects and motives of the men who formed our Constitution. They had themselves passed through the perils of the Revolution, and the equal perils of the Confederation. They knew what were the future dangers to be apprehended. They were unwilling to subject their offspring and their brethren, who should emigrate to the West, to the tyranny and oppression of the old States; but determined, in the spirit of liberality which common suffering had produced, that the American people, whether at the West or at the East, should be one—one out of many—one out of many in interest, one in affection, in protection, and one in glory and honor. They resolved, by an overwhelming vote, that the revenues derived from imposts should be placed, in trust for the whole, in the hands of the general goverment; and to enable it to apply those and all other general funds, they gave to the same government the power "to regulate commerce with foreign nations and among the States"; and the occasion and manner of giving this power, as well as the arguments for and against it, demonstrated *what they meant* by "commerce among the States."

There are other facts and occurrences in the debates which confirm this conclusion; but I am unwilling to detain you by quoting them, and prefer to let the great incident which has been quoted stand out in all its strength and force, as a landmark of the Constitution.

In seeking for the meaning of the framers of the Constitution in the use of the term, "regulate commerce," we have a right to interpret it as it has ever been understood in all treaties, laws, and public documents; and that interpretation has universally given to the word "regulate" the utmost latitude of power, and the most complete control of the subject, which any other word or set of words in the language can impart. In this sense it was familiar to those who thus used it.

Another source of construction is to be found in the acts of the government, particularly when it was composed of those wise and good men who had been members of the Convention. Exactly one month after the government began under the Constitution, namely, on the 7th of April, 1789, an act was passed by Congress, and approved and signed by Washington, "for the establishment of light-houses, buoys, beacons, and public piers," which directs that such of the said works as had been constructed by the States should be maintained by the federal government; and it authorized a new light-house. The further history of legislation on those subjects I propose to give in the language of a departed president, General Jackson, in his message of December, 1830: "The practice of defraying, out of the treasury of the United States, the expenses incurred by the establishment and support of light-houses, beacons, buoys, and public piers, within the bays, inlets, and harbors, and ports of the United States, to render the navigation thereof safe and easy, is coeval with the adoption of the Constitution, and has been continued without interruption or dispute."

Such, then, are the facts of the case; such has been the

unvaried construction of the power to "regulate commerce." To what respect and confidence is it entitled? I prefer again to give you the answer in the language of General Jackson, in his message returning the Maysville-Road Bill: "For although it is the duty of all to look to that sacred instrument (the Constitution) instead of the statute-book, to repudiate at all times encroachments on its spirit, which are too apt to be effected by the conjuncture of peculiar and facilitating circumstances, it is not less true that the public good, and the nature of our political institutions, require that individual differences should yield to a well-settled acquiesence of the people and confederated authorities in particular constructions of the Constitution on doubtful points. Not to concede this much to the spirit of our institutions would impair their stability, and defeat the objects of the Constitution itself." I do not quote this because it is new or extraordinary, but because, coming from such a man, whose heart was always in the right place, whatever may have been the errors of his head, who will not be suspected of any disposition to latitudinarian doctrines, it may be received with more confidence by many than if the same sentiment had been quoted from other eminent statesmen and writers.*

We have now seen the construction given to this power "to regulate commerce" in its application to harbors on the rivers of the Atlantic coast. We claim the same construction of the same power in favor of harbors on the interior lakes and navigable rivers, upon the ground that such harbors are necessary to "com-

---

* At a subsequent period of the proceedings of the Convention, a delegate offered a resolution declaring the necessity of amendment to the Constitution, to enable Congress to make appropriations for "internal improvements;" and stated that it was taken from the same message of General Jackson, in relation to the Maysville Road, which has already been quoted from by Mr. Spencer. To which Mr. Spencer replied that the message referred to was the veto of a bill making appropriations for a *local turnpike*, and that it was in reference to *such* internal improvements that General Jackson deeemed an amendment to the Constitution necessary, but that his suggestion was not intended to apply to appropriations for objects connected with commerce among the States.

In further illustration of the point of difference, it is proper to observe, that in his message of December, 1830, General Jackson states explicitly that he should not withhold his assent to bills making direct appropriations for light-houses, beacons, piers, etc., upon navigable rivers and harbors within collection districts established by Congress, and where, of course, ports of entry would be located. The existence of a collection district, established in good faith, would be evidence of foreign commerce, or commerce among the States, being carried on from the ports of such district, so that vessels would be registered, or enrolled, and licensed there. And thus it will be seen that his idea of the meaning of the power to regulate commerce among the States was really the same with that maintained in the remarks of Mr. Spencer, and in the propositions of the Convention.

merce among the States." There is nothing in the terms of the grant to justify any difference; and the only question is, What is "commerce among the States?" I have endeavored to show what the framers of the Constitution intended, and what must be comprehended within the term, in order to carry out their design of applying the means derived from imposts to the equal benefit of the interior States; and that, unless the power to improve the means of commercial intercourse between two or more States be given to the federal government, it exists nowhere. The inference, then, seems irresistible and conclusive, that such power is vested in Congress, and that its limitations are to be found in those provisions of the Constitution which forbid alliances between States, or, in other words, that where all authority on the given subject is denied to the States, by denying to them the modes of action essential to its exercise, or where no one State has the requisite jurisdiction over the locality, or over the incidents essential to the contemplated improvement, then it results, of necessity, that the authority must be exercised by the general government. Again, as expressed in the second proposition reported by the committee, wherever the expense of the undertaking ought to be equitably borne by two or more States, it would be fairly within the scope of the power given to Congress. Still, the contemplated undertaking should be such as to form a link in the chain of communication between two or more States. Every improvement or facility to commerce must necessarily be local; a light-house or a pier must be at some place, and that place must be within some State or Territory. Its locality in itself does not necessarily determine its purpose; that is to be ascertained from the circumstances of its position in reference to communications between and among different States. And a sound judgment, aided by common honesty, will encounter no greater difficulties in determining upon the facts of the case, what is the fair and legitimate purpose of the proposed improvement, than such as must be met in legislating upon any subject within the competency of Congress; and, being thus eminently and peculiarly a question of fact, its determination appropriately belongs to the legislative department of the government, which possesses the means of ascertaining the facts. But, in truth, the disputes respecting the extent and limitation of this power have been theoretical rather than practical, and have arisen from dealing more with words than with things. Let it be our object to bring the discussion back to the few elementary principles and the plain facts upon which alone it should be considered.

There are some collateral facts and considerations to strengthen and confirm the conclusion that the power to "regulate commerce among the States" authorizes appropriations for the improvement of harbors and the navigation of rivers in the interior, when such improvements fall within the limitations already mentioned. One of these is the fact that the federal government has established light-houses at various points on the lakes and at the mouths of rivers emptying into them, and that this has been done without a murmur of objection from any quarter, in or out of Congress, of any want of constitutional authority. This authority can be derived only from the power to regulate commerce, for there is no other that has any connection whatever with the subject. The authority to exercise exclusive legislation over places ceded by the States for forts, magazines, and other needful buildings, is not an authority to erect such buildings, but proceeds on the assumption that such authority already existed. It therefore gives no power for the building of light-houses; but it does contain a most important implication, namely, that Congress may authorize the erection of forts, magazines, and other needful buildings, although no explicit power for that purpose is to be found in the Constitution. The practice of the government from its foundation, "without interruption or dispute," under the power "to dispose of and make all needful rules and regulations respecting the territory and other property of the United States," has a conclusive bearing upon the question. Under this power money and land have been appropriated to construct roads, clear out rivers, connect streams, and in various ways to improve communications through the territories; and one of the latest acts of the kind appropriates land to the amount of $700,000 to connect the Wisconsin and Fox Rivers. Now, it is very true that the federal government, as a great land proprietor, is bound to enhance the value of its own property by improvements, and it would be monstrous if it did not possess the power. Still we are bound to inquire, In what part of the Constitution is such power found? It is to be found only in the clause quoted, "to make needful rules and regulations;" for a grant of money from the treasury for such purposes can not, without violence to all reasonable construction, be considered an act under the power "to dispose of" the territory or other property.

Another consideration in favor of the construction for which we contend, arises from the acts of the federal government in extending its jurisdiction, for other than revenue purposes, over the interior rivers and lakes. I have never heard a doubt expressed, and certainly none was intimated in Congress, of the constitutionality of the act of 1838, to provide for the security of the lives of passengers on board of vessels propelled by steam. By this act, steam vessels navigating the sea, or the lakes Champlain, Ontario, Erie, Huron, Superior, and Michigan, which are specifically named, or any bays, lakes, rivers, or other navigable streams of the United States, are required to be inspected by officers appointed under the authority of the United States, and to take out licenses from them, and are subject to forfeiture and heavy penalties for violating the provisions of the law. No one will doubt the wisdom, nay, the obsolute necessity, for such a law, a necessity arising not only from the ignorance and recklessness of those having charge of steam vessels, but a still stronger necessity that such a law should be passed by the federal government, and enforced by its tribunals, arising from the utter inability of the States separately to regulate the subject. And here is a remarkable instance and proof of the extent which must be given to the power "to regulate commerce among the States," in order that the general government may fulfill the duties and perform the functions for which it was created.

A similar instance is furnished by the more recent act of 1845, giving jurisdiction to the district courts of the United States in matters of contract and tort, "arising in, or upon, or concerning steamboats and other vessels of twenty tons burden and upward, enrolled and licensed for the coasting-trade, and at the time employed in business of navigation and commerce between ports and places in different States and Territories, upon the lakes and navigable waters connecting such lakes." Here is a description of commerce among the States essentially like that for which we contend, and here is an assertion of the authority of the United States to exercise admiralty and maritime jurisdiction over that commerce. The difficulties and embarrassments experienced by the United States courts in enforcing contracts, and punishing wrongs and trespasses made or committed in the cases described, are familiar to professional men; and it is equally well known that the State courts were totally inadequate to afford any remedy in that class of cases. And this law may also be cited as a most happy illustration of the extent of the meaning of the power under which it was enacted, of regulating commerce among the States.

There are other instances of the exercise of similar jurisdiction, particularly the laws requiring hospital money from mariners navigating the lakes and interior rivers, but it is not deemed necessary to dwell on them.

Here, then, we take a position which we believe to be impregnable. By these acts, the absolute necessity of which is undeniable, the federal government has asserted, and rightfully maintained, its jurisdiction over that "commerce among States" which we contend is within the grant of the power of Congress. This jurisdiction has been actually exercised by its courts, without question or dispute, and no one has had the hardihood to question the constitutionality of these laws.

If, then, Congress may thus regulate commerce among the States in these various modes, by what authority and under what pretext shall its power be circumscribed to these modes, and prevented from operating in any other mode of regulating the same commerce? Those who would maintain such a limitation of the power of Congress must be driven to the point of denying the constitutionality of the laws quoted, and thus rendering our whole form of government "a mockery, a delusion." And to the federal government have we not a right to say, you have gone too far in regulating commerce among the States to recede from your position, or to justify you in refusing to advance in the same line, as far as the exigencies of the subject and the paramount interests of the people require. You are precluded by your own acts. You have acknowledged this commerce among the States to be a national subject; you have "regulated" it as such in various modes, and, to be consistent, you must proceed in your regulation to afford the necessary facilities to that commerce, or you must renounce the jurisdiction you have assumed, and leave the citizens of the United States in a worse condition than that in which they were at the adoption of the Constitution.

Here, then, I rest the argument in favor of the power of Congress to regulate our internal commerce by granting it facilities to the full extent already indicated. Such a power is absolutely necessary to the well-being of any people; it is not possessed by the States; it ought to be vested in the federal government; the framers of the Constitution intended so to vest it; the government itself has received and exercised it with the sanction of the whole people, in a manner that defines its extent; and the whole legislation of Congress upon the most important rights and interests of the citizens must be overturned, and the direst anarchy and confusion must ensue, if the principle be abandoned.

But I am not disposed to leave our adversaries in possession of ground which they have appropriated to themselves, as I believe, unwarrantably. They vindicate the appropriations made for the improvement of harbors and rivers on the Atlantic coast, on the ground that it is legitimately within the power to regulate commerce with foreign nations, because such commerce is national, and they deny this character to commerce among the

States. But we maintain that whatever subject is within the jurisdiction of the federal government, is, by the very fact, national; that the union of the States is national, not only in its relations to foreign countries, but equally so in its relations to the several States; and it would by no means follow that a subject ceased to be national by its want of connection with our foreign commerce. The conclusion does not flow from the premises; but the premises are unsound. Foreign commerce consists of two parts, imports and exports, and, *ex vi termini*, exports not only constitute a portion of foreign commerce, but are the elements by which alone it can be conducted.

Upon what principle will you stop short in the protection of foreign commerce—at the wharf at which your exports are put on board a ship bound to a foreign port? Is not that cargo as much an export while it is descending a navigable stream to reach the wharf as it is when it arrives there? and if the same cargo is obliged to be transported over our great lakes, to be carried to its destined wharf, is it therefore any less an export? and does it lose its character by being transmitted down a river emptying into a lake for the same purpose?

Again: When does an importation from abroad lose its character of an import in a commercial sense? Is the hogshead of molasses, or the bale of woolens, any less an import at Cleveland, where it is broken up and retailed, than it was at New York, where it was entered at the custom-house?

The truth is, internal trade is but the extension of foreign import, distributing its freights. And it is also the beginning of our foreign exports; and, practically, they are one and the same, and any discrimination in the protection of the government to one in exclusion of the other, is as absurd as would be a law to protect the body by cutting off all nourishment; and a dispute between them would be equal, in point of reasonableness, to a quarrel between the arm and the hand.

Our simple, plain, and precise ground therefore is, that the same considerations which justify and require appropriations for facilitating foreign commerce are equally applicable to internal trade, embraced in the term "commerce among the States."

The propositions submitted by the Committee state that there are peculiar dangers in the navigation of the lakes from the want of harbors, and of many of our rivers from snags and other obstructions. To such an audience, and at such a place as this, it would be a mere waste of time to dwell on these dangers. But as these remarks may reach others not so well informed, allow me to make some brief quotations from a report of the brave, gallant, and lamented Captain Williams, who fell so nobly at the taking of Monterey, made by him in 1842, to the chief of the Topographical Bureau:

"Chicago," he says, "is the only harbor on that lake (Michigan), the shores of which comprise a development of coast of about nine hundred miles. Milwaukee affords no shelter for vessels during a storm, and even in calm weather it is difficult of access. At the mouth of Kalamazoo River, a large ship (the Milwaukee) was driven from its moorings, where it was taking in a cargo of wheat, and wrecked in the vicinity, with the loss of nine of her crew. Thus, from the time a vessel leaves Chicago, she has no place of shelter till she reaches the northern outlet of the lake at the Straits of Mackinac, or by taking refuge under the lee of the islands at the northern part of the lake. After passing the Straits of Mackinac, proceeding eastward, we enter Lake Huron, which extends two hundred and twenty miles in a south-westerly direction, yet upon the whole coast there is not a single harbor construction effected."

We all know the difficulties of the flats in the St. Clair River, which so seriously impede navigation, and which can be so easily made navigable.

From the head of Lake Erie to Buffalo, a distance of three hundred and thirty miles, there is but one place of security for vessels during a gale, and that is at Erie, where they may lie under the lee of the islands. All here know that vessels, during storms, have been driven back to this place for the whole distance from Buffalo, in consequence of the hazards of entering the nominal harbors on this lake.

Captain Williams remarks that there is greater danger in navigating the lakes than the ocean, because "upon the lakes there is at all times a dangerous proximity of coast, upon which vessels are liable to be thrown in a long-continued gale, while on the ocean there is room to drift until the storm be over." The only remedy is obviously harbors with spacious entrances?

Not having accurate information of the details, I can only allude in general terms to the immense losses of vessels and property, and the destruction of human life, which annually occur, particularly during the latter part of the season of navigation. I have heard it estimated that the value of property thus lost, in five years, would improve all the harbors on the lakes to the necessary extent. This is, in itself, sufficiently afflicting; but what shall we say of that neglect which consigns to watery graves the gallant sailors whose exposure to accidents is always so great and imminent? I will not trust myself to speak on this point, for fear that I may forget the decorum due the occasion. But I commend it to the consideration of all who have human sympathies.

The danger of the navigation of the Mississippi and its tributaries are so notorious and so appalling, that I need but thus briefly allude to them.

The consideration of these dangers in the navigation of the lakes leads to the mention of another and undoubted source of power in the federal government to provide harbors of shelter on these lakes. No one can say how soon the elements of discord may convert into belligerents the nation whose citizens and subjects reside on the different sides of those great waters; and when the shock of arms comes, as many suppose it must come, the contest there must be carried on by ships and steamers. How can that contest be urged without harbors for the shelter of our navy? It is not necessary to suppose that the stars and stripes may be pursued by superior force, but it is indispensable that the vessels which bear them aloft should have places of rendezvous, and refitting, and refuge against gales and storms. The harbors required for such a purpose can not be constructed in a day; and when the time arrives for their use, it will be too late to prepare them. Does not ordinary prudence require that the power to maintain a navy should be promptly exerted in view of possible events, and especially when the interests of commerce so imperiously demand their immediate construction?

The amount of the trade carried on upon the lakes west of Buffalo has been the subject of some inquiry by Colonel Abert, the distinguished and very able chief of the Topographical Corps, in pursuance of a suggestion which I made to him when we were officially connected. In his last report on the subject, made November 1, 1845, he estimates, from returns made to him, that the import and export trade of the various ports on the lakes was $100,000,000. This estimate does not include Lake Ontario nor Lake Champlain.

The President of the United States, in his msssage of December, 1846, states the value of all the exports of the United States at $102,141,893.

It is by such comparisons only that we can form an idea of the vast amount of this portion of our internal commerce. Is it not an interest demanding, in tones which can not be disregarded, the equal and just protection of the government?

From a very able statistical report furnished us by the delegates from Missouri, we learn that the amount of cargoes received at New Orleans, in 1846, from the upper country, transported on the Western rivers, was $77,193,464, and that the number of steamboats running up the Western rivers during the same year was 1190, whose aggregate value was more than $16,000,000.

These statistics, imperfect as they necessarily must be, give us some idea of the mighty torrent of trade which is rushing from the fertile and boundless West to satisfy the wants of man, and to exchange for the products of other climes.

Can any one be so infatuated as to suppose that this vast rolling volume can be impeded by the mere caprice and whims of visionaries, who seem to be reading the stars while the world is running past them?

One of the propositions reported complains of the disproportion between the appropriations made to improve the facilities of commerce in the harbors, rivers, and bays of the Atlantic coast, and those made for similar purposes on the interior lakes and rivers.

A report of Colonel Abert, made to Congress in December last, of all the appropriations made since 1806 for roads and the improvement of harbors and rivers, shows an aggregate of $17,199,000, of which $2,861,964 were for the harbors of the lakes and the improvement of the rivers at the North-West—about one-sixth of the whole. It is needless to speak of the gross inequality of this apportionment of common funds to those who know the vast and teeming population which is occupied or interested in the navigation of the Western lakes and rivers.

You were doubtless surprised at one of the propositions reported, which contains such an obvious truth that it is scarcely required to be stated. It is that which declares our inability to distinguish between a harbor for shelter and one for commerce. This is introduced to meet an idea of Mr. Calhoun in his report to the Senate of the United States on the memorial of the Memphis Convention, in which he admits the constitutional power of Congress to appropriate money for a harbor for shelter, but denies its power to aid a harbor for commerce. It is impossible here to give you the process of reasoning by which he arrives at this result. It is one of the instances in which a brilliant genius has made captive all common sense. A habit of theoretic speculation, indulged until it has obtained the mastery of all other faculties, has rendered this gentleman, who, with all his errors, is one of the jewels of the Nation, so impracticable as a statesman and a legislator. The committee propose to meet his speculation with a plain matter of fact, for which they appeal to the common sense and ordinary observation of all men.

Another idea of Mr. Calhoun's, contained in the same report, seems also, to the committee, to demand some notice. It is, that with the assent of Congress a law may be passed by one State, or by two States, imposing a tonnage duty on vessels arriving at or departing from a port or harbor for its construction or improvement.

Observing merely in passing that it is difficult to perceive how a tonnage duty can be levied on vessels to raise the means of constructing harbors before there is any harbor or any vessels entering it, the committee have deemed it best to meet the idea by showing its injustice. We claim that the common funds of the Nation, being contributed by all the people and belonging to them, and the proceeds of the sales of public lands, are held in trust for the equal and common benefit of all. And maintaining, as we do, not only the power, but the duty of the federal government to apply these funds in a just and fair proportion to the improvement of interior rivers and harbors, we hold that we can not be called upon to put our hands in our pockets, and, by the addition of special burdens upon ourselves, perform the work of the government, so long as it has our common resources in its hands. If we are compelled to contribute our private means to a public, general, and national purpose, we shall find other means of doing so than by laying burdens on a trade already sufficiently discouraged by the neglect, of those whose duty it is to cherish and foster it; and we submit the proposition simply that such a special burden would be unjust and oppressive.

The propositions before you have been drawn and presented in the spirit of harmony, with the desire of exhibiting plain and practical principles as a common ground on which all may conscientiously and consistently unite. They are broad enough to cover the ground necessary to attain the objects for which we have assembled, and are yet so limited, by carefully abstaining from any other terms than those employed in the Constitution itself, as not to give color to vague and indefinite construction. The entire unanimity with which they have been reported by the most numerous committee yet appointed by this Convention, furnishes in itself strong evidence that they are adapted to our case, and have taken positions which will meet the united and cordial assent of this vast assembly.

The following letters were received by members of the Corresponding Committee, and were not read to the Convention, but have since been handed to the Publishing Committee, who, as a matter of record, embody them in the proceedings of the Convention:—

DETROIT, *July 3d, 1847.*

GENTLEMEN:—My public duties will not admit of my attendance at the Chicago Convention, and I am restrained from expressing my views of the constitutionality and expediency of constructing Harbors, and removing obstructions to commerce on our Lakes and Rivers, by the consideration that I am a member of an independent department of the Government, whose province it is to give, in the last resort, a construction to the Constitution. With the expression of an ardent desire for the attainment of the great objects of the Convention, I am, Gentlemen,

Your friend and fellow-citizen,

JOHN MCLEAN.

George W. Meeker, N. B. Judd, Wm. B. Ogden, E. W. Tracy, and S. J. Lowe, Esqrs., Committee, etc.

DETROIT, *May 20th, 1847.*

MY DEAR SIR:—I have had the pleasure to receive your very friendly letter of the 10th instant, transmitting to me an invitation from the Chicago Committee of Correspondence, to attend a North-Western Harbor-and-River Convention, to be assembled in that City on the first Monday in July next, without regard to distinctions of party.

I understand the objects of the Convention to be to promote the improvement of Lake-and-River Harbors, to secure the safety of Lake-and-River Navigation, on the navigable waters of the United States, and to urge the passage of laws through Congress, making appropriations for these purposes so essential and invaluable to the advancement of our commercial prosperity in these immense and expanding north-western regions.

In this great object, and in the requisite measures for its accomplishment, I most cordially concur. It is the peculiar duty of the General Government, it may be said to be their exclusive right and power, to promote and protect the commerce and navigation of our magnificent inland seas. They alone have authority to regulate the commerce, to collect imposts, duties, and taxes, on these waters; and I am incapable of comprehending upon what just national ground they can, compatibly with their constitutional obligations, refuse to exercise the power. We must persevere, amidst all the discouragements we have to encounter, until we triumph in this great cause. These were my sentiments in the Senate; they are my sentiments now; they will continue to be my sentiments forever.

I deeply regret that the approaching term of the Circuit

Court of the United States, and my official and professional engagements during its continuance, will prevent my attendance at the Convention. I pray, however, that its proceedings may be guided by the patriotism and wisdom which distinguish the Northwest, and that they may result in the signal advancement of the benificent objects for which it is to assemble at your prosperous City. Indeed, upon these points no doubt is entertained.

My cordial thanks are due to the Committee for their obliging invitation, and to yourself personally for the exceedingly kind terms with which its transmission was accompanied. All the friendly feelings disclosed in your note are gratefully reciprocated by   Your friend and fellow-citizen,
JOHN NORVELL.
GEORGE W. MEEKER, Esq.

AMELIA, VA., *July 26, 1847.*

GENTLEMEN:—Your invitation to me, to attend the "Harbor-and-River Convention," at Chicago, on the first Monday of the present month, owing to my absence from home, did not reach me in time to receive an answer before the meeting of that Assembly. Conceiving the design of the invitations issued on this occasion to public men at a distance, to have been, not so much to procure their attendance, as to elicit their opinions on the interesting subject of the purposes of the Convention, I have deemed it not too late, through the medium of the acknowledgment which I owe for the honor of your invitation, to express my sincere concurrence in those purposes.

Of the importance of the objects sought to be accomplished, or of the disproportion of the expense required, to their value, there can, I presume, be but one opinion; the sole diversity of opinion relating to the constitutional difficulty, as regards the authority of the Government to execute the works proposed. On this point, I have to say in the fewest words that regarding the power of the Federal Government as unquestionable to expend the public money on objects conducive to commerce between States of the Confederacy, I can see no just ground for distinction, in this respect, between Fresh Water or Tide Streams, Lake Harbors or Ocean Harbors, which are or may be rendered really subservient to these ends.

In this view, I have, whilst a member of the Senate of the United States, given my vote for the appropriations proposed for the improvement of the Mississippi and its tributaries. I have withheld my vote at the same time from the Harbor bills presented, because I had, on every occasion, cause to entertain the belief that subjects had found insertion in the Bills by what is denominated log-rolling and jobbing, which had no just title to their place from their intrinsic utility, and I could not conceive any object of value enough to authorize the sanction of such an abuse, and the mischief of introducing it as an example and a precedent. It has been with regret that I have been constrained to yield to the paramount force of this objection.

You will, I am sure, appreciate justly the motives to this late reply to your letter, and I beg you to believe me to be

With much respect, yours,

W. S. ARCHER.

Messrs. JUDD and others, Committee.

ABRAHAM LINCOLN, the only Whig representative to Congress from this State, we are happy to see is in attendance upon the Convention. This is his first visit to the commercial emporium of the State, and we have no doubt his visit will impress him more deeply, if possible, with the importance, and inspire a higher zeal for the great interest of River-and-Harbor improvements. We expect much from him as a representative in Congress, and we have no doubt our expectations will be more than realized, for never was reliance placed in a nobler heart and a sounder judgment. We know the banner he bears will never be soiled.—*Chicago Journal*, July 6, 1847.

FALLEN.—It becomes a melancholy duty to chronicle the death of one of our oldest citizens, Samuel Lisle Smith. He expired at his residence, on Sunday last, [July 30, 1854, aged 37,] surrounded by his family and friends. The departed had lived among us for a period of sixteen years, and his name is ineffaceably associated with the growth of our City, in which he experienced a peculiar pride, and over which his brilliant talents shed a lustre. The memory of the eloquence of the gifted orator will not soon fade from the public mind, which he could sway at times as with the wand of a magician. The remembrance of his virtues will ever live in the hearts of those who communed with him as a friend. For those who mourn the sudden rupture of the most tender ties, there is no language to express their grief; how applicable to their case is the following beautiful passage which fell from his own lips but a few days since, in speaking of the death of James H. Collins, [July 14, 1854,]:

"There is no styptic to staunch the artery of domestic love now bleeding. There is one and only one Comforter. To Him let us commend the widow and the orphan, that to them he may give beauty for ashes, the oil of joy for mourning, and the garments of praise for the spirit of heaviness."—*Chicago Democratic Press*, August 5, 1854.

JESSE B. THOMAS, late Judge of the Supreme Court of Illinois, and one of the most distinguished men of the West, died in Chicago on Feb. 21, 1850, and the *Democrat* of the 22d, says:

He had been for some days suffering under an attack of erysipelas, which a short time previous to his decease assumed the malignant form. He was conscious of his dissolution from the commencement of the attack, and accordingly set himself to prepare his temporal affairs in anticipation of his departure.

Judge Thomas was in the 44th year of his age. He leaves a large and interesting family, and, we are happy to learn, through his exertions, in easy circumstances.

HORACE GREELEY'S REPORT.

[From the *New-York Semi-Weekly Tribune*, Saturday, July 17, 1847.]

The Great River-and-Harbor Convention at Chicago—Railroad to the Pacific—Internal Improvements and Party Politics, Etc.

Editorial Correspondence.

CHICAGO, Illinois, July 5—4 P.M.

Chicago has been filling up with Delegates to the People's Convention for the last ten or fifteen days, but it was not until Saturday that the pressure became burdensome. When we arrived, on the *Oregon*, at sunrise, yesterday morning, there was scarcely a spare inch of room in any public house save in a few bedrooms long since bespoken. But the citizens had already thrown open their dwellings, welcoming strangers in thousands to their cordial and bounteous hospitality; the steamboats, as they came in, proffered their spacious accommodations and generous fare to their passengers during their stay; and though four or five boats full freighted came in yesterday, and two more, with a thousand or fifteen hundred each, came in this morning, I believe there are none left in doubt as to their chance of shelter to-night at this present writing. At all events, the people of Chicago have earned a noble reputation for hospitality and public spirit.

The grand parade took place this morning, and, though the route traversed was short, in deference to the heat of the weather, the spectacle was truly magnificent. The citizens of Chicago, of course, furnished the most imposing part of it—the Music, the Military, the Ships on wheels, ornamented Fire Engines, etc. I never witnessed anything so superb as the appearance of some of the Fire Companies with their Engines drawn by led horses, tastefully caparisoned. Our New-York Firemen must try again: they have certainly been outdone.

I think New York had some 300 Delegates on the ground—among them, John C. Spencer, J. Depeyster Ogden, Thurlow Weed, James L. Barton, Seth C. Hawley, George W. Patterson, Alvin Bronson, John E. Hinman, etc. From New England the number present is smaller, but still considerable; I notice among them, Hon. John A. Rockwell, of Conn., Hon. Elisha H. Allen, now of Boston, etc., etc. From New Jersey there are 6 or 8; from Pennsylvania I think 50 to 100; among them Hon. Andrew Stewart. Senator Johnson, of Erie, etc.; from Ohio, the number may not be much greater, but among them are Hon. Tom Corwin, Gov. Bebb, Ex-Gov. Morrow, Hon. R. C. Schenck, Hon. John C. Wright, etc. From Georgia, there are at least two here, and one of them is Hon. Thos. Butler King; there is one even from South Carolina; Indiana, Missouri, and Iowa are well represented; Michigan and Wisconsin have a large regiment each, while Northern Illinois is here, of course, *en masse*. A judicious estimate makes the number present to-day 20,000 men, of whom 10,000 are here as Members of the Convention.

The morning was very hot, and the Procession, though not long in its course, was long in getting in motion—of course, the waiting was tedious; though we had a pleasant square on the Lake shore to form in and something of a breeze to temper the sun's fervor. But for a gentle shower last evening, the day would have been extremely dusty; it was sufficiently so as it was. The afternoon is more breezy and pleasant.

The citizens had provided a spacious and beautiful tent, about 100 feet square, pitched in an open square near the centre of the City, radiating from a tall pole in the centre, and well provided with seats. It holds about 4000 persons comfortably. The rest of the gathering were constrained to look in over the heads of those seated.

[Mr. G. here gives an account of the preliminary organization of the Convention, but this part of his letter was anticipated by our Express.]

On reassembling in the afternoon, the Convention was briefly addressed by Rev. Mr. Allen, of Mass., mainly on the influence of the Puritans of New-England on the settlement and character of the great West. When he had closed, a very general call was made for Hon. Thomas Corwin, of Ohio, which could not be stilled. Mr. Corwin was finally sought out in the body of the Convention, and conducted to the stand by Hon. John Wentworth. Although coming to the stand reluctantly, Mr. C. addressed the Convention for nearly an hour in his own inimitable manner on the relations and relative character of the Puritans, so eloquently eulogized by the preceding speaker, and the people of the West—on the wants and just demands of the West—the absurd folly of considering Harbor Improvements on salt water Constitutional and on fresh water not so—the mighty strides of the West to greatness and dominion, and the certainty that she who now implores will soon be in a condition to command, etc., etc. The vast assemblage was electrified by this admirable effort.   H. G.

SECOND DAY.

CHICAGO, July 6, 1847.

The attendance at the sessions of the Convention to-day has been very numerous, indicating undiminished interest. The first business was the appointment of a Committee of two Delegates from each State represented to draft and report Resolutions expressive of the general views and commendatory of the objects of this vast deliberative body.

Various propositions, which were offered, were referred to this Committee, which immediately retired to the Court House to enter upon the discharge of its duties.

In its absence, the letters of Hon. Thomas H. Benton, Henry Clay, Silas Wright, Martin Van Buren, Lewis Cass, Gov. Felch, of Mich., Hon. B. R. Wood, of Albany, Hon. Joseph Grinnell, of Mass., etc., etc., were read. These I dispatched you in proof-slips last evening, and I hope they will have reached you in advance of this. The shortest and most significant of these is that of Gen. Cass, who is content to say he can not (*i. e.* will not) come, without the least expression of sympathy with the objects or desire for the success of the Convention. The letter excited much astonishment, and was read twice at the urgent call of many Delegates. The general expression of sentiment thereupon, though not boisterous, was by no means flattering to Gen. Cass. Messrs. Wright and Van Buren's letters, especially the former, though full of qualifications and reservations, wore a favorable aspect, and were received with hearty cordiality. Mr. Wood's letter is the gem of the collection. Its straight-out advocacy of Harbor-and-River Improvements, without equivocation or compromise, and its plain-spoken denunciation of the objects and character of the present War on Mexico—coming from a Loco-Foco Member of the last Congress, who has had the best public and private opportunities for observing the machinery by which that war was got up and is sustained, I hope it will be every where read and heeded. The letters, having been deliberately read, were ordered to be printed along with the proceedings of the Convention. It having been understood that a characteristic letter had been received from Hon. John M. Botts, of Virginia, a very urgent and general demand was made for its production and reading; but it appeared that it was a private letter, though referring to the meeting and objects of the Convention, and that the gentleman who received it had seen fit to withhold it from the Committee, as possibly calculated to give offence to some portion of the

Delegates present. It will doubtless be published after the adjournment of the Convention, and will be every where current. It is said by those who have seen it to be particularly spicy.

Hon. Andrew Stewart, of Pa., was next called out, and made a vigorous and animated speech in favor of Internal Improvement generally, on comprehensive grounds and in the most catholic spirit. It was perhaps a little too plain and thorough-going for the weak stomachs of some present, who had but recently begun to profess friendship for Internal Improvement, and who did not wish to lose caste with their party while desirous of doing something for the people. It pleased right well a majority of the Convention, but brought up in opposition Mr. David Dudley Field, of our City, who favored us with an able and courteous speech in favor of "Strict Construction" and of such River and Harbor Improvements only as are consistent therewith. He was sharply interrogated by different members, and, in reply to their questions, denied the right of the Federal Government to improve the navigation of the Illinois River, since that River runs through a single State only, or of the Hudson *above a port of entry!* The Convention, or rather a portion of its members, manifested considerable impatience during the latter portion of this speech, which is to be regretted, for Mr. F. was perfectly courteous, not at all tedious, and fairly called out by the speech of Mr. Stewart. For my part, I rejoiced that the wrong side of the question was so clearly set forth. When he had concluded, the Convention adjourned to dinner.

In the afternoon, Hon. Abraham Lincoln, a tall specimen of an Illinoian, just elected to Congress from the only Whig District in the State, was called out, and spoke briefly and happily in reply to Mr. Field. As he closed, the Committee came in, and through its chairman, Hon. J. C. Wright, reported a series of fifteen Resolutions, which were read by Charles King, of N. J., and advocated in a most able and interesting speech by Hon. John C. Spencer, of New York—a constitutional argument, evincing deep research and great power. They are as follows: [We published these Resolutions in our last, under the title of "Declaration of Sentiments."]

These Resolutions having been read and accepted, Mr. D. D. Field very fairly objected to the last clause of the fifth resolution, affirming substantially that the "common understanding" of the Constitution, through a long series of years, "has become as much a part of that instrument as any one of its most explicit provisions." This ought to have prevailed, but it did not—Mr. Spencer suggesting that it was almost a literal extract from Gen. Jackson's Maysville Veto Message. A motion to amend the 14th resolution, which was thought to affirm anti-Tariff doctrine, prevailed—though the objection seemed to me rather superfluous. The resolutions were then adopted—the other thirteen with absolute unanimity. A sixteenth resolution, proposing the appointment of an Executive Committee, to transmit the proceedings of this Convention to the President and to Congress, to collect and publish facts calculated to enforce the views of this Convention, etc. This resolution was unanimously adopted.

Hon. Thomas Butler King, of Ga., was now urgently called out, having declined a call to speak until the resolutions should be adopted, and made a most admirable speech in favor of River-and-Harbor Improvements, and Internal Improvement generally. It was really a great speech, thoroughly National in its spirit, and looking to the benefit of each section through the good of all. I do hope this excellent speech will be reported, for I am sure it will be generally read and approved. When he had closed, Gov. Bebb, of Ohio, was called for, but did not appear, and the Convention (6½ o'clock) adjourned to 9 A. M. to-morrow.   H. G.

THIRD AND LAST DAY—RAILROAD TO THE PACIFIC, &c.

CHICAGO, Ill., July 7, 1847.

To-day has been mainly devoted to speaking and hearing, with the transaction of such minor business as was left unfinished yesterday. A Committee of two from each State to collect and prepare evidence of the importance and urgent necessity of River and Harbor Improvements, as also to lay before the President and each House of Congress the proceedings and resolves of this Convention, was appointed by the Chair, on the suggestion of the Delegations from each State. I believe the two members from our State are John C. Spencer, of Albany, and Samuel B. Ruggles, of New York. The printing of the proceedings in pamphlet form, with such reports and documents as should be deemed advisable, was also ordered. Resolutions of thanks to the President were moved by Hon. Thomas Corwin, and adopted with enthusiastic unanimity; so was a vote of thanks to the citizens of Chicago for their courteous hospitality and kindness to the Delegates generally. But the Convention came together thoroughly resolved that no topic should be entertained which might mar the harmony and hearty unanimity with which the Resolutions of the Grand Committee had been received and adopted yesterday; so that successive efforts to get before it the project of a Railroad to the Pacific, the Free Navigation of the St. Lawrence, etc., etc., were promptly and decidedly thwarted by the undebatable motion to lay on the table; and at about 11 o'clock A.M., being the first practicable moment, a motion to adjourn was made, seconded, put and carried by an overwhelming vote.

Previous to putting the question, however, the President of the Convention, Hon. Edward Bates, of Missouri, returned thanks for the honor done him in a speech which took the Convention completely by surprise—so able, so forcible, and replete with the soul of eloquence. I will not attempt to give an account of this wonderful speech, of which I regret to know that no full notes were taken. No account that can now be given will do it justice. In the course of it, Mr. B. remarked that when he emigrated, in 1812, to the French village of huts called St. Louis, which has now 50,000 inhabitants, he was obliged to hire a guard against hostile savages to accompany him across the unbroken wilderness which is now the State of Illinois, with a civilized population of 600,000 freemen.—His speech was greeted at its close by the whole Convention rising and cheering long and fervently.

The Convention was now adjourned *pro forma*, but instantly reörganized as a Committee of the Whole on the State of the Union, when Gov. William Bebb, of Ohio, was constrained to come forward. In a brief speech, he forcibly set forth the just subordination of all physical and material to mental and moral improvement—to the diffusion of Intelligence, the purification of Morals, and the Melioration of the Social condition of Man. Vain, said he, will be all your Canals and Railroads, your River-and-Harbor Improvements, if the condition of the Toiling Millions be not thereby or therewith sensibly meliorated—if there shall still be constrained to delve twelve to fourteen hours per day for the bare necessaries of physical life. I hold, said he, that this need not and ought not to continue—that Society may be so revised that ten or eight hours' faithful labor daily will secure to every industrious man or family a fully supply of the necessaries and comforts of life, so that each may have ample leisure to devote to the cultivation and perfection of his Moral, Social, and Intellectual powers. Let us never forget that this is the great end of all physical improvement, and that such works as we are met to urge upon the attention of our rulers and fellow-citizens are essential only as conducive thereto.—[Gov. Bebb's remarks were warmly and generally responded to by the thousands present; two-thirds of whom were doubtless Whigs; for, though the principal editors respectively of the *N. Y. Express, Utica Gazette,* and *Buffalo Com. Advertiser,* with one of the editors of the *Courier & Enquirer,* were among those present at the Convention, it doth not appear that their journals have ever been much circulated or pondered in this part of the country. Should they see fit hereupon to read Gov. Bebb out of the Whig party, it will be necessary to have their bull of excommunication copied into some journal or journals circulating Westward, or they will hardly have the desired effect.]

Hon. A. W. Loomis, of Pittsburgh, Pa., Gen. Levi Hubbell, of Milwaukee, Wis., S. Lisle Smith, of Chicago, Ill., Anson Burlingame, of Mass., (late of Mich.), Hon. E. H. Allen, of Boston, Mass., and H. Greeley, of New York, were called out in succession, when each briefly and acceptably addressed the vast concourse. The speech of Mr. Smith, of this City, regarded as an oratorial effort, was the best of the many good speeches made here within these three days. It was beautiful, thrilling, highly poetic, enchaining and enrapturing the audience. I will not attempt to sketch it. Mr. Allen's remarks were very happy, in a very different vein—these two affording striking illustrations of Western and Eastern popular speaking respectively.

Mr. Wm. M. Hall, of Buffalo, N. Y., next rising to advocate a series of resolutions offered by him concerning the proposed Railroad to the Pacific, the Committee of the Whole (1 P.M.) adjourned over to 3 o'clock, at which hour the meeting reassembled and listened to a long and forcible argument of Mr. Hall against the respective plans of Mr. Whitney and Dr. Carver for constructing the great Pacific Road,* and in favor of the counter proposition that the Railroad shall be constructed and owned by the Nation, its directors being chosen by the people of the several States, the lands along the route withheld from the clutch of the speculator, etc., etc. When he had concluded, the meeting, after some desultory discussion, adopted his resolutions, with a preamble explaining that this was the act of a Mass Meeting of citizens at Chicago after the adjournment of the River-and-Harbor Convention.—And then (5 P.M.) the meeting adjourned without day.

—Thus has met, deliberated, harmonized, acted, and separated, one of the most important and interesting Conventions ever held in this or any country. It was truly characterized as a Congress of Freemen, destitute of Pay and Mileage, but in all else inferior to no deliberative body which has assembled within twenty years. Can we doubt that its results will be most beneficent and enduring? H..G.

INTERNAL IMPROVEMENT AND PARTY POLITICS.

CHICAGO, Thursday, July 8, 1847.

The great North-Western Convention has completed its labors and adjourned—its members are now wending their several ways homeward; its deliberations and acts are on record, and are, or soon will be, before the people, by whom I trust they will be generally and thoughtfully considered. Those who were not present can not see, but may imagine, the feverish and incessant anxiety manifested that nothing done or said in the Convention should seem to wear a *party* aspect, be dictated by party considerations, or obnoxious to party prejudices—the continual, unsparing disparagement of party ends and operations, and the exertions on all sides to bury party ties and feelings in oblivion. If to be a partisan and to be a thief had been synonymous, Party could hardly have been more studiously descried and reprobated.

This was partly right and partly wrong. Whoever manifests zeal for River-

* Wm. M. Hall's Resolutions and Speech will be found at page 91.

and-Harbor Improvements, or labors to promote their construction and magnify their importance, *for the sake of Party*—to subserve the interests of Party—acts a sinister, unworthy part, deserving severe reprobation. "Let every tub stand on its own bottom." But this labored renunciation and denunciation of Party seem to me neither just nor honest. If there be any man who regards Party but as a means of advancing sordid and selfish ends, that man does well to seem ashamed of Party when he appears as the advocate of any enterprise looking to ends of general and enduring beneficence. Let me for one, however, be understood and recorded as not less uniformly zealous, consciencious, open and ardent in my politics than in anything else whatever. I very willingly strike hands with political opponents who may agree with me in favoring this or any other good work, and in all sincerity say, "While on this sub-"ject we will put aside and forget our partisan differences: we will remember "only that we are fellow-citizens ardently desiring a liberal and systematic "improvement of our Rivers and Harbors." This is right, honest, practicable. But if any one chooses to manifest his zeal for River-and-Harbor improvement, or anything else, in any such language as this—"Politics and "Party differences are all folly, nonsense, insanity—'the madness of the many "for the gain of the few'—we renounce and repudiate Party as an idle or un-"clean thing,"—I beg that it be understood that he speaks for himself and those who agree with him, and not at all for me.

Nor can I even assent unqualifiedly to the doctrine of one of the Resolutions reported by the appropriate committee and adopted by the Convention, deprecating all association of the subject of River-and-Harbor Improvements with Party Politics. I have already stated what I understand to be the truth in this direction. But suppose one of the great parties which divide the Country be proved to manifest an inveterate and radical hostility to the Improvements in question—a hostility tempered only by considerations of local necessity and to the extent of such necessity—while its antagonist approves itself, through a long series of years, the steadfast and efficient champion of such Improvements, is it just or honest to say, "Party Politics have nothing to do with this matter: Vote for one party or the other as prejudice or fancy "may dictate—it will be all the same as far as Rivers and Harbors are con-"cerned?" I do not so understand it. Doubtless, many an individual will virtually say, "Though I want the Rivers and Harbors improved, I shall still "act and vote with the Party I well know to be mainly *un*favorable to such "works, because of other and paramount considerations"—this is every man's own business, and, wise or unwise, Conventions can not meddle with it. But he who says that this River-and-Harbor question stands utterly aside from the general Politics of the Country speaks for himself, and in pointed opposition to *my* understanding and convictions.

For who that reads the leading journals of the day—not to mention the journals of Congress—can be ignorant that the elemental notions and popular maxims of one of the great parties of our time evince the most radical and invincible hostility to all such undertakings by Government as that of River-and-Harbor improvement? "The world is governed too much"—"The best Government is that which governs least"—"*Laissez faire*" ("Let us alone,") etc., etc.—does anybody that *has* eyes pretend to shut them to the bearing of these maxims on such topics as those which have occupied the Chicago Convention? Undoubtedly, there are individuals of the Loco-Foco party who on this, as there are some who on other subjects, act earnestly in opposition to the spirit and obvious dictate of these maxims—for instance, Hon. John Wentworth, M. C. from this District, of whom, said in substance, Mr. Corwin in his speech on Monday:

"This subject unites men most opposed in Politics—for instance, the Hon.

Member from Northern Illinois and myself. When we two agree in favor of a public measure, it must be right. He is among the most zealous and thorough champions of these Improvements, and not at all troubled with Constitutional scruples in regard to them. He may be considered even latitudinous on the subject, which [glancing round at 'Long John's' ample proportions] is probably owing to his longitude. He goes his length."

True: But has anybody ever heard of a Loco-Foco representing a District *not* specially interested in such Improvements, who went his length for them? If anybody knows the whereabouts of that unicorn, let him be trotted out.

No man can read even the letters addressed to this Convention, in answer to invitations to attend it, without being struck with the palpable difference of tone and spirit which separates the statesmen of the two great parties. On the Whig side all is frank and unqualified—as for example, Mr. Webster's characteristic letter which was only received here on Tuesday night, and the reading of which yesterday called forth three spontaneous and hearty cheers from the Convention. Nobody is left to guess at the position of Mr. Webster, or will read his letter twice to learn what it means. Turn from this to the letters of eminent Loco-Foco statesmen, beginning with that of Gen. Cass, long a citizen of the West, a U. S. Senator from harborless Michigan, and an aspirant to the Presidency, *via* South Carolina. Did mortal man ever before see such a letter from one who is by position and was by profession friendly to the objects of the Convention? It was listened to with hardly less astonishment than indignation. I was forcibly reminded by it, with "a few more of the same sort," of an anecdote I lately heard of the renowned battle-field of Bladensburgh, which a lanky, lop-sided Marylander, who saw the affair, is in the habit of showing and illustrating to visitors (not often Americans) for a consideration. A British officer was lately his customer, and, on examining the ground where our militia stood—or rather did n't stand—he could not conceal his surprise at the historic suddenness of their departure. "Why," inquired he, "how came your countrymen to run away in such numbers from such a position as this?" "Why," replied Maryland, rather puzzled by the directness of the query, "*they did n't seem to take no interest.*" Ditto of Gen. Cass and company.

Turn from this to the letters of Silas Wright & Co., who form the other wing of the Loco-Foco array. These appear to be really desirous that something should be done for Rivers and Harbors, but extremely fearful withal that the expression of this sentiment will compromise their Political orthodoxy. The critical navigation on which they are embarked may well awaken them to sympathy for the mariners on our Western Lakes and Rivers. How cautious! how full of reservations and qualifications! Gov. Wright is careful to tell us that he has a deep local interest on the right side of the Improvement question, and he is very careful also to exhibit his fears that too much will be done in the way of improving Rivers and Harbors. The ship of State must be well supplied with anchors ere she is sped upon that perilous coast. Millions on millions are annually voted without hesitation or scruple to maintain armies and armaments, forts and navies; nobody expresses fears that our Constitution or our Liberties will be periled by that: but a few thousands squeezed out semi-occasionally for purposes really, palpably, enduringly beneficent—these suffice to throw into hysterics even those who profess to be favorable to the objects thus promoted. We must take care—look sharp—watch narrowly, or the Constitution will be subverted and Freedom crushed by the building of a few piers and the clearing out of the channels of certain rivers! Was ever such a cause of apprehension conjured up before?

But look at Gov. Wright's timidly suggested limitation to River Improvements. They must be confined to Rivers and parts of Rivers whereon Commerce already exists, and not extended to those previously unsusceptible of navigation. For instance, the Red River of the South-West is (or was) utterly obstructed by the famous Raft not far above its mouth, and, of course, so long as that absolutely prevented all navigation above Shreveport, its removal was unconditional. But if it had only been half as injurious as it really was—if it had not utterly prevented navigation, but allowed small, hardy steamboats to work through or dive under and thus vanquish it, then it might do to let the Government pull it in pieces and remove it! Its extreme injuriousness affords the reason for preserving it, in deference to the immortal "Resolutions of '98," and in view of the fact that nothing is said of the Red-River Raft in the Federal Constitution. I believe it is one of Dryden's heroes who in a stilted drama paradoxically exclaims,

"My wound is great because it is so small,"

on hearing which a wag in the pit sung out,

"Then 't would be greater were it none at all."

Gov. Wright has evidently studied logic and constitutional law in this school.

In the same mistaken spirit, Mr. David Dudley Field of our City, when arguing before the Convention in favor of a "strict construction" and displaying the awful perils of latitudinarian views and policy on this subject being asked, "Do you consider an appropriation for the improvement of the Illinois River Constitutional?"—"Does it not run through more than one State?" was his Yankee answer. "No! No!" responded a hundred voices. "Then I do *not* consider it Constitutional," was his response. Now the principle here aimed at may be sound, yet the application be flagrantly blundering. A river may be wholly in one State, yet its navigation be immensely important to a dozen—as the Hudson, for example—while another may run through two or more States, yet its navigation be far less important to any or to all. Thus the Chesapeake and Delaware Canal, only a few miles long, lying wholly within the limits of the smallest State in the Union, is plainly a work of great National importance; while the Delaware and Hudson, ten times as long, and penetrating two great States, is palpably local in its character and uses. Mr. Field's distinction is ill taken and worthless.

"But do you hold that the Hudson may be Constitutionally improved?" was the next question. "*Below a Custom-House* it may," replied Mr. Field. Here was revived in essence the very distinction between salt and fresh water improvements which Mr. F. had just before most emphatically repudiated! And is it not a most fallacious and irrational distinction? Consider its practical effect in filling the country with inland Custom-Houses—at St. Louis, at Albany, at Pittsburg, etc.—to the pernicious multiplication of offices and the sensible increase of our public burdens. Who can seriously regard it as more Constitutional to improve the Ohio with a Custom-House at Pittsburg than if the goods had paid duties at Cincinnati, Louisville, or even New Orleans? Who does not see that the doctrine here enunciated makes the improvement of our rivers subordinate entirely to the raising of revenue, while the facilitation of commerce and the promotion of National well-being are made the merest incidents of the taxing power. Instead of raising revenue for purposes of general benificence, we tolerate such purposes as incidental to the raising of revenue. I protest.

"But may the Government make a Harbor at Chicago?" Mr. F. was asked. "Was there any Harbor here already?" he queried in turn. Here is Mr. Wright's distinction again. But just consider it for a moment. Suppose there had been originally a dozen perfect Harbors on the southern coast of Lake Michigan, with half a dozen needing some work to render them safe and accessible, these latter being needed only for local accommodation, might not their improvement have been very fairly deferred to local and personal enterprise, on the ground asserted by Col. Benton that they in truth "harbored nothing but the interests of their owners?" Now take the actual case of the entire coasts of Lake Michigan, nine hundred miles in extent, and covered with commerce, yet without a single natural harbor or place of refuge for vessels in a storm, who can doubt that the construction of one or more Harbors is imperatively demanded by considerations of National and general well being? No matter if they have to be made entirely—scooped out of the shifting sands and fortified by expensive piers—the very fact that they *must* be expensive puts them beyond the reach of private enterprise or local exertion. The greater the natural deficiency—the necessity for Harbors being obvious and conceded—the more palpable the necessity and thus the Constitutionality of National interposition.

I must close abruptly, being summoned to the day's journey before me. Will not each considerate reader follow out the train of thought suggested and draw the fitting conclusions? H. G.

THURLOW WEED'S REPORT.

[From the *Albany Evening Journal*, Wednesday, July 14, 1847.]

A Trip to Chicago—Lake-and-Harbor Convention—A Run through the Lakes—Niagara Falls—"Maid of the Mist"—Captain Van Cleve and his "Cataract," Etc.

From the Editor.

STEAMBOAT EMPIRE, June 30, 1847.

I am afloat, for the first time, on Lake Erie, in that magnificent Steamer, the *Empire*, Capt. Randall, who had steam up and was waiting the arrival of the cars. In ascending to her beautiful saloon, we found some three hundred ladies and gentlemen grouped around upon sofas, divans, etc., as luxuriously as on board of our own splendid *Isaac Newton* and *Hendrik Hudson*. Immediately Capt. R. commenced working his way, by slow and tortuous movements, out of Buffalo Harbor, the insufficiency of which, for the vast commerce of these inland oceans, forcibly impressed us with the importance of the Convention about to assemble at Chicago. That Convention will, by its deliberations, it is hoped, awaken not only the whole American people, but their Government, to the magnitude of an interest that has heretofore been almost entirely neglected, saving the people from the mortification and the Government from the disgrace of again seeing the implements and the materials prepared for the construction of Lake harbors, sold at "public vendue!"

At least two-thirds of our cabin passengers are Delegates to the Convention. These, however, are but the stragglers of an army of delegates that had left Buffalo earlier. The number of delegates, therefore, will be legion. Our great commercial metropolis, though deeply interested, will, I fear, be but feebly represented. The only Delegates with us, from New York, are Mr. Brooks of the *Express*, and Edwin Burr, Esq., a friend with whom I traveled in Europe, and with whom it is always pleasant to meet. Very few of the large number of Delegates appointed have appeared. Albany has shown more spirit, though her delegation is not as large as was expected. Hon. John C. Spencer, Mr. Croswell, and Mr. Thomas L. Greene are here, bringing up our rear guard. Gen. Davis is, I believe, the "sole representative" of the city of Troy.

July 1.

We have a calm, delightful night, and at sunrise was a few miles above Conneaut, Ohio, gliding rapidly along some six miles from the shore. At 8 o'clock, nearly three hundred passengers were seated in the *Empire's* spacious saloon, to an ample and well-served breakfast.

During the forenoon, our friend, Seth C. Hawley of Buffalo, called our attention to a circumstance which was particularly unpleasant to American eyes, and which proved, far more conclusively than argument or even figures can prove, the impolicy and wretchedness of our "Financial System of Forty-Two." The eye, at a single glance, took in a commercial fleet, consisting of fifteen sail, all from Cleveland, and the neighboring ports, and all heading directly for the Welland Canal.

We reached Cleveland at 1 o'clock, where we lay an hour, which hour we improved by riding, first through its busy, bustling streets, and then along one or two of its broad avenues, adorned with tasteful mansions, surrounded by a profusion of fruit trees, shrubbery, and flowers. Cleveland, as the outlet of the Ohio Canal, is fortunate in possessing an accessible, safe, and "snug" harbor. The fact that since the opening of navigation 1,300,000 barrels flour, and 1,200,000 bushels wheat have been shipped at Cleveland "speaks for itself."

Hon. John W. Allen, a former Representative in Congress, and one of the most useful, as well as one of the most deservedly esteemed, citizens of Cleveland, with several other Delegates from that town, joined us. Mr. Allen, after completing his law studies at Oxford, Chenango Co., came to Cleveland in 1825, in a schooner of less burthen than an Erie canal-boat, and landed in a yawl on the beach, there being then neither harbor nor dock there.

In the afternoon, we passed in view of the scene of Perry's sanguinary naval battle and glorious victory. It commenced only a few miles south of the mouth of the Detroit River, near a group of islands known as the Sisters, the respective fleets drifting, during the action, several miles toward Put-in-Bay. Gen. Proctor, with Tecumseh and several British officers, stood on a point at the mouth of the Detroit River, below Malden, watching the progress of the battle.

We entered the river at ½ past 8 o'clock P. M., and at ½ past 10 was along-side of the wharf at Detroit, having traveled from Albany to Detroit (nearly 700 miles) in FIFTY-ONE HOURS! We are, they tell us, the only persons who ever performed the journey between Albany and Detroit in so short a time.

We lay but an hour at Detroit. Mr. Corwin and Gov. Bebb of Ohio, left Detroit this morning for Chicago, in the Steamer *Oregon*.

This evening, soon after tea, the saloon was arranged for dancing, and the hours were passed very pleasantly in the mazes of the cotilion and the whirlings of the waltz.

July 2.

The officers of the boat held a council of steam yesterday, which resulted in a determination to attempt a moonlight flitting over the "St. Clair Flats," a point of navigation which corresponds with our "Overslaugh" in its worst state, before its obstructions were partially removed. This is a feat not attempted with large vessels by night, and bets were made against its success. An experienced lake captain maintained that we should go through, saying that whatever "Bartholomew," our sailing-master, "does not know of that channel is not worth learning."

The difficult passage was reached about 2 o'clock P. M. The boat felt her way carefully along the winding channel until all the worst points were passed, when, just before reaching deep water, where two stakes had disappeared, she struck, and lay "hard aground" until 6 o'clock this morning.

At 8½ o'clock this morning we came alongside a dock upon the Canada shore to "wood." An hundred-and-six cords of wood (hickory, maple, beech, and oak) was seized by the deckhands, steerage passengers, etc., and soon transferred from the dock to the boat, and at 12 o'clock we were under way. I learn that the *Empire*, in a single trip, consumes over 600 cords of wood. This requires for each trip the clearing up of over ten acres of well-wooded land! The wood which was taken on board to-day cost $1 per cord.

The St. Clair River is the trunk through which the waters of Lake Huron discharges itself into Lake Erie. It is a broad, beautiful river, looking out on either side upon a rich, fertile soil, and most of the way, on the British side particularly, the water and the land presenting a surface so even that another puncheon of water would apparently overflow the land. There is a current of something less than four miles an hour running through this outlet for the mighty Huron. The country along the St. Clair River, strikes me as a most desirable residence. To-day, at any rate, everything looks bright and smiling. St. Clair is the principal village. Here commences the pine-timber region, for the sawing of which steam-mills are numerous. Here, too, is the gigantic frame-work of a steamer, building by Capt. Walker, that is to be the Leviathan of the Lakes.

Early this morning, we passed the Steamer *Illinois*, Com. Blake. She is owned by my old friend, Oliver Newberry, whose intelligence and enterprise is associated with all the improvements of this New World.

Passing out of St. Clair River into the broad and deep Huron, and stretching along an arm of the State of Michigan which helps to form Saginaw Bay, you *begin* to comprehend something of the vastness of the West. Visions of the coming greatness and grandeur, and of the ultimate destiny of this continent, fill the mind with amazement. That America is to be the "seat of empire," and that too at no distant day "is a fixed fact." A wisdom above that of man has prepared for the inhabitants of worn-out, impoverished, and overburthened Europe, a fresh, fertile, primeval land, whose virgin soil and graceful forests will wave over millions of people. Those who are here are but the seeds of an emigrant population which are destined to multiply indefinitely. I say let them come, for there "is ample room and verge enough" for all. And in their labor, developing the riches of the earth, consists the elements of national prosperity.

July 3.

We had another calm, beautiful night, and Lake Huron, this morning is scarcely moved by a ripple. The evening was again passed in conversation and dancing. And here let me say a word about the mode of "killing time." I had heard much about gambling on the Lakes. But if this habit continues, the *Empire's* passengers form an exception to the rule. The time, so far, has been most rationally appropriated. Many volumes of "cheap literature" have been devoured. Lakes, harbors, and river improvements have been freely discussed. But cards seem to have gone out of fashion.

We reached Mackinaw at 12 o'clock M. Here is an old town with four or five hundred inhabitants and a well-constructed fort, from which you have a fine view of Lakes Huron and Michigan. Having added some fifty cords to our supply of wood, and replenished our larder with an abundance of salmon-trout and whitefish, we are again under way, passing from Lake Huron into Lake Michigan, whose waters present an unrippled surface. From Mackinaw our course is south, the westerly or northwesterly course leading to Lake Superior. At 7 o'clock this evening we touched at one of the Manitou Islands for wood. At this point all the steamers "wood." This island, some three miles by ten in extent, is only inhabited by the few persons employed in cutting and hauling wood. It is not even inhabited by animals. I saw none of the feathered race. Reptiles are seldom seen. And in the absence of all these, musquitoes, finding nobody to torment, come not to the Manitou Island!

July 4.

This is the 71st Anniversary of the Declaration of American Independence. Its sun dawns upon us in the middle of Lake Michigan, "the blue sky above and the blue waters beneath us," but no land in sight. It is a bright day. We are steaming onward rapidly, headed for Milwaukee, yet some seventy miles distant.

The great and good men who, seventy years ago, carved out a republic, could have had but imperfect conceptions of its even yet unappreciated magnitude. They did not dream that in territory then unknown to them, there would now be a population greater than that of the old thirteen colonies. They could not, in their wildest imaginings, have supposed that on these then unexplored Lakes there would now be a commerce exceeding, in tonnage and value, that of our Atlantic States. Yet these things are more than realized. And in reference to the population and resources of the West, we have only seen "the beginning of the end."

The works of nature away out here, where "the sun sinks to rest," are indeed upon an extended scale. Here are a succession of mighty Lakes, emptying themselves one into another, until, nearly three thousand miles from their head, their waters mingle with those of the Atlantic. And upon the shores of these Lakes is an extent of country capable of supporting and destined to receive, in the course of half a century, at least a quarter of a million of inhabitants.

At 10 o'clock to-day, our steamer's bell was tolled for the purpose of assembling the passengers in the saloon for divine service. The Rev. Mr. Stimpson of Greenbush, officiated. The Services were impressive—the audience large and attentive. During the services, a bird "on weary wing" flew into the saloon, hovered around among the congregation, and then passed out to find a resting-place upon the shoals.

We have now been nearly four days "at sea," and everything has gone just right. The steamer is well managed. Though nearly three hundred passengers draw around the table, the fare continues as abundant and extensive as it could be if Fulton Market was at hand every morning.

The *Empire* was built at Cleveland, three years ago. She is over 1200 tons burthen, and extremely well arranged for freight, steerage, and cabin passengers. Capt. Randall is himself the largest owner. He was formerly engaged upon the Hudson River, and came here twelve years ago. His enterprise, industry, and energy promise him the reward which such qualities deserve.

We are now, at 1 o'clock P. M., approaching Milwaukee, only seven miles off. My first view of Wisconsin is a very pleasant one. I come prepared to believe it a most desirable residence. That within a few years it will become an important member of the confederacy there is no doubt.

CHICAGO, July 5, 1847.

The Convention assembled at 12 o'clock, under a spacious awning in a public square. An immense throng of citizens formed around the seats provided for the Convention. An army of reporters were seated on either side of the President.

Hon. Mr. Curtiss, the mayor of Chicago, on behalf of the Illinois Delegation, welcomed the Delegates from the different States of the Union, in a brief address, explaining the objects of the Convention.

While the Mayor of Chicago was speaking, the very beautiful 4th-of-July procession, of which I shall speak again, came into the field and formed around the Convention.

On motion of Mr. Ogden of Chicago, James L. Barton, Esq., of Buffalo, was appointed chairman *pro tem*. Mr. Chambers of Missouri, and Mr. Crocker of Wisconsin, were, on the same gentleman's motion, appointed secretaries *pro tem*.

The Rev. Mr. Allen of Massachusetts, then invoked the blessing of heaven upon the deliberations of the Convention.

Let me here say that the firemen's display in this infant city to-day excited universal admiration. I never saw anything got up in better taste. The companies were in neat uniforms. Their machines were very tastefully decorated. There was, also, a miniature ship, manned and full-rigged, drawn by 12 horses, in the procession. While moving, the crew on board *The Convention* made, shortened, and took in sail repeatedly.

S. Lisle Smith, Esq., of Chicago, submitted a plan of organization, which after an amendment submitted by David Dudley Field, Esq. of New York, was adopted.

The States were then called alphabetically, and lists of Delegates from such as were represented were handed to the secretaries.

This is undoubtedly the largest deliberative body that ever assembled. In looking around the sea of faces turned toward the Chair, I recognize, from various parts of the Union, men of distinguished talents. Among the most prominent are Senator Corwin and Gov. Bebb, Ex-Gov. Morrow of Ohio, Andrew Stewart, Joseph R. Ingersoll of Pennsylvania, Thomas Butler King of Georgia.

The gentlemen were then appointed a Committee to report Officers of the Convention. * * *

And then, on motion of Mr. Wells of Wisconsin, the meeting adjourned till 4 o'clock P. M.

There is an immense concourse of people in the City. The hotels having overflowed, private mansions were thrown hospitably open to Delegates. We had several invitations, but having excellent quarters on board the *Empire*, we remained there. There are four fine boats here, *viz.*: the *Baltic*, the *St. Louis*, the *Empire*, and the *Sultana*, all of which are crowded with guests. Our State is well represented, with the exception of *the* City.

I have met many old friends from the Empire State, now residents of the West.

4 o'clock P. M.

When the Delegates assembled, the Committee not being prepared to report, the Rev. Mr. Allen, a Delegate from Massachusetts, addressed the meeting with a view to show that the land of the Puritans was the hive from which swarmed the intelligent and enterprising settlers who were now developing the agriculture of this boundless and fertile region. He also insisted that education and religion were intimately connected with the prosperity and happiness of the indomitable West. But the settlers from New England, in the great works in which they are engaged, find themselves associated with not only citizens from other States, but from the nations of Europe. Coming, as the inhabitants of the new States do, from all parts of the world, to fix their habitations permanently here, they have a common interest.

After Mr. Allen closed, there was a spontaneous call for "Corwin," who was not, it was thought, present. But he was soon observed and pointed out in the crowd; and then a tremendous shout went up for "Corwin," "Corwin," who finally came forward amid deafening acclamations.

Immediately after reaching the stage, a profound stillness pervaded the assemblage. From five to six thousand faces, indicating intense interest, were turned upon the speaker, who riveted their attention.

Mr. Corwin closed a most impassioned and eloquent speech of half an hour, by deprecating the introduction of any political tests here. Let nothing be said or done to recall the past, to mar the harmony of the present, or to jeopard the prospects of the future. Let the bugles of party sound a truce to politics while this Convention is in session.

When Mr. Corwin closed, there was a general call for "Greeley," whom Mr. Wentworth introduced to the Convention. Mr. Greeley remarked that he had hoped that his reputation as a bad speaker would have saved him from the embarrassment of addressing so vast an assemblage.

Mr. Greeley then spoke for half an hour with much effect in favor of the objects of the meeting. He was listened to with great attention, and warmly cheered in concluding. Every word that Mr. Greeley uttered was full of truth and wisdom.

The committee appointed to nominate officers of the Convention, now, through Maj. John Biddle of Michigan, reported. * * *

After the report of the Committee had been read, Mr. Charles King of New Jersey, from the Committee, moved that the report be amended by substituting the name of Thomas Corwin instead of that of Edward Bates, as president of the Convention.

Mr. Corwin immediately rose, and peremptorily declined to serve, even if chosen, under such circumstances.

The report of the Committee was unanimously accepted.

Mr. Bates, in taking the Chair, made an able and impressive exposition of the objects and duties of the Convention.

Mr. Schenck of Ohio, from the same Committee, reported sundry resolutions in relation to the forms of proceeding, which elicited a long debate.

Upon a resolution for the appointment of a committee to prepare an address, a constitutional debate sprung up, in which David Dudley Field of New York, Robert C. Schenck of Ohio; Mr. Stringham of Buffalo; Judge Thomas and Senator Judd of Illinois; and Mr. Hone of New York, participated. The resolution was laid on the table.

The debate was continued till a late hour, but as the mail is about to close, I can not give even the result.

July 6, 1847.

The Convention met at 9 o'clock A. M.

Prayer by the Rev. Mr. Allen.

The President announced the arrival of Delegations from the States of Kentucky and Rhode Island.

The President then announced the appointment of the Committees on Resolutions. * * *

D. Gardner, Esq., of New York, rose and stated that he held in his hand a set of resolutions representing the voice of some 70 Delegates, which he asked the privilege of reading. The resolutions were referred to the Committee on Resolutions without reading. It was requested that all those Delegates having propositions prepared, submit the same to the Committee on Resolutions.

Mr. Allen of Missouri, read a letter from Hon. Thomas H. Benton, a copy of which I send. * * *

The President then announced the reception of letters from other distinguished men, all of which were ordered to be read. That of Ex-Gov. Wright was first read. That of Henry Clay was next read. It was only a brief note explaining why he was unable to attend the Convention. Letters were read in succession from Hon. Washington Hunt of Lockport, Daniel S. Dickinson of Binghamton, Lewis Cass of Detroit, Thomas B. Curtiss of Boston, Joseph Grinnell of New Bedford, Bradford R. Wood of Albany, George P. Barker of Buffalo, Alpheus Felch of Ann Arbor, Martin Van Buren of Lindenwald, R. McClelland of Michigan, Charles Butler. * * *

The letters of Col. Benton and Gov. Wright were well received; those of Messrs. Hunt, Grinnell, and Wood elicited warm expressions of admiration. That of Mr. Cass elicited strong expressions of disapprobation. Its second reading was called for, and, upon its second reading, renewed and increased expressions of disapprobation were manifested. A profound silence succeeded to the reading of Mr. Van Buren's.

The Convention called up Hon. Andrew Stewart of Penn., who addressed it at length, with much effect, upon the subject which brought it together. He took strong ground and was warmly cheered.

David Dudley Field of New York, followed, expressing the views entertained by those who were partial to the doctrines which led to the veto of former Harbor-and-River Improvement Bills. Mr. Field was more liberal than others of his sect, but his views were in conflict with those entertained by the Convention. * * *

CHICAGO, July 7, 1847.

You will find full reports of the proceedings of the Convention in the Chicago papers. The resolutions, which were reported and adopted unanimously, are all that could be desired. They were well considered and forcibly discussed by Hon. John C. Spencer.

The Convention has this moment (12 o'clock) adjourned. The reply of the President to a vote of thanks, which was excellent, drew forth six most enthusiastic cheers from the Convention, over three thousand delegates being present.

A letter from Mr. Webster was read to the Convention this morning, which elicited three hearty cheers.

This Convention was composed of enlightened, discriminating men. Its action was deliberate, but emphatic, and can not fail to be effective. I venture to predict that no more Harbor-and-River Bills will be vetoed or "stolen."

The Convention was fortunate in the selection of its president, though when called to the Chair, but few were aware of his fitness to discharge its duties. Mr. Bates was a member of Congress in 1824 and 1825. Then the sole representative from Missouri, he felt it to be his duty to cast the vote of his State for Mr. Adams. This lost him the popular favor of his State, and he has since been in retirement, greatly respected at St. Louis as a distinguished member of the Bar.*

If Gen. Cass had any hold upon the confidence of the people of the West, his cold, formal, and almost disrespectful letter to this Convention, has forever blasted his hopes. Its first reading occasioned a general, broad laugh. The second reading changed the expression into one of withering scorn. And this was scorn of men who wield the political power of Michigan, Illinois, Wisconsin, and, to a good degree, of Ohio.

Chicago is destined to be a large and beautiful city. It is regularly laid out, with its broad avenues, and, out of the business part of the city, it is thickly planted with trees, which will soon, in addition to adorning the city, furnish a grateful shade. It has four admirably-conducted public-schools, much larger than ours, and filled with children. The various religious denominations have large houses of public worship. The River, extending well through the City, furnishes an ample and excellent harbor.

All are looking forward anxiously to the completion of the Canal. That done, Chicago will eclipse even its own past magic-like growth. In ten years, Chicago will contain more inhabitants than Albany.

* See page 172.

We rode a few miles out yesterday, to get a glimpse of the prairies. In doing so, we found the road all the way occupied with an almost unbroken line of wagons, drawn generally by two yokes of oxen, bringing wheat to the City. These teams are called "prairie schooners." That eccentric member of Congress from Alabama, Felix Grundy McConnell, among his last acts, asked the House of Representatives to "*Resolve*, That this is a great country, and constantly increasing." One needs to visit Chicago to realize and confess that the proposition is one of undeniable truth.

It is said here, that the article in the *Union*, throwing cold water on the Convention, kept Senators Breese and Douglas, with other leading Loco-Focos, away. But a large number of the "bone and sinew" of the Democracy of the West are here.

We leave this evening in the Steamer *St. Louis*, Capt. Wheeler, for Sault de St. Mary. Senator Corwin, Gov. Bebb, and Hon. Robert C. Schenck of Ohio, Roswell L. Colt of Patterson, N. J., Trumbull Cary of Batavia, Thos. C. Love, Seth C. Hawley, Dr. Foote, and George W. Clinton of Buffalo, with a large number of ladies and gentlemen, are of the party.

The following is a sketch of the remarks of Senator Corwin and Mr. Greeley, on the first day:—

As the Rev. orator took his seat, *Tom Corwin* was loudly called for from all parts of the assemblage. With his proverbial and characteristic modesty, he seemed anxious to hide himself among the crowd, but he was too well known, and being speedily discovered, was fairly lifted from his seat, and forced to the stand. He was greeted with an outburst of applause, which showed how deeply seated was the admiration and respect all felt for the wagon-boy of Ohio.

Mr. Corwin said he would have been most happy could he be excused from answering at this time to the imperative call which had brought him before the audience. He complimented the Rev. gentleman who had preceded him, and united with his tribute to the Puritans; one of whom he presumed the gentleman was himself (a laugh). As for himself, he thought it must be evident to every one who saw him from a *prima-facie* view, that he could not be descended from the same stock (a laugh). It almost seemed as if he was brought forward directly after the Rev. gentleman to produce a sort of discord by comparison. Yet, however much we may have been indebted to the hardy and noble sons of New England for much that elevates and ennobles the West, he would venture to say that if any one would enter the interior of Illinois and Iowa, he would find many of the strong-armed sons of Pennsylvania, many from the good old State of Kentucky, and *huge swarms* (turning to Mr. Allen) from Ohio.

Gentleman had all heard of Ohio—he resided there himself—if they doubted the existence of such a place, and would put him upon the stand, he would prove it to them—yet there are some in our wide world who have not a very clear idea of it. He once met a Frenchman who complained bitterly of our *diplomats*. He inquired what was the matter with them? were they not dignified and gentlemanly in their deportment? Yes, but they spoke no language at all—What, not their own mother vernacular? No, they spoke a kind of *patois;* he believed they called it *Ohio* (a laugh).

He spoke of the involuntary impulse which had gathered together from all parts of the Union, men of the highest respectability and most exalted worth. In this remark he meant by no means to be egotistical (a laugh). They had here united, forming a great *Congress of the American People.* It is a far nobler patriotism than conquering distant nations with your war-clad armies, thus to assemble to secure the blessings of a free government. There is no people under the wide heaven who would have exhibited, as you do to-day, so keen and true an estimate of this great truth. This impulse had moved men from every part of the land to this gathering point.

Away from distant *Massachusetts*, from the city of the merchant princes, the old Bay State has sent her sons.

And from the old colony of William Penn, come representatives to this Congress of American People, without any *per-diem* allowance or mileage, to marry the good old drab city of Philadelphia to the young city of Chicago.

And from distant Savannah comes one, to learn here whether our glorious republic is destined to be composed of widely-disjointed fragments, or whether it is to become, and remain united until the "last syllable of recorded time."

Was not this a noble Congress? He had been for many years a member of another Congress, but could he transplant this one to the Ten Miles Square, he would gladly *swap* the old one for it.

Congress has power to regulate commerce between the several States. If you send a cargo of wheat from Chicago to Buffalo, a distance of 1000 miles, crossing lake after lake, stretching away in their magnificent length, would not one naturally think that this might be called *commerce?* But no, that is a mistake, we are told. What is it then, my brother? Why that is *trade* (a laugh). But if you send the same cargo from New York to New Orleans, what is it then? Well, then it is *commerce.* Why is it not in the first instance as well as in the last? Oh! it is not on salt water (a laugh).

He begged gentlemen would notice this nice distinction between *commerce* and *trade.* If we are engaged in business upon salt water it is *commerce.* If upon fresh water, then it is *trade* (a laugh).

Such is the beautiful construction of that clause in the Constitution, as given to it in various parts of the Union. If you are desirous of knowing the construction of that clause, recollect! you are not to ask the opinion of some able *lawyer* or erudite *statesman*, but you must seek some distinguished *chemist* and have the water carefully analyzed to discover whether it is *salt* or *fresh* (a laugh).

It would be interesting to inquire what influence *commerce* has had in producing the success of your own good city, and in building up the abodes of civilization where, but yesterday as it were, the wild savage ruled your prairie land. Without *commerce* it would never have existed, and we should not be assembled here to-day. *Commerce* and *Christianity* have marched hand in hand—the pioneers of the West. It is *commerce* which builds up and enlarges a nation. Countries are prosperous, as an almost universal rule, exactly in the relative proportion of the seaboard to the inland extent of territory. Africa at this day is as dark and desolate as ever, her seaboard is only one square mile to 900 inland. Even our New England, without *commerce*, notwithstanding her stern and heroic sons, would have sooner become barbarous than what she is now.

He spoke of the future greatness of the country between the East and the Rocky Mountains—it would at no distant day become the arbiter of the destinies of the Republic—it would make our Presidents and enact our laws. (Turning to Mr. Allen). It is well, sir, that you have come among us to see your future masters (a laugh)—its rights will be maintained; the ballot-box will secure us the same privileges accorded to our brethren, I have never seen a disease in the body politic that could not be cured by the ballot-box. Shall treasure be poured out for the ocean mariner? and shall not a dollar be given to remove impediments from our Lakes and Rivers? No, we do not believe this. The same indomitable energy that brought our Pilgrim forefathers through the snows of winter and the perils of the deep, is fast bringing their descendents hitherward, with their *notions* (a laugh).

He need not argue more on this occason. Every man present had an opinion in accordance with his own. In this Congress there would not be a dissenting voice.

Let us not then allow any discord to creep into our councils, to mar the harmony of the present, or jeopard the vast interests of the future. Let the bugles of party have no sound in this Convention. Let there be here no Whig, no Democrat—nothing but Americans. Let us here form a new party, and let it be the boast of us all in future years, that we aided harmoniously in urging on this great movement.

Turning to Mr. Wentworth, the Representative in Congress from this District, he continued:—

Gentlemen, when he and I can agree on any subject, there must be harmony. He had the pleasure to know that that gentleman was warmly enlisted in favor of the objects of this Convention. He might say he was *latitudinous* upon the subject; perhaps this was owing to his longitude. He goes his whole length (a laugh).

If any of the empires on earth injure or assail us, we are ready to arm ourselves to the teeth and go forth to do battle, to spend immense treasures, and draw upon all our resources; but here upon these Lakes, and in our Western Rivers, thousands of lives are lost, more than have fallen in the Mexican war, for want of a small appropriation. A single ship-of-the-line destined to protect our foreign commerce, costs us more than a million of dollars. That same gallant ship which bore the name of his own State, Ohio, cost a million and half of dollars. Four of these ships have cost us more than has been expended for our Western Harbors since the formation of our government. Every gun that you will find on board these ships costs you fourteen thousand dollars. Would it not be better to take some of these fourteen thousands and improve our Harbors at Chicago, Milwaukee, and other places, or to remove snags and sawyers from the Ohio and Mississippi?

It is a curious fact that 82 per cent of our revenues have gone to supply our armies, our forts, and our ships, leaving 18 per cent to be invested for the purposes of peace. He thought this state of things had better be reversed. There is no fear that this country will be invaded. He did not think there was a country in God's creation which would invade a land that the Yankees had already invaded.

He alluded also to the fact that these obstructions of the Lakes reacted to the great injury of the farmer, as well as commercial men. If the farmer raises any more produce than he desires to use himself, he wants a good market for the surplus. If he can not sell his produce to advantage he is prevented from giving good education to his sons and daughters, who are to be the future voters and the future mothers in the land.

Our Union ought to be so connected and consolidated that all parts can be accessible to all. It should be bound together, hooped round with railroads, as with iron ribs. The true definition of a commonwealth is that land where all parts are equally protected and equally accessible.

It is said that Thomas Jefferson violated the Constitution to acquire Louisiana, his design being to prevent what he feared might take place—that the West, at some future day, would seek to divide the Union, making the Alleghanies the separating line. If a railroad had then extended from East to West, we should not have needed to acquire Louisiana for any such reason. The sons of the Pilgrims *will* look out upon Asia, and have commercial associations with her. If proper appropriations are not made to bind the growing West to the distant East, their swarming Puritans will build up on the shore of the Pacific an independent Republic of Anglo-Saxon blood.

But this great work on which we are engaged will be accomplished. Since these same Puritans have taken it in hand, they will never rest nor sleep until it is done.

He thanked God that he had the assurance in this vast and intelligent assemblage that the hopes of the West were not to be disappointed.

After Mr. Corwin had closed, John Wentworth was called for. He declined addressing the audience, and introduced Horace Greeley, editor of the *New-York Tribune.*

Mr. Greeley said that he was somewhat humbled in being called upon to address this assemblage. He had cherished the hope that his reputation as a bad speaker had become national, and regretted to discover that it was only local. He had seen as large assemblages before, doubtless composed of men of as great respectability, but he had always before been saddened by the reflection that the assemblage was in opposition in its views and actions to a large portion of its fellow-citizens. It was a subject of gratification to all, that this Convention was not an adversary to any portion of the Union.

He was pleased to see an assembly so much larger than he had anticipated. He believed that when the Delegates returned to their homes, they had only to tell the country what they had seen here, what they saw to-day, and every one, no matter what might be the crotchets of the political leaders of his section, would be anxious to facilitate communications with this garden of the Republic.

He was accustomed to look to the results of such meetings as these. His ears heard coldly the shouts which ascended in commemoration of victorious battles, but he loved to hear the triumphs of such victories as the Erie and Welland Canals, etc.

Returning thanks for their attention, he closed.

The President of the Convention, on taking the Chair, remarked that he could not say, as is often said on such occasions, that he was grateful for the compliment paid to him, for he feared that in appointing him president, an unfortunate mistake had been made in the outset.

It could not be expected of him to enter into any argument, called upon as he had been, to his own utter astonishment, to preside over their deliberations. He had hoped that some one would have been selected who was tall enough to be seen across the Alleghanies: some one whose fame was confined to no locality, but like that of the gentleman from Ohio, everywhere illustrious.

He could not but reiterate his regret that he, who had for twenty years been strictly confined to his legal duties, should have been selected to mar, by his blunders, the deliberations of the Convention. He felt that he had not a name and character in the Union sufficient to render him worthy of this position. But let it be so. He trusted that indulgence would be shown him, and his errors pardoned.

He would simply say, that not only the present race who peopled this broad land, but all the vast generation whose home it was to be in future years, demanded of them to perform their whole duty wisely and cautiously. They had all been called together by the everywhere-pervading feeling that they had been injured by defective legislation.

He believed that the constitutionality of the objects of this Convention needed no proof. That was proved when the Constitution was written.

He closed with an allusion to Mr. Corwin's remark, that the West was destined to become the ruler of this continent, trusting that when it came into power it would rule in righteousness.

LAST DAY.

Although we have already given the official proceedings of the Convention to its close, there is much of interest yet behind. The brief sketches of the debates which we give to-day, merit attention.

After the introduction of the Resolutions on Tuesday afternoon, June 6, which we gave in our paper of Saturday, the Convention proceeded with the business as follows:—

The President remarked that he would not take the question upon the adoption of the resolutions, until after some remarks from Hon. John C. Spencer of New York, in their support and elucidation.

Mr. Spencer was heartily welcomed by the Convention.   *   *   *

Mr. Gardiner of Troy, N. Y., was then called for.

Mr. Gardiner had but a few observations to make. He expressed the entire concordance of his own view with those expressed in the resolutions.

Mr. Gardiner dwelt very ably and eloquently upon the true definition of the term, *nationality*. He stated that the aggregate amount of the commerce of the lakes was now between $600,000,000 and 700,000,000, while our foreign trade, both exports and imports, amounts to only $230,000,000. He asked if an interest so vast as this was not a *national* interest, what is nationality?

Mr. Gardiner described the immense circle of interior trade, sweeping from the East to the Gulf of Mexico, around the valley of the Mississippi to the waters of the north, and asked if this vast interest had not the stamp of *nationality?* He spoke of the time when future generations—the sons of those before him—should dwell on the shores of the far *Pacific*. Would they not then wish for some line of intercommunication stretching from one shore to another?

He spoke of the resolutions as precursors to other resolutions, when Congress should be supplicated to establish a railroad from Chicago to the shores of the Pacific.

David Dudley Field congratulated the Convention that the resolutions would bring the Convention upon common ground. He had little fault to find with them; they had his cordial assent, and affirmed precisely what he himself had affirmed in the morning, that the seaboard and inland waters are under the same category for constitutional action. He had, however, a desire to offer an amendment to the 5th resolution, by moving to strike out the last clause, and would therefore move the question be taken upon the resolutions separately.

Mr. Green of Ohio, wanted to reflect before he voted. They could as well be taken to-morrow morning as then.

Mr. Bigham, of Penn., said he was going to leave in the boat that night with several hundred other Delegates, and was anxious to have an opportunity to vote upon them before leaving, he hoped they would be passed.

Judge Thomas proposed that they be acted upon *seriatim*.

Mr. Fenno moved that all be passed at once, except the resolution objected to by Mr. Field.

Judge Thomas made a brief address in support of the unanimous passage of the resolutions. He believed that when they were read one by one, and every word scanned, there would be no dissenting voice. They embodied general principles, and did not invite attack by specific declarations. He had the honor of being placed upon that Committee, a majority of whom were politically opposed to him, yet all their action had been courteous and conciliatory, and in a common spirit of harmony and peace they had been offered.

To illustrate the courtesy of the Committee, he would relate an incident connected with their proceedings. It happened that in one of the resolutions the word *repudiate* was used; but upon his suggesting that some other word had better be used, it was immediately withdrawn, and no such word appears in the resolutions.

The resolutions were then passed *seriatim*, and without opposition, except to the 5th, which, however, was unavailing, and the whole report of the Committee was adopted as the voice of the Convention.

One or two additional resolutions were then submitted and adopted.

Mr. Redfield, desired to offer an amendment to one of the resolutions of the Committee. It was, he said, in the language of Gen. Jackson.

Laid on the table.

The assemblage called upon Thomas Butler King of Georgia, for a speech. That gentleman came forward in answer to the call.

Mr. King said he knew it was not for anything he had to say, as coming from him, that this assemblage wished him to speak, but they were anxious to hear what were the opinions and views of the free and independent citizens of Georgia, who have sent me here to meet you, upon the questions for whose consideration you are gathered together.

He came as no party man. There was a time when both the political parties of his State were opposed to internal improvements. But that time had long since passed by. They have grown more intelligent, and better know their own interest.

As he was on his way hither in the cars, it was whispered around him that there was a delegation in the cars from the State of Georgia to the Chicago Convention—and he overheard the inquiry, "What the devil has the State of Georgia to do with that Convention?" (A laugh.)

He would reply that the State of Georgia was one of the old Thirteen, and that it had a great interest in the welfare of all its bright and glorious daughters.

It would seem as if a prophetic spirit dwelt in the hearts of our eminent men of old, in relation to the future destinies of the West.

He mentioned the suggestions made by Mr. Gallatin, Secretary of the Treasury in 1808, for improvement of the routes—from the Hudson to the great Lakes—from the waters of the Chesapeake to the head of navigation on the Ohio, and from the head waters of the Savannah to the head waters of the Tennessee. The first two of these routes have been successfully accomplished, and the last will be within the space of twelve months. This last route will be extended by railroad to Cincinnati, and probably to St. Louis. We like our Northern brethren exceedingly, and we bid them God speed in all their enterprises, but we of the South desire also to come in for our share of the benefits to be derived from these great interests, and we intend to offer you a Southern outlet, and we shall welcome you in our orange groves, when the snows of winter render your homes less pleasant than ours.

We give fair warning to the Empire State that we intend to rival her in bearing off the products of the West. We do not say she should enlarge her Erie Canal. That is left for the decision of her own wise men, better capable of judging than himself. He only gave her fair warning. The South is wide awake. But there will be no necessary rivalry among the different parts of the Union for your exports—all the railroads and canals which can be built will not afford outlets sufficient for your productions.

We too have our harbors and rivers, and we are anxious that yours should be improved, for we desire your coöperation to secure the improvement of our own.

It is for the interest of the Union that you should receive these appropriations in another point of view. In our next contest with John Bull—and a contest must come as sure as this great world rolls round, the theatre of action will be upon these inland Lakes—when that time comes he wanted our harbors ready for our navies, he disliked hard blows as much as any man, but if he had got to fight, he wanted to be able to strike a little harder than his enemy. Governments wants safe harbors on these Lakes for naval depots, as you do for commerce.

Mr. King remarked that as long as he held a seat in Congress, they might always count upon his vote for the harbor-and-river interest. Justice has been long delayed, and he wondered not that the West rose to demand it. Some of our politicians had held to the dogma, "Give liberty, and you give anarchy." He spurned such a doctrine as totally unworthy any freeman of this country.

He was pleased with the distinction drawn by the gentleman from Ohio, between *commerce* and *trade*, but he must say, if all salt-water navigation was entitled to the name of *commerce*, he believed these Lakes were clearly under the provisions, for so many cargoes of salt had been sunk in them that their water might safely be given to a *chemist* to be analyzed.

He supposed if the Pilgrims had first come up the Mississippi instead of landing at Plymouth Rock, and the West had been first settled, we should find this ground reversed, and that *fresh*-water navigation would be under the provisions, and we poor Atlantic States should be now demanding the same that you request.

One great truth has been asserted here—that when a cargo leaves any part of the West for a foreign port, it comes under the head of foreign commerce from the moment it is embarked, as much at Chicago as at New York.

Delegates had assembled to scatter old puerile notions, and he hoped they would never fail to assemble year after year, until their great objects were accomplished.

Even Mr. Calhoun, in his Memphis Report, says the mouth of the Mississippi must be improved at any cost. What difference is there in this respect between the mouth of the Mississippi and the mouth of the Chicago?

Mr. King spoke at length on the subject of public lands. He wondered not that the West on this subject were sensitive. It was the great domain on which they lived, and they naturally feel that it should be used for their benefit. He had voted in Congress, and would again, to grant to the States alternate sections along the canals and railroads; it would serve to bind them together still more closely. He went for internal improvements, because it would bind the East to the West—the North to the South.

He alluded to the great railroad to the Pacific. Such a line of communication was necessary and expedient. The United States would never give up Oregon, and it was fortunate that we had a constitutional way pointed out to us to accomplish such works—pointed out, by the most thoroughgoing of Southern abstractionists.

Mr. Calhoun says it would be constitutional to contract beforehand for 25 years to transport mails on great public lands.

He thanked the Convention for its attention to his discursive remarks. He himself, and all whom he represenented, would act in zealous good faith with them in carrying out the great objects of the Convention. Adjourned to 9 o'clock next morning.

Wednesday Morning.

Convention met pursuant to adjournment.

Provisions were then made for the publication of the proceedings and their distribution among the people.

Hon. Thomas Corwin of Ohio, then offered the usual resolution of thanks to the Chairman.

Thereupon, the Chairman, Mr. Bates of St. Louis, arose and, in one of the most appropriate speeches, returned his thanks to the Convention.

The speech, if ever published as delivered, will be pronounced one of the richest specimens of American eloquence. He was interrupted continually by cheer upon cheer; and at its close, the air rung with shout after shout, from the thousands in attendance.

The Convention adjourned at half-past eleven to-day, with more harmony, if possible, then it commenced. Never have we witnessed such a harmonious meeting, from beginning to end. Its proceedings have been worthy any people and any cause. And the interest of the public was continued throughout all the sittings. Up to the last hour the crowd was a dense one, and every Delegate staid to the end.

This Convention must rank as one of the most respectable, and we hope it will prove one of the most useful, ever assembled on the continent. This is a strong expression, we know. But we ask those who may be inclined to doubt it, to first hear before they judge. * * *

The President announced the following named gentlemen as composing the committee to gather statistics and present the same to the consideration of the Congress of the United States:— * * *

THE COMMITTEE OF THE WHOLE.—After the adjournment of the great Convention yesterday, on motion, the assemblage resolved itself into a "committee of the whole," Horace Greeley of New York, in the chair. Gov. Bebb of Ohio, Mr. Loomis of Penn., Gen. Hubbell of Wisconsin, S. Lisle Smith of Illinois, Mr. Burlingame of Mass., Mr. Allen of Mass., and Horace Greeley were successively called upon, and addressed the meeting on general subjects connected with the cause which brought them together.

Some of the most soul-stirring speeches that have been made in the three days past were evoked by this occasion.—*Chicago Com. Adv.*

STEAMBOAT ST. LOUIS, July 9.

Soon after leaving Chicago, on Wednesday evening, a meeting of the passengers was called, to determine our route. The chair was taken by Philip Hone of New York. After an expression of views and wishes by the passengers, a committee, consisting of Hon. Mr. Schenck of Ohio, Hon. Wm. Mosley of Buffalo, and another individual, was appointed, to obtain information from Capt. Wheeler, whom we regretted to find ill in his berth. Upon learning from the Captain how much time would be consumed in the excursion, and what points were most attractive, we reported to the meeting, when it was determined that the boat should, after touching at Milwaukee and Sheboygan, proceed to Green Bay, for the purpose of cruising for a day among its picturesque islands.

There is a much larger number of passengers than was expected. Several hours before leaving Chicago, the officers of the boat refused to promise staterooms or even berths. But the interest of the excursion and the reasonableness of the fare, combined, were irresistible. The boat goes where the passengers direct, and remains as long as they choose, for $2 per day, including board.

I mentioned, I believe, that Mr. Corwin, Gov. Bebb, and Mr. Schenck of Ohio, were with us. There are several other gentlemen of distinction from Ohio, and among them, Hon. J. C. Wright and Judge Hall of Cincinnati, and Mr. Parkhurst, G. W. Davis, and Mr. Thurston, with many ladies. Hon. Thomas Butler King of Georgia, is with us. Hon. Edward Bates, President of the Convention. Thomas Allen, Esq., formerly of the *Madisonian*, Mr. Chambers of the *Republican*, Mr. Treat of the *Union*, Mr. Keemle of the *Reveille*, and Doct. Simpson all of St. Louis, are here. They go up Lake Superior to the Falls of St. Anthony. Mr. Foote of the *Buffalo Commercial Advertiser*, Mr. Williams of the *Detroit Advertiser*, Mr. Green of the *Cincinnati Herald*, and Mr. Camp of the *New-York Police Reporter*, are of the party. From Buffalo we have N. K. Hall, S. C. Hawley, G. W. Clinton, T. C. Low, Col. Barton, Mr. Spalding, etc.

Charles King of the *Courier & Enquirer*, left us at Milwaukee, where he remains a day or two with his son, editor of the *Sentinel*, and in whose prosperity it is needless to say that I take a deep interest. It is peculiarly gratifying, therefore, to see and to know that Gen. King, so long "part and parcel" of the *Evening Journal*, is known for his worth, and "heard for his cause," throughout the growing West. His talents, integrity, and patriotism are acknowledged by all. His intelligence and public spirit, in forming and fashioning the institutions so essential to mental and moral cultivation, is proverbial. He is just such a man as is wanted in Wisconsin.

Mr. Cramer, who was formerly in the *Argus* establishment, is now publishing the *Daily Wisconsin* at Milwaukee, and is also a gentleman of education and talents, with great purity of purpose, and of amiable character.

I had not the opportunity I desired of seeing Milwaukee leisurely, as our boat remained there but two hours. Next to Chicago, it is to be the great city of the Far-West. Mr. Croswell and Mr. Corning, with their ladies, are at Milwaukee.

Mr. Hone, one of whose daughters accompanies him, left us at Sheboygan, where he owns property that is becoming very valuable. This place, like all that I have seen of Wisconsin, is delightful. The Sheboygan River is navigable for the largest vessels two miles, but for the want of a few thousand dollars to improve its mouth, all its usefulness is lost. But this state of things can not last.

We left Sheboygan at 7 o'clock last night, and at 6 this morning were at "Death's Door," a narrow straight, with several reefs, (where it is said a large tribe of Indians, endeavoring to escape from a hostile tribe in canoes, were all drowned), which forms the entrance to a group of wild, picturesque islands, around which we have been coasting for eight hours. The weather is delightful. Our captain and mate are familiar even with this out-of-the-way and seldom-visited region. These waters are seldom traversed, and human footsteps are rarely set upon these islands. A single light-house, with an occasional land-mark, is all that we have seen, indicating that our Government has recognized the existence of this most interesting portion of our common country.

Having completed our run through these islands, our boat was headed for the North-Manitou Island, which, being only thirty-five miles distant, we reached long before sunset. On the northwest side of this island the sand-banks rise, in some places, full two hundred feet above the surface of the Lake, and what is singular, this island of sand is without its "sand beach." The shore is almost as bold, where the banks are high, as that in our Highlands.

We were told that there is a large lake upon the summit of this island, abounding with trout, but on landing, I found that this lake was upon the level part of the island, and even with the surface of Lake Michigan.

This sand soil produces nothing but wood, though I do not understand why a soil that sustains a maple and a beech forest should not bear wheat, corn, and vegetables. There are some forty men employed here in cutting and hauling boat-wood, for which $1.75 per cord is paid. The only family here is from Granville, Washington Co. Among the privileges they regret, is that of voting a Whig ticket. From the last of October until May, they know nothing of what is passing in the world.

Saturday, July 10.

We left the Manitou Island at 8 o'clock last evening, and were called at five this morning to take a view of the beautiful approaches to Mackinac, or "Michilimacinack," that "hard word," the spelling of which has so severely tried the patience of some teachers, and has cost so much birch with others.

The early part of the night was rendered anxious by the severe illness of our friend, Trumbull Cary of Batavia, who, I am happy to say, is much better this morning. Mr. Colt of New Jersey, has been quite ill for three days.

He leaves us here, for the benefit of repose and the healthful atmosphere of this island.

The Steamboat *Baltic*, leaving Chicago 15 hours after us, was here when we arrived, she having come direct. I observe, among her passengers, a number of the Albany and Troy Delegates.

Here our party separates for the day. Most of the ladies and two-thirds of the gentlemen go on shore to enjoy a "pic-nic," for which ample provision has been made by Mr. Bloomer, our indefatigable steward.

At 10 o'clock the steamers got under way for Carp River, a distance of 12 miles, where there is said to be excellent trout fishing. We now lay at anchor at the mouth of the river, and some forty gentlemen, "armed to the teeth" with rod, reel, line, hook, fly, angle-worm, etc., etc., are intent upon beguiling and capturing the wary trout. We shall see with what success.

Our boat rides at anchor in a broad bay, from which we look out upon a broader wilderness, apparently as unbroken and fresh as it was the day that Columbus discovered this continent. Solitude—vast and sublime solitude—is the striking feature of these mighty waters and these boundless woods. Lake Michigan occupies more surface than the State of New York, and the productive, unoccupied lands bordering it. would sustain a population greater than that of all the New England States. And yet there are hundreds of miles of coast, upon this Lake, whose waters float hundreds of vessels burdened with millions of dollars, where the Government has not yet expended the first dollar for a harbor! There is a light-house, to be sure, on Washington Island in Green Bay, which warns the mariner of that danger, but if he is in a gale, or needs a harbor, he may run over an hundred miles without finding one.

4 o'clock P. M.

The boats have just returned from the Carp River. The enterprise was not all that was expected. The party were beset by merciless mosquitoes, and, if possible, still more ferocious flies. Trout were abundant, but fastidious. They were probably not acquainted with, or possibly objected to, the city mode of being caught. An hundred and fifty were taken, of which Mr. Clinton caught 39. But though the fish were shy, the mosquitoes and flies bit magnificently, as is apparent in the stung, swollen, and blood-besmeared faces of the anglers.

We are now preparing to return to Mackinac to receive our "pic-nic" friends on board, then to depart for Sault de St. Marie.

STEAMBOAT ST. LOUIS, MACKINAC, July 10, 1847.

This island, though the abode of peace, and peaceful in all its parts now, has been the theatre of many and horrible atrocities. One of its most appalling tragedies was enacted in 1763, when a small fort was garrisoned by 70 British troops, and afforded a shelter for half-a-dozen English traders, among whom was Alexander Henry, a most intelligent and enterprising trader. Mr. Henry had been adopted as a brother by a Chippewa Indian by the name of "Wawatam," who, on one occasion, when the Indians obtained a quantity of liquor, fearing that while intoxicated he should not be able to restrain them, took Mr. Henry to a cave, where he lay concealed two days and nights, until the debauch was over, when his Indian brother came for him.

Subsequently Mr. Henry's Indian brother, under various pretexts, urged him to leave the island. This effort was repeated with much earnestness, for several successive days, after which the Indian himself disappeared; and the following night a general massacre of the British soldiers and traders took place. Mr. Henry secreted himself in the house of a Frenchman, but two days afterward was discovered and given up. Eight others who had secreted themselves were found, and while the Indians were preparing for a war-dance, at which they were to be sacrificed, "Wawatam" returned with a pipe, which he smoked and then handed it to the principal chief, who also smoked, and then "Wawatam" addressed the chief, saying that he had been sent away from an apprehension that he would disclose to his white brother their intention of massacring the British for the purpose of plunder and spoil; that they had promised him that his brother should be protected; that in violation of that promise they were now about to kill him; and then reminding them of the sacredness of the relation that existed between him and his brother, claimed that he should immediately be released.

The chief, in reply, admitted the truth of "Wawatam's statement, to whom Mr. Henry was restored, and received by the other members of the family with more than Indian emotions of joy. Soon afterward, Mr. Henry saw the dead bodies of his fellow-prisoners brought from the fort to be cut up and eaten. One body was cut into five parts and placed in five kettles. Invitations (small bits of cedar-wood for cards) were sent for guests to the feast. "Wawatam" was a guest. He took his dish and spoon, and returned with a human hand and a large piece of flesh.

This is a brief account of one of the scenes of horror which used to be enacted upon this now quiet island. Its early history presents scarcely an unstained page. During our late war with Britain, Col. Croghan attempted to retake the island from the British, but with an inferior force, and was repulsed, Lieut. Holmes being among the killed. We have now an expensive fort here; and one which, in passing up, I supposed would command the island. But, upon examination, it seems to have been designed rather for ornament than defence. There is a point in the rear of this fort, of such decided advantage, that an enemy, landing at any of the exposed parts of the island, with very little trouble, and two or three guns, without any loss or danger to themselves, could utterly destroy this apparently strong fortress.

The "pic-nic" realized all the enjoyment that was anticipated. A delightful spot, with a natural bower, had been selected. Mr. Bloomer had taken care to provide a dainty repast, having with him, also, the cook, waiters, etc. After visiting the "Sugar Loaf," "Arch'd Rock," and other points of interest, the band being in attendance, dancing upon the green commenced. Other rural exercises and sports were resorted to, and kept up with spirit, until dinner was announced. The "chowder," as one or two Bostonians affirm, was one over which Mr. Webster, without loss of culinary character, might have presided. After dinner, the sports of the day were concluded by a grand "steeple chase," in which ladies and gentlemen participated. The ground selected for the chase, though apparently of an even surface, proved to be undulating! The consequence was that several gentlemen who left the starting-post with *spirit* and confidence, were either down, or distanced by the ladies. One gentleman attributed his fall to the circumstance that Mr. Bloomer, in compounding his "lemonade," had substituted champagne for water! For the offence, the steward was immediately arraigned, but Mr. Corwin, who undertook the defence, obtained a verdict of acquittal, not so much upon the merits of the case as by showing that the services of the steward were indispensable to the continued enjoyment of all parties. The party returned, greatly delighted with their excursion, at 7 o'clock P. M. In the evening, a large party of ladies and gentlemen were rowed about the harbor, for the purpose of hearing the "Canadian Boat-Song" from *voyageurs*.

At Mackinac we learned that Gov. Seward and family, who were to have been with us, passed up the night before. His attendance as a Delegate to the Convention was prevented by professional engagements at Canandaigua.

The fort here is garrisoned by a detachment of the "Brady Guards," from

Detroit. The other members of this corps are in charge of the fort at the Sault.

Sunday, July 11.

We left Mackinac at sunrise this morning. The day is calm and intensely hot. At breakfast, this morning, the trout taken yesterday in Carp River were served. They were done to a turn; and larded, as they were, with delicate slices of salted pork broiled to a crisp, I need not say that the repast was a delightful one.

At 9 o'clock we found ourselves gliding through and around an apparently interminable group of islands. We were in a broad bay, with no land except that of islands in sight. These islands, thickly wooded with hemlock, cedar, and spruce, presented a deep evergreen foliage. They were of various dimensions and in all forms. While some contained 1000, 500, 300, 200, 100, 50, and 25 acres, others were but a few rods square, and several were mere tufts, all, however, covered with trees and foliage. This splendid bay forms the head of Lake Huron. The islands are all uninhabited. They stand up amid these mighty waters, silently but impressively teaching the wonders of Nature to the children of man—having been spoken into existence by an all-wise and omnipotent Creator.

At 10 o'clock, the passengers were summoned to attend Divine service. The Rev. Mr. Allen officiated. During the service, our boat had passed through this magnificent archipelago and entered St. Mary's River. This river, you know, is the outlet for Lake Superior. It is something more than forty miles long, with a current of three miles to the hour. Its banks are low and thickly wooded. Midway between the mouth of this river and the Sault, is St. Mary's Lake. Upon the shores of the river and lake, we saw numerous Indian lodges, whose inhabitants seemed enjoying the repose of the Sabbath. The smoke from these wigwams curled very gracefully through the forest. But one white family was seen along the river, until we approached the Methodist Mission House, which is in the vicinity of the Sault.

Our pilot having but an imperfect knowledge of this river, it was not deemed prudent to proceed very near the Sault with a vessel drawing so much water as the *St. Louis*. An anchor was cast nearly thirty miles from the Sault, shortly after which the *St. Clair*, a boat that plies between the Sault and Mackinac, on her way to the latter place, came alongside, received our passengers, and put back, landing us at 8 o'clock P. M.

So large a number of visitors had never before landed here in a body. A rush for apartments ensued. The "Van Anden House" and the "St. Clair Hotel" were filled to an overflow. Mr. Corwin and several other gentlemen found quarters in the fort. Those who were unable to get accommodations at the hotels, remained on board the *St. Clair*. Mr. Van Anden gave us up his family room. At 9 o'clock, we (some fifty) supped upon deliciously broiled whitefish that were caught after our arrival.

Monday, July 12.

We were astir at sunrise this morning. An hour was consumed in walking about the town, which has a population of 1000 or 1200, chiefly French and half-breeds. After breakfast, three of us started for the head of the Rapids, where a bark canoe, in charge of three *voyageurs*, had been engaged for the day. Above the rapids lay three fine schooners that had been moved by land over this carrying place. Here is a broad and beautiful bay, out of which you pass into Lake Superior. The *Julia Palmer* (formerly the ship *Julia Palmer*), a steamer that had been moved on ways from the River St. Clair into Lake Superior, was off for Copper Harbor, nearly two hundred miles up the Lake.

We seated ourselves in the bottom of our canoe, upon mats, and glided up and across the Bay some three miles above the rapids, into her Majesty's dominions.

In consequence of a painful occurrence in running the rapids, some three weeks since, when a boat was dashed against the rocks and three visitors drowned, we were told that the *voyageurs* would not take us over, and many who promised themselves the excitement of running through these boiling waters, relinquished the enterprise. But in returning, our crew headed directly for the rapids, through which we passed pleasantly and safely, avoiding the rocks over which the water bubbled, on either side of us, by a dexterous and graceful use of the paddles. The distance is three-quarters of a mile, over which the current swept us in seven minutes. After this, several other parties chartered canoes and came down in the same manner.

Arrangements were then made for trout fishing. Ladies and gentlemen supplied themselves with tackle, and more than an hundred anglers sallied forth. But the day was so clear and bright that the trout rose reluctantly, and but few were taken. While others were fishing, we rambled about on the Canada shore, visiting the establishment of the Hudson-Bay Fur Company, etc., etc.

There is nothing at the Sault which strikes a visitor so forcibly as the fact that our Government has neglected to construct a ship-canal around these rapids, connecting the waters of the mighty Superior with those of the lower Lakes, and thus perfecting a chain of Lake-and-River Navigation more than three thousand miles in extent. It is not possible to select a point more favorable to a ship-canal. The distance is but three-quarters of a mile! The elevation is but 22 feet! This great work might be completed for less than a quarter of a million of dollars. And yet it has not been done. I shall be disappointed if Messrs. Corwin, Butler King, and Schenck, who are with us, do not press this improvement in the next Congress.

Large quantities of copper, some in masses and some in barrels, lay upon the wharves here. I observed much virgin copper blocked out from the mines in pieces weighing from one to two thousand pounds. I was happy to learn that a copper mine, in which our friend Greeley has a large interest, is promising to be very valuable.

Tuesday, July 13.

We turned our faces homeward this morning. The passage down the St. Mary's River, and again through the Bay of Islands into Lake Huron, was truly magnificent. Presque Isle, upon the Michigan side of the Lake, is the first landing. Here we took in wood, ice, and fish. Along here is a coast of nearly two hundred miles almost wholly uninhabited. Upon an uninhabited island, some fifty miles from Presque Isle, a son of Senator Backus, who resides at Saginaw, Michigan, has a fishing-station, where he is now engaged with a dozen fishermen, and where he expects to put up 3000 barrels of whitefish during the season.

Wednesday, July 14.

We came out of Presque Isle last evening with a breeze which promised to freshen into something lively, but before 11 o'clock the wind subsided, and the Lake became as it has been for a fortnight, calm and unruffled. At 2 o'clock this afternoon, we passed Fort Gratiot, at the outlet of Lake Huron, and soon entered the beautiful St. Clair River, for which my admiration is, if possible, increased. I have never seen a water-and-land view combining so much that is rich and beautiful. They tell me that the winters here are long and severe. But the wheat, corn, vegetables, etc., look vigorous and healthy, and are well advanced.

We reached the St. Clair Flats at 4 o'clock. This spot, as I have remarked, reminds an Albanian of the Overslaugh. Here vessels arriving in the night are detained until morning, as there are no lights or beacons to enable them to discern the channel. And vessels other than steamers are compelled to lay here for a favorable wind.

There are now over SEVEN HUNDRED steamboats, propellers, brigs, and schooners navigating these Lakes. In July, 1846, as Capt. Mills, who had charge of the dredge, reports, 71 steamboats, 37 propellers, 59 brigs, 128 schooners, and 81 coasting craft passed the St. Clair Flats. Thirty-one of these vessels were compelled to employ lighters in crossing, and all were more or less obstructed and delayed. And yet, though a few hundred thousand dollars would remove these obstructions, Jackson, Van Buren, and Polk have opposed, resisted, and defeated appropriations!

Time has passed very pleasantly upon the *St. Louis* since we left Chicago. Though the number of passengers was too large for a pleasure excursion, yet the efforts of the officers to accommodate and please, and the disposition of passengers, generally, to be pleased, has been successful. The passengers breakfast, as at the Astor House, whenever they please, between the hours of 7 and 11 A. M. There is a lunch at 12. At half-past 2 we dine. A substantial tea is served at 7; and at 10 the supper-table is spread. And the fare is not only uniformly abundant, but the cooking excellent. The table is loaded with meats, viands, delicacies, etc., all served in good taste.

Our evenings are uniformly gay and joyous. Immediately after tea, the tables are removed from the saloon, the band appears, and "the ball opens." Of our party, which numbers about two hundred, nearly one-third are ladies —agreeable and accomplished ladies, whose conversation, music, and accomplishments invest the excursion with an interest which ladies only can impart to society, and without which it would have been robbed of half its enjoyment. Dancing commences at 8 and continues till 11 o'clock, with much spirit, not only by the young ladies and gentlemen, but by many of the elder and graver personages, to whom the occasion has brought back something of the freshness and inspiration of youth.

The *St. Louis* left Buffalo on the 29th ultimo, expressly for a pleasure excursion, taking the Chicago Convention in its way. The following list of "stores" consumed (taken from the steward's bills) will give an idea of what has been going on among us:—

16 quarters fresh Beef,	3 bbls. Corned Beef,	30 dozen Ale,
22 Lambs,	2 " " Pork,	16 " Porter,
11 Sheep,	15 boxes Soda Biscuit,	24 baskets Champagne,
9 Calves,	4 barrels Crackers,	16 dozen Madeira,
18 Pigs,	4 large Cheeses,	9 " Port,
600 Chickens,	12 kegs Pickled Oysters,	15 " Claret,
5 doz. Turkeys,	12 " " Lobsters,	18 " Congress-Water,
40 Hams,	6 barrels Flour,	14 " Cider,
128 live Lobsters,	2 " Indian Meal,	7 boxes Lemons,
450 lbs. Bass, Trout, etc.,	20 " Apples,	2 barrels Crushed Sugar,
150 lbs. Halibut,	1 " Mackerel,	4000 segars,
60 Beef Tongues,	8 boxes Raisins,	6 wheelbarrow loads of
125 Sweetbreads,	6 " Oranges,	Mackinaw Trout, White
800 doz. Eggs,	45 dozen Soda,	Fish, etc., etc.

The preponderance of "sack" over the "bread," in this bill, is not as great, by any means, as in that presented by Dame Quickly against Sir John Falstaff. And yet the liquids bear at least a fair proportion to the solids. It is due, however, to those who were seen most frequently at the bar, to say that they assigned the "shocking bad water" of the West, or the "excessive heat," as a reason for preferring "punch," "julips," "cobblers," "smashes," "fixins," etc., to "such horrid water."

Thursday, July 15.

We reached Detroit last evening in season to get a view of the harbor which is an admirable one, and to walk before dark through its principal avenues, which presents a broad, pleasant, and business-like appearance. The U. S. Steamship *Michigan* is laying off the City, and I regretted that we had not time to accept Capt. Champlain's invitation to go on board. This veteran is worthy of his command. He, it will be remembered, was the sailing-master who took Com. Perry's fleet so handsomely into the battle of Lake Erie, and who conducted himself with marked coolness and courage throughout the fight.

The Detroit people had heard of the contemptuous reception which the letter of Gov. Cass met with at Chicago, and were anxious to learn particulars. But it was a scene which can not be described. The letter excited laughter, derision, and scoffing. But these marks of scorn were not as withering as those expressed by the leering eye, the curled lip, and the sneering countenances of at least six thousand intelligent, independent freemen. It seemed as if every delegate present wanted to spit upon a man who, though high in station, and owing so much to their favor and support, had written them an insulting letter.

Mr. Wales, an old Monroe-County friend, keeps an excellent hotel at Detroit. After taking leave of our Batavia and Lockport friends, who have lodgings for a day or two at Wales', we repaired to the City Hall, to enjoy, for an hour before our boat left, the melody of Christy and his minstrels. The room (a large one) overflowed with an admiring audience.

We reached Sandusky at 7 o'clock this morning. Its harbor, though requiring improvement, is one of the broadest, most secure, and commodious, that I have ever seen. The City, after struggling for twenty-five years with formidable difficulties, is overcoming them all, now looks prosperous, and is no doubt flourishing. The Mad-River Railroad, which owes much of its success to the efforts of the late Gov. Vance, is nearly completed. Running, as it does, from Sandusky to Cincinnati, it is destined to become one of the great thoroughfares of the Union. Already much of the travel of the Southwest comes over this road. We called early upon Oran Follett, Esq., editor, many years ago, of the *Buffalo Journal*, and now a member of the Ohio Board of Public Works. He has a splendid mansion, embowered with rose, honeysuckle, etc., and surrounded with delicious fruit. May he live, in the enjoyment of these luxuries, "a thousand years."

Senator Corwin, Hon. Mr. Schenck and lady, and other agreeable people, leave us here. It is a privilege to have made Mr. Corwin's acquaintance under circumstances so favorable to its cultivation. I had long admired, without having seen, this distinguished statesman. The desire, previously entertained, of seeing this "favorite son of Ohio" advanced to a higher station, is increased by personal observation of his claims to the confidence of his fellow-citizens. He is, really and truly, a conscientious, unselfish. true-hearted politician, who will not, even for the Presidency, compromise principles, nor sacrifice rights. His anti-Mexican War speech, last winter, was an honest expression of indignant impulses. The War *is* an atrocious one, yet I can not but regret that, being in, our statesmen do not see the wisdom of waiting until it has been fought out, before holding the administration to its responsibilities.

I learn here that the produce speculators from the East have been making wild purchases of flour, wheat, and corn, in anticipation of more favorable news by the steamer that is now due. They will be sadly disappointed. It is strange how entirely the judgments of men are clouded by their cupidity. Nothing is more certain than that the next intelligence from England will show a further decline in breadstuffs.

Friday, July 16.

We arrived at Cleveland before sunset last evening, and enjoyed another view of this thriving City. Among its striking features is the "Weddell House," one of the most magnificent hotels in America. This building looms up like the Astor House, and is furnished with every attainable luxury. The furniture would compare favorably, in value and beauty, with that of the drawing-rooms of our "merchant princes." The house was built by Mr. Weddell, who had accumulated a large fortune in business at Cleveland. When returning from New York, last spring, where he had been to purchase furniture for this house, he took a severe cold, from the effects of which he died. The house is well kept by Mr. Barnum, who was formerly with his uncle in "Barnum's Hotel" at Baltimore.

We are now approaching Buffalo, after an absence of sixteen days, having traversed Lakes Erie, St. Clair, Huron, Michigan, and St. Mary's; run through the Detroit, St. Clair, and St. Mary Rivers, and *looked* into Lake Superior. The distance from Buffalo to Chicago is 1054 miles. From Chicago to the Sault, *via* Green Bay, the distance is about 800 miles. From the Sault to Buffalo the distance is over 700 miles. We have journeyed, therefore, more than 2500 miles upon Lakes and Rivers whose waters are whitened with the canvas and blackened with the smoke of vessels and steamers greater in number and exceeding in value the vessels and commerce of any one of the nations of Northern Europe. And yet our Government refuses to recognize this great interest as a part of the Commerce of the Republic!

The weather, during this long excursion, has been most auspicious. There has not been wind enough to disturb the most sensitive stomach. Nor has the slightest accident occurred. The Steamboat *Empire*, in going up, and the *St. Louis*, in going the rounds, behaved admirably. Capt. Wheeler and his officers were constant and untiring in their efforts to render the excursion, what it really has been, one of instruction and enjoyment. Mr. Bloomer, who acts as clerk, steward, "chief cook," and "head-waiter," (for he makes himself generally useful), is just the man to take charge of these various departments.

The *St. Louis*, though not one of the fastest, is among the best built, stanchest, and most commodious steamers on these Lakes. She is owned by the Messrs. Hollister, a family of brothers and sons who have been long known at Buffalo, and up the Lakes, as enterprising and liberal merchants, public spirited, and useful citizens, and efficient, reliable Whigs.

The following well-merited tribute to Captain Wheeler and his Officers was very cheerfully signed by the passengers of the *St. Louis:*—

The undersigned, passengers on board the Steamboat *St. Louis*, on her recent passage from Buffalo to Chicago, and thence back by way of Green Bay and Sault Ste. Marie, a voyage now about being terminated, in justice to their feelings and sense of right, can not separate without bearing emphatic testimony to the kind and courteous treatment they have experienced throughout the whole voyage, and warmly commending the *St. Louis* to all, who, for business or pleasure, may have occasion to traverse the Lakes. Fortunately, the uniform and delightful serenity of the weather has called for no striking display of seamanship, but all the officers of the boat, by their careful attention to their duties, and unremitting exertions to promote the safety, comfort, and enjoyment of all on board, have shown that they could be relied upon in any emergency.

Our thanks are especially due, and are tendered to Capt. Frederic S. Wheeler, W. Kennedy, the Mate, S. A. Stebbins, the Engineer, and T. T. Bloomer, the Steward, who, in their respective departments, have proved themselves worthy of their proverbial reputation. With a boat so stanch and well found as the *St. Louis* under us, and with such skilful and attentive officers to watch over our safety and provide for our enjoyment, traveling becomes a pleasure. We most cordially and unreservedly commend the *St. Louis* to the public.

Wm. A. Mosley,	Buffalo,	T. M. Foote and wife,	Buffalo,	Seth C. Hawley,	Buffalo,
Bela D. Coe,	"	N. K. Hall and wife,	"	George W. Clinton,	"
T. C. Love and wife,	"	Dr. Walter Cary,	"	A. P. Thompson,	"
Miss Julia Love,	"	Charles R. Gold,	"	Wm. Laverack,	"
George M. Love,	"	Geo. H. Bryant,	"	George W. Bull.	"

Miss C. E. Putnam, Buffalo,	Miss Evans, Lockport,	J. G. Lowe and wife, Dayton,
Miss A. E. Lacy, "	Miss Spalding, "	E. W. Davies & wife, "
Miss A. A. Allen, "	George Evans, "	John W. Vancleve, "
Miss H. V. Allen, "	J. J. Hollister, Monroeville, O.	Dr. Edmund Smith, "
Harrison Bristol, "	Thos. Butler King, Georgia.	Henry V. Perrine, "
Miss C. N. Bristol, "	Thomas Corwin, Lebanon, O.	Miss Harrison, Cincinnati, O.
P. G. Alvord, "	A. B. Dunlevy & wife, "	R. Buchanan and wife, "
James L. Barton, "	Miss F. Dunlevy, "	John C. Wright, "
Benjamin Barton, "	W. R. Edwards, "	James Hall, "
I. J. Hathaway & wife, "	Miss Reeve, Detroit, Mich.	S. C. Parkhurst & wife, "
Edward Bates, St. Louis, Mo.	Junius H. Hatch, "	John Ross, "
S. Treat, "	T. C. Sheldon, "	Stanley Mathews, "
J. N. Converse, "	A. S. Williams, "	Robert L. Deane, "
A. B. Chambers, "	J. N. Elbert, "	W. Greene, "
Robert Simpson, "	James Bemis, "	B. B. Hastings, Cleveland, O.
L. V. Bogy, "	Jno. G. Camp & wife, Florida.	Joseph R. Williams,
Wm. Simpson, "	Ward Barker and wife,	Constantine, Mich.
D. B. Morehouse, "	Sandusky, O.	Joel Buttles, Columbus, O.
H. S. Coxe, "	A. M. Porter, "	A. B. Buttles, "
Thomas Allen, "	Wm. Jones, Milan, O.	Jno. B. Martell, S. Ste. Marie.
Charles Keemle, "	Rev. Dr. Wm. Allen, "	L. P. Converse, Unionville, O.
Milton Knox, "	Northampton, Mass.	S. S. Osburne, Painesville, O.
John G. Priest, "	Miss Sarah Steele,	J. H. Moseley, "
T. Cary & wife, Batavia, N.Y.	Saratoga Springs, N.Y.	Jas. B. Wakefield, "
Miss Lucinda Cary, "	Miss M. E. Clement, "	P. A. Ladue, Detroit, Mich.
H. J. Redfield, "	Robert A. Wilson,	Dwight Kellogg, Ann Arb. M.
Miss Jane Redfield, "	Woodstock, C.W.	A. S. Story, Sheboygan, W.T.
Benj. Pringle, "	Hugh Richardson,	H. H. Conklin, "
Miss J. Redfield, Syracuse,	Toronto, C.W.	W. Smith "
Samuel Larned, "	Dr. E. H Merryman,	Dr. Wm. Wamplee, "
Philip Hone, New York City,	Springfield, Ill.	E. S. Thorp, "
Miss M. Hone, "	Charles A. Davis,	H. Camp, "
Wm. Burger & wife, "	Cape Girardeau, Mo.	J. B. Allen, "
Levi Beardsley, "	Wm. L. Smith, Chicago, Ill.	H. S. Anable, "
Theo. F. McCurdy, "	O. F. Niles, Mishawaka, Ia.	C. O. Loomis, Pittsburg, Pa.
Edwin C. Burr, "	Robert C. Schenck and wife,	A. W. Loomis "
Enoch E. Camp, "	Dayton, O.	Joy Mix, Logansport, Ia.
T. Weed and wife, Albany.	Mrs. W. S. Schenck, "	P. McMartin, Jers. City, N. J.
C. Joy and wife, Ovid, N.Y.	H. G. Phillips & wife, "	Ros. L. Colt, Patterson, N. J.
C. Evans and wife, Lockport.	Miss Kate Phillips, "	July 14, 1847.

NIAGARA FALLS, July 17, 1847,

We arrived at Buffalo last evening just in time to take the cars for Niagara Falls. The railroad from Buffalo to the Falls, since I was here last, has, much to the advantage of the public and the stockholders, changed hands. Instead of the rickety rail over which we were then drawn by horse-power, we were now taken through upon a substantial road in an hour and ten minutes.

Much has been done, since I was last here, to adorn Goat Island, to facilitate access to the Falls, and to enhance, if possible, the grandeur and sublimity of the views. Gen. Whitney has enlarged and improved his magnificent hotel. Mr. White, in the "Eagle," presents every possible luxury and enjoyment that "mine inn" can furnish to visitors. Mr. Hooker, who has been here almost as long as the Cateract, is still at hand, in no otherwise changed than that instead of "Hooker, Guide to the Falls," upon his hat, it is now "Hooker & Sons, Guides to the Falls." The "Indian-curiosity" business, which, twenty-five years ago, was in its infancy, has grown into a large, and from the price asked for the first article we looked at, a profitable trade. For a cigar-case intrinsically worth twenty-five cents, but for which we were prepared to pay fifty, as a fancy piece, the "Injun" (as they spell the word at Mackinac) Bazaar man had the modesty to demand $2.50! As our "curiosity" was not quite sharp enough for such a bite, we left the bargain open for the next fool.

But the grand new feature here is the Steamboat *Maid of the Mist*, that runs, three times a-day, from the Rapids, a mile below the Cataract, up that wild, fierce, whirling current, to and along the base of the mighty column which rushes from the summit "down below."

This was a bold and expensive enterprise. The steamer was placed under the Falls last year, but without sufficient power to stem the current. This discouraged some of the proprietors. But Mr. John Fiske of Rochester, went to work this season, with indomitable energy, to overcome all obstacles, and he has succeeded triumphantly.

You are taken in carriages, nearly two miles, to the steamer. The road down the bank starts from the point on the American side which has been fixed upon for a terminus to the Suspension Bridge.

As the "Rapids" and "Whirlpool," in the former of which a boat would be torn to pieces preparatory to being swallowed up by the latter, are just below the *Maid's* wharf, this voyage has a nervous look. But the precautions and guards against accident are so well and carefully provided as to inspire full confidence. The steamer has two engines, so that if one fails the other can be put in gearing in a minute and a half. She is found with two anchors and chain-cables. She has also a small boat, by means of which a strong line can be run ashore the moment a necessity for doing so exists. The *Maid of the Mist* is commanded by Capt. Filkins, who, like his engineer and pilot, keeps both eyes open and all their wits about them. Without this excursion upon the *Maid of the Mist*, a view of the Falls of Niagara is incomplete.

STEAMBOAT CATARACT, LAKE ONTARIO, July 18.

We intended to have returned to Buffalo, for the double purpose of visiting friends and seeing the extent of the commercial, manufacturing, and mechanical wonders that intelligence and enterprise have wrought in a youthful city which is destined to be second only, in the Empire State, to its great commercial emporium, since 1840. But learning that our old friend VanCleve was at Lewiston with his new boat, the *Cataract*, that temptation was irresistible. At 4 o'clock this afternoon, therefore, having come over the Niagara Falls and Lewiston Railroad, passing a succession of wheat fields whose waving straw, bristling beard, and well-filled heads, all "fully ripe," and inviting the embraces of the reaper, resembles the gold which is far less intrinsically precious, we found ourselves seated upon the beautiful promenade deck of the *Cataract*, viewing Brock's Monument upon the heights which American valor conquered; the spot where VanRensselaer fell; seriously wounded; and the sanguinary field in which Scott and Wool so gallantly fleshed their maiden swords.

The British Steamboat *Admiral*, that runs to Toronto, and evidently a craft in which John Bull takes pride, was also at Lewiston. Both boats had steam up, and the moment their passengers were on board, both "let go." They were in for a "trial of speed," though Capt. VanCleve was taken by surprise. It was, however, but a short race. The *Cataract* having gained nearly a mile upon the *Admiral* in running seven, when the latter drew off.

The *Cataract* was built at Ogdensburg, under the immediate superintendence of Capt. VanCleve, whose experience, judgment, and taste enabled him to correct many defects, and suggest many improvements. She is 225 feet long 28 feet beam, and 11 feet hold. Her main saloon is 170 feet long. She has 51 spacious, airy state-rooms, with doors opening into the saloon and out upon the guards. She has also 190 large, commodious berths. Her ladies' saloon and dining-cabins are in excellent keeping with the accommodations in other respects.

There is a neatness and beauty in the furniture, hangings, tapestry, etc., etc., of the *Cataract*, which can not fail to strike and charm passengers. Everything is arranged with an eye, as well to fitness and propriety, as to enjoyment and ease. The rooms are all richly, but not gaudily, furnished.. And every part of the boat is arranged with a view to the comfort and quiet of passengers.

When summoned to tea, the table, its furniture, and the repast itself, excited general admiration. Innumerable delicacies were served with most appetizing taste.

The *Cataract* runs with less noise and motion than I have ever known. In her model, the line of nautical beauty has been preserved, and in her construction, arrangements, and finish, she seems as nearly perfect as science and art, combined with experience and taste, could make her.

Capt. VanCleve, though yet a young man, is a veteran on Lake Ontario, where he has been in command of steamers more than twenty years. He is a capable, vigilant, and efficient officer, possessing, in an eminent degree, all the other qualities which make men respected and popular.

Lake Ontario has its full share of perils. Its navigation is often rough, difficult, and dangerous. But Capt. VanCleve, during his long career, through all seasons and all weather, has never met with an accident which seriously damaged his boat or injured his passengers.

Among the passengers on board, I notice Hon. Alvin Bronson of Oswego, and Hon. Myndert Van Schaick of New York. These gentlemen were former members of our State Senate, where, by their business habits and practical knowledge, especially in reference to the various questions of finance, they rendered valuable public service. They are both of another political faith, but I do them no more than justice in saying that they discharged their duties, as representatives of the people, upon all questions not political, with an intelligence and integrity which senators, in all coming time, may imitate with great advantage to the people.

We are now, at 10 o'clock, gliding up the Genesee River, having run down from Lewiston (over 80 miles) in six hours, showing a speed of nearly 15 miles to the hour.

[From the *Albany Evening Journal*, Friday, July 23, 1847.]

MR. BATES, PRESIDENT OF THE CHICAGO CONVENTION.

"The editor of the *Albany Evening Journal*, writing from Chicago, refers to the early history of Mr. Bates, president of the Convention. He states that Mr. Bates was the member of Congress from Missouri in 1825, when Mr. Adams was elected President by the house of representatives, and adds that the political career of Mr. Bates was brought to a violent end by his voting for Mr. Adams, the people of Missouri preferring Gen. Jackson. With all due deference to the *Journal*, knowing his usual accurate historical and political information, we submit that he is mistaken in this matter. Our own recollections are entirely different, we have not the record before us or any documents to which we can refer, but we are quite certain that Mr. Bates came into Congress for the first time in 1827. Mr. Scott represented Missouri in 1825, and his vote for Mr. Adams was the subject of much animadversion both then and thereafter. Mr. Scott was sent by Mr. Clay on some diplomatic errand, the nature of which we now forget, to the Havana; and it was allowed by the opponents of the administration that this was evidence of a corrupt understanding between Clay and Scott. It was by like unsupported charges persisted in against the most conclusive repudiation, that the heterogeneous combinations rallying under the Jackson flag were able to prostrate the purest administration which the country has ever seen since Washington's first term.

"With respect to Mr. Bates, we have a distinct recollection of his course in Congress in 1827, '28, and '29. He was elected in the summer of 1826 or

'27, against Mr. Scott, and in the expectation that he would oppose the administration of Mr. Adams. He voted for Andrew Stephenson, for Speaker, against John W. Taylor, on the organization of the House, and was placed by universal consent in the ranks of the opposition, but, a clear-headed, sagacious, and patriotic man, he early discerned the unworthy motives of the demagogues who were striving to break down Mr. Adams, and convinced of the purity and integrity of the administration, zealously, and efficiently sustained its leading measures.

"Mr. Bates soon attained an important position in the House. He spoke occasionally, only, but always with point and effect. He came there with a high reputation for firmness and intrepidity, and it soon became universally known that he was an unsafe and unsatisfactory man to run against. There were many indications of this fact. A single circumstance which occurred in the winter of 1827 will illustrate his character in this regard.

"It was toward the close of the day's session, after a protracted debate, when the House was restless and impatient, for the question, that Mr. Bates obtained the floor in the midst of a scene of tumultuous excitement, then rather rare, but common enough since locofocoism has desecrated the halls of legislation. There were cries of 'question? question? order! Mr. Speaker! Mr. Speaker!' and all sorts of ejaculations from every part of the House. Mr. Bates addressed the Chair, but his voice was drowned in these multitudinous exclamations.

"'Mr. Speaker,' said he, pitching his voice at its highest tone, 'I demand the protection of the chair.' Rap, rap, went the Speaker's hammer, 'order, order! gentlemen will observe silence. The gentleman from Missouri is entled to the floor.'

"Mr. Bates again essayed to speak, and the uproar was increased tenfold.

"'Mr. Speaker,' said Mr. Bates, in a voice whose peculiar intonations produced instantaneous and universal silence, 'the chair evidently can not protect me in my rights on this floor, as the representative of the sovereign State of Missouri, Sir,' said he, drawing himself up to his full height, and looking menacingly round the House, 'let me see the man who dares to interrupt me.'

"Mr. McDuffie, occupying a seat near to Mr. Bates, threw back his angry look and immediately shuffled with both his feet, crying 'question! question!' Mr. Bates promptly addressed a hostile note to Mr. McDuffie, with a very distinct intimation that, unless he disclaimed any personal intent, the bearer was instructed to make the necessary arrangements, etc. Mr. McDuffie replied, not only disclaiming all feelings of disrespect toward Mr. Bates, but professing the highest regard and esteem—and there the matter ended.

"Mr. Bates retired from public life at the end of Mr. Adams' administration, whether voluntarily or not we are not certain, but incline to the opinion that it was upon compulsion. He was at one time regarded as the great rival of Col. Benton, and a personal difficulty was apprehended between them. We are not apprised of the relations now subsisting between these gentlemen, but from the imperious temper and unforgiving disposition of Mr. Benton, and the high-toned independence of Mr. Bates, it is hardly to be believed they are very cordial."—*Buffalo Morning Express.*

The *Buffalo Express* is doubtless correct. Mr. Bates broke suddenly upon the Convention, and, at the moment, remembering him as a former representative from Missouri, we fell into the error of placing him in the wrong Congress.

The fact that a gentleman of such eminent ability, who stands so deservedly high at home, was almost wholly unknown to such a numerous and intelligent class of citizens as composed that Convention, shows how widely the different

States of the Republic are separated, and how important was the mission which had brought the sons of Maine, of Georgia, and of Missouri together, upon common ground, to confer upon interests valuable alike to all.

When the name of "Edward Bates" was announced as president of the Convention, the inquiry of "Who is he?" and "What are his politics?" was general. Many asked, but few could answer. But when the labors of the Convention closed, and six hearty, spontaneous cheers rent the air in honor of their president, more than four thousand delegates separated to return home and speak of Edward Bates with enthusiasm, as one of the ablest and most eloquent men they ever heard. It was the occasion of deep and universal regret that his masterly speech was not reported. It was made at the close of the session, when some of the reporters had retired, and others had put away their materials. After Mr. Bates was fairly upon his feet, all were too intent and absorbed as listeners, to think of reporting.

After leaving Chicago for the Sault of St. Marie, we had the pleasure of sharing the Captain's state-room with Mr. Bates. And then we pressed him to supply what the reporters had neglected to furnish, by writing out his remarks. But he insisted that the Convention, in its kindness, had greatly overestimated their value. His mind, he said, during the sitting of the Convention, had become deeply imbued with the spirit of its deliberations. What he had seen and heard of the magnitude of the interests involved; the number, intelligence, and patriotism of the Delegates; the courtesy, self-respect, and dignity which distinguished their action; superadded to their cordial and hearty demonstration of kindness to himself, impelled him to the utterance of such thoughts as his feelings prompted, without order, arrangement, or preparation. They were spoken, and with the impulse that produced them, gone, not to be recalled. The evening of our arrival at the Sault, Mr. Bates took a severe cold, and until he left us, three days afterward, was too much indisposed to permit us to reiterate, as we intended, a request for at least a sketch of this lost treasure.

In reference to another allusion of the *Buffalo Express*, it may not be improper to say, that after a long alienation, produced, we believe, by political differences, there was recently, on some public occasion at St. Louis, a reunion between Col. Benton and several prominent Missourians, Mr. Bates being present and participating in the "era of good feeling." Though we conversed freely of Col. Benton with Mr. Bates, the latter awarding to the former great credit for the service he had rendered the country upon the annexation and Oregon questions, it was from another member of the St. Louis Delegation that we received the information in relation to the "reunion."

Mr. Bates is a native of Virginia, about 55 years old, and, we need not add, possessing great intellectual strength. "There is a good time coming," and we look forward with confidence to a political revolution which will restore Edward Bates to the public service. The Nation can not afford to be deprived of so much integrity, talent, and patriotism.

STATISTICS CONCERNING THE CITY OF CHICAGO:

REPORT OF HON. JESSE B. THOMAS AS A MEMBER OF THE EXECUTIVE COMMITTEE APPOINTED BY THE CHICAGO RIVER-AND-HARBOR CONVENTION.

CHICAGO, ILL., *Dec. 1st, 1847.*

HON. JOHN C. SPENCER,
Chairman, Select Committee, of the Executive Com., Chicago Convention:

DEAR SIR:—Having had the honor of an appointment, as a member of the Executive Committee of the Chicago Harbor-and-River Convention, instituted for the purpose of collecting and reporting to the National Legislature statistical information in aid and furtherance of the great measures of Internal Improvement, proposed by that numerous and enlightened body; and having subsequently had assigned to me specially, by said Committee, at their meeting in Chicago, and afterward by ratification, at that held in the city of New York, the task of collecting such portion of the desired information as might tend to exhibit the claims of the ports in Indiana and Illinois, on Lake Michigan, to the pecuniary assistance of the General Government, in the improvement of their respective harbors, etc., I have the honor to report to you, as the Chairman of the Select Committee, appointed to prepare the Report to the general meeting of the Executive Committee, my actings and doings in the premises, as required by resolution.

Deeply impressed with the importance and magnitude of the duties assigned me, it would have been to me a source of unqualified gratification could I have given to their performance my undivided attention; but this, under the circumstances, was impossible. On the contrary, my official duties have drawn so constantly upon my time as to leave me almost entirely destitute of any leisure for other purposes. For this reason, while duly appreciating the high honor conferred upon me, in associating me with so many of the most illustrious and distinguished men of the Union, in the performance of labors, inevitably destined, if faithfully executed, to redound so greatly to the benefit of the whole country, it would, nevertheless, have been gratifying to me had some other gentleman, having more time and ability than myself, to devote to the promotion of the public weal in this matter, been appointed in my stead. And, under the operation of the same restrictive influences, I have since been denied the pleasure as well of attending the session of the Committee of the 15th of Sept., as of meeting Messrs. WEATHERLY of Cleveland, O., NOBLE and WILLIAMS of Michigan, and KING of Milwaukee, for comparing and digesting the results of our several operations, as required by resolution to do.

However, I am gratified to have it in my power to say, that my agency will not prove entirely barren. Deeming it proper to seek through the labors of others the information which I was required, but had not time myself to collect, I took steps, shortly after my appointment, for doing so. The result has been, that all of the desired information, connected with this City, has been gathered together, and will be found embodied in the Report hereinafter submitted; while I am in daily expectation of receiving from the other points in my district, Little Fort and Michigan City, the statistics peculiar to those points.

Were it not that I am compelled to leave home immediately, on official business, I would further await their arrival, that I might thus consolidate all the returns from the district assigned to my inquisition. As it is, I will provide for their transmission to you as soon as received, and in the meantime commit to your charge the material already in my possession, for the purposes of the Report to be prepared by the Committee, from the various sources of information to be made therefor available. An examination of this Report however will show, that, while all of the information contained in it directly affects this City and involves its best interests, there is much of it equally affecting every other port upon Lake Michigan; and indeed common in its application to every portion of the country bordering the entire Lake coast, and as touching the matter of National welfare, made up as it is of the aggregate of individual prosperity of the entire confederacy.

It contains an array of facts, exhibiting, in our view, a list of shipwrecks, and other marine disasters, on our Lake alone, so numerous, and as involved in their train, a loss of property so ruinous, and a catalogue of human lives destroyed, so appallingly swollen, as to appeal at once to the sympathies of the whole country. And, it is confidently hoped that, when the history of these disasters, and others equally mournful, and more numerous, happening on the Lakes, constituting the remaining links in the entire chain, having been written and published, shall be traced, as by the testimony in this Report, and suppletory evidence to be found in other similar documents, they, to a considerable extent will be, to the almost entire destitution of good and sufficient harbors on our coasts, the necessary measures will at once be adopted, so far as by human agency it may be done, to prevent the recurrence in future of similar calamities—that the promptness and efficiency of future legislation, in this respect, will be exhibited in admirable contrast with the tardiness and inefficiency of the past, while in the benign results of the former will be found, if not a remedy for the past evils growing out of the latter, at least a preventive of their repetition. That pecuniary appropriations, entirely adequate for that purpose, will at once be made for establishing, on the shores of our great Inland Seas, wherever the interests of Commerce may demand it, safe and convenient places of refuge from the fury of the elements—then, and not otherwise, will this important and interesting branch of the common welfare be promoted; property and life involved in enterprises connected with it, adequately protected; and the guaranties of the Constitution in that behalf, preserved unimpaired. Accompanying this, will be found the Report referred to.

I have the honor to be, very respectfully,

Your most obedient servant,

JESSE B. THOMAS.

CHICAGO, ILLINOIS.

This City is deeply interested in the improvement of Rivers and Harbors. Her geographical position is at the head of the great northern Lakes, at a point nearest and easiest of access to the West, and is the dividing point between the two sections of the Union, and the key to the northern and principal route of communication between them. This point is the commercial metropolis of an immense extent of country abounding in agricultural, manufacturing, and commercial resources; and is already the centre of a large and growing trade in produce, lumber, salt, coal, and other staples of the region, and merchandise imported for its consumption. A glance at the origin, progress, and present condition of the place, will, perhaps, best illustrate its commercial importance and claims, in common with the other cities of the Union, upon the fostering care and protection of that paternal Government, established, as we are informed, in the Constitution, for the express purpose, among others, of promoting the general welfare.

In 1832, Chicago was scarcely a village, situated far beyond the extreme western limits of civilization. As a city, it has consequently seen but fifteen summers. Its history, prior to this period, can be compressed in a few words. The French, during their wanderings in the West, often visited the place, and, some say, they built a fort here. In confirmation of this fort, *Chicagou*, is found Fon old rench maps of that period. They discovered the passage from Chicago River into the Des Plaines and Illinois, and often benefited by the discovery, passing in their canoes from one valley into the other. Although often here, there is no evidence that the French ever made a permanent settlement at this point; nothing more, probably, than a temporary station for trading with the Indians. They, however, foresaw the future importance of the situation pointed out in their writings, the practicability of a canal connecting the Lakes with the Mississippi; regarding this, from their knowledge of the country, as the point easiest of access to the navigable waters of the great valley. They had singular sagacity in this matter.

In 1796, at the Treaty of Greenville, Gen. Wayne purchased of the Indians, six miles square of land, at the mouth of *Chikajou* Creek, within which the present City is situated. This purchase was made at that time with the view of establishing here a military station, for the protection of the frontier, and the security of the fur trade. Fort Chicago was built, and occupied by a garrison in 1804, and about the same time an Indian agency was established and a light-house built.

In 1812, the Government, apprehensive of the safety of the post, ordered its evacuation. The attempt to carry this order into execution proved fatal to nearly the whole party, some seventy in number. This is known as the "Massacre of Chicago," and took place about one-and-a-half miles below the Fort, near the present southern city-limits. This unfortunate event was followed by the burning of the Fort and the temporary dispersion of the settlement. The Fort was rebuilt in 1817, when it took the name of Fort Dearborn. It was occupied by a small force as late as 1837.

Thus, it will be perceived, that Chicago, though visited by the French nearly two hundred years ago, and perhaps marked out by them as one of the links in their immense chain of posts connecting the St. Lawrence with the Gulf of Mexico, and for a period of nearly thirty years afterward, occupied as a frontier military post, and a trading-station connected with it, could not, previous to the period we have named, 1832, have had a permanent existence as a town. The united population, never exceeding one hundred, came here for temporary purposes, and not with the design of remaining permanently and settling the country. No attempt was made to cultivate the soil; supplies of all kinds were brought at great expense from the East. The country around, in every direction, was unsettled and full of Indians. Illinois, it is true, had been admitted into the Union in 1818, with a population of about 30,000; but they were confined chiefly to the southern part of the State, immigration having been derived principally from Virginia and Kentucky.

The Black-Hawk war occurred in 1832, and it was this event, more than anything else, which first brought Chicago and this region into notice, and laid the foundation for a permanent settlement. During the progress of this brief contest, many persons attached to the army, and others, visited this place, and explored the country between the Lakes and the Mississippi. Being highly pleased with the country, on their return to the East, they naturally communicated their impressions to others, and created a general desire to remove and settle here, which in process of time was carried into an execution. The successful issue of the war removed danger from the frontier, and immigration was safe. It was besides, as will be remembered, a period of unusual prosperity throughout the country, when enterprise was stimulated to extraordinary activity. These causes combined, in the latter part of 1832 and the spring of 1833, produced immigration. Lands and town-lots were eagerly sought after; speculation naturally resulted; which soon became the ruling passion of the period, and was only arrested by the universal crash and bankruptcy of 1837-8. Chicago became the centre of speculating operations, and enjoyed or *suffered* during its continuance, and inflated prosperity. Thousands flocked here from all parts of the country and the place was thronged with new citizens and strangers.

Although we have been induced to regard 1832 as the period from which to date the commencement of Chicago, still it should be stated, measures intimately connected with the place, originated at an early period. Soon after the organization of the State government, at the second session of the legislature, an act was passed to construct the Illinois-and-Michigan Canal; and the subject continued to be legislated upon at almost every subsequent session down to the present time. In 1826-7, Congress donated each alternate section of land, for ten miles in width, along the line, to aid the State in the construction of the work, and at the same time granted the right-of-way. The principal part of Chicago was included in this grant, and in 1829, commissioners appointed for the purpose, laid out the Original Town, amounting to about half-a-section on both sides of the River; and the next year, 1830, sold a few lots to pay the expenses of the survey. The Original Town is now the centre and most valuable portion of the City. Prices of lots at this sale were very moderate, from $5 to $20. A few hundred dollars would then have purchased the whole of Lake Street, now worth millions. Few persons here at that period probably dreamed that a place of 17,000 inhabitants would grow up here in the short space of seventeen years, although some may have foreseen its ultimate importance. The external appearance of things was far from encouraging. There were a few log and two or three frame-buildings scattered over the town site; besides a few more in different parts of the County of Cook, amounting to some twenty in all, besides the Fort. A small beginning it must be confessed for the Garden City; but it was fifteen years ago.

Down to 1837, as before intimated, very little was done at Chicago but *operate* in real estate. Very little or nothing was raised. Domestic wants of the community even, were supplied from the East. Vessels rarely came here, and the arrival of a schooner off the town was an event of the greatest importance. There were no roads and scarcely any travel. A weekly mail on horseback, was first received from Niles, Mich., in 1832; a one-horse wagon succeeded in 1833, followed in 1834 by a four-horse stage-line, and a daily mail in 1837. Scarcely any domestic improvements of a durable character were attempted, except dwelling-houses, although the Lake House, and two or three other substantial brick-blocks, and several warehouses date at this period. The harbor was commenced in 1833, and the first work done on the canal on the 4th of July, 1836. In 1833, the *Chicago Democrat*, and in 1835, the *Chicago American*, two weekly newspapers, were started. The School Section, one mile square of valuable land, within the City limits, was sold about this time for some $40,000. In the winter of 1836-7, the legislature passed the act incorporating the City.

In 1837, speculation having run its career, the bubble burst, and brought ruin to thousands who had become identified with it and risked their all upon its chances. It was a severe calamity to Chicago. Without capital; without a currency; with undeveloped resources; without trade; the dissipation of this fatal illusion, left her citizens nothing but a mountain of indebtedness; and the lands for which it had been incurred, now worse than valueless. Every thing remained stationary until about 1840, when times had improved; population had come in; farms had been opened in the country; trade had revived; and especially by the wise interposition of law, the fetters were removed from business men, and enterprise permitted to act untrammeled for the advancement of private interest, and the welfare of the community. The condition of things during this period would have been more deplorable than they were but for the partial benefit derived from the Canal, which was in progress of construction, and the Harbor, upon which several appropriations were expended.

About 1840, Chicago experienced the first healthy growth and real, substantial prosperity; not, however, so strikingly perceptible previous to 1843, as the four years following. From 1843 to the present time, the place has advanced with a rapidity unexampled in the history of cities. Capital, to some extent, has been introduced; the country is generally settled; the soil has been brought to furnish productions for export; real-estate, both lots and lands, has become valuable; our citizens, many of them, have become wealthy; and population and trade, both export and import, have, during the short period of four years, more than doubled—very nearly trebled.

The most satisfactory evidence we can furnish, not only of what Chicago now is, but of what she has been, and may reasonably become, will be found in the following statistical tables of population, trade, etc., to which attention is directed for that purpose.

POPULATION.

Table showing the total population of the City of Chicago, and the population of each ward in 1840, 1843, and 1845, and the increase of each period, and total increase:—

	1840.	1843.	Increase	1845.	Increase	Total.
First Ward, ...	1,197	1,986	789	3,238	1,252	2,041
Second Ward, .	1,467	2,231	764	3,460	1,229	1,993
Third Ward, ..	251	509	258	1,009	500	758
Fourth Ward, .	179	414	235	830	416	651
Fifth Ward, ...	436	600	164	1,052	452	616
Sixth Ward, ...	1,323	1,840	517	2,499	659	1,176
Total, ...	4,853	7,580	2,727	12,088	4,508	7,235

Population of the City of Chicago, and the several precincts in Cook County in 1845; showing the number subject to military duty, the value of live-stock, and the amount of grain and the number of pounds of wool produced:—

COOK COUNTY. Precincts.	Population.	Subject to Military Duty.	Live-stock.	Bushels Grain Produced.	Value other Agricultural Productions.	No. Lbs. Wool.
Chicago City, ..	12,088	3,037	44,834		9,000	
Chicago, ...	575	160	1,354	4,583	3,134	33
Athens, ...	593	125	8,695	2,062	1,094	
Blue Island, ...	234	49	8,735	5,201	815	10,728
York, ...	346	73	10,043	11,365	2,651	524
Monroe, ...	786	200	18,625	11,497	4,471	324
Lake, ...	699	141	13,156	7,518	2,473	659
Lyons, ...	554	164	10,290	4,755	985	3,600
Summit, ...	619	299	3,370	1,670	600	
Desplaines, ...	999	276	18,295	19,155	6,080	1,598
Gross Point, ...	738	204	8,670	6,335	3,893	150
Hanover, ...	710	170	23,240	28,130	3,019	2,402
Barrington, ...	594	118	15,405	25,260	1,910	769
Bridgeport, ...	449	147	6,999	800	960	
Thornton, ...	546	109	12,940	11,550	1,915	1,423
Salt Creek, ...	1,073	268	24,975	24,731	6,045	4,204
Total City & Co.	21,581	5,540	241,793	164,835	42,045	26,414

The total population of the City, according to the census of 1846, was that year, 14,199. The census of this year, just completed, gives us, on the first day of September, 1847, in round numbers, 17,000.

STATISTICAL REPORT—JESSE B. THOMAS.

Table showing the several branches of business, trades, and professions in the City of Chicago, Nov. 1st, 1847:—

Architects, 2	Dyeing Establishment, 1	Newspapers, 4 daily, 6
Attorneys, 56	Engravers, 2	weekly, & 4 monthly, 14
Auction & Com. Stores, 8	Fire-Engine Comp'ies, 10	Oil, Soap, & Candle man. 8
Bandbox Manufactory, 1	Flour Stores, 2	Packing Houses, 6
Bankers and Brokers, 6	For., Storage, & Com. 18	Painters and Glaziers, 8
Barbers, 15	Foundries, 6	" Orna. & Min., 2
Bath-House, 1	Fruit Stores, 9	" Portrait, 2
Billiard Saloons, 3	Fanning-Mill makers, 2	Pawnbrokers, 3
Blacking Manufactory, 1	Glove-&-Mitten man., 2	Physicians, 31
Blacksmiths, 12	Grinder and Cutler, 1	Potteries, 1
Bookbinders, 2	Groceries, whol. & ret., 65	Printing-Offices, 11
Booksellers, 5	Gunsmiths, 2	Printers' Wareroom, 1
Boot-and-Shoe Mak'rs, 25	Hardware Stores, 17	Reading-Room, 1
Bowling Saloons, 5	Hat, Cap, etc., Stores, 6	Starch manufactory, 1
Brass-Smith, 1	Hotels and Taverns, 25	Steam Planing-Mills, 2
Brewers, 3	Hydraulic Companies, 2	Schools, Public, employ-
Builders, Master, 17	Ink Manufactory, 1	ing 10 Teachers, and
Cabinet & Chair man., 12	Ins. Com. & Agencies, 13	numb'g 1500 scholars, 4
Churches, 20	Justices-of-the-Peace, 5	Schools, Private, employ-
Clothing Stores, 11	Land Agencies, 4	ing 20 Teachers, and
Coffee-Houses, 9	Land Offices, 2	numb'g 1000 Pupils, 15
Colleges, 3	Leather Store, 1	Saddle and Harness, 8
Commission Houses, 3	Libraries (12,500 vols), 3	Ship Builders, 3
Cradle-maker, Grain, 1	Liquor Store (wholes.), 1	Ship Chandlers, 2
Confectioners, 4	Livery Stables, 7	Societies, 33
Coopers, 14	Locksmith, 1	Tailors, 25
Crockery Stores, 3	Looking-Glass man., 2	Tanneries, 2
Dentists, 5	Lumber Dealers, 24	Theatre, 1
Depositories, 3	Mill Wrights, 2	Tob. and Cigar man., 3
Door Factories, 4	Marble Factory, 1	Undertakers, 2
Drug Stores, 10	Markets, 15	Upholster, 1
Dry, Fancy, & S. Goods, 8	Millinery, 15	Wagon Makers, 13
Dry-Goods and Grocery	Mills, 5	Watch Mak. & Jewel., 7
Stores, about 300	Notaries Public, 6	

TRADE AND COMMERCE.

For several years after the commencement of the place, provisions for domestic consumption were imported from the East, as well as goods and merchandise. Exports previous to 1839–40, were merely nominal. A small cargo of beef was shipped in 1833, and was followed each successive year by a small consignment of the same article and pork; but not a bushel of our great staple, wheat, was shipped previous to 1839.

Table showing the value of Exports and Imports to and from Chicago, from 1836 to 1847, inclusive:—

EXPORTS.

1836, $1,000.64	1840, $228,635.74	1844, $785,504.23
1837, 11,065.00	1841, 348,862.24	1845, 1,543,519.85
1838, 16,044.75	1842, 659,305.20	1846, 1,813,468.00
1839, 33,843.00	1843, 682,210.85	1847, 2,296,299.00

IMPORTS.

1836, $325,203.90	1840, $562,106.20	1844, $1,686,416.00
1837, 373,677.12	1841, 564,347.88	1845, 2,043,445.73
1838, 579,174.61	1842, 664,347.88	1846, 2,027,150.00
1839, 630,980.26	1843, 971,849.75	1847, 2,641,852.52

Table showing the exports of leading articles from Chicago, in six years, from 1842 to 1847, inclusive:—

	Wheat. Bush.	Flour. Bbls.	Beef and Pork. Bbls.	Wool. Pounds.
1842,	586,907	2,920	16,209	1,500
1843,	628,967	10,786	21,492	22,050
1844,	891,894	6,320	14,938	96,635
1845,	956,860	13,752	13,268	216,616
1846,	1,459,594	28,045	31,224	281,222
1847,	1,974,304	32,538	48,920	411,488

Table exhibiting the amount of goods, wares, and merchandise received at Chicago, from the opening of navigation in the spring of 1847, to Nov. 1st, near the close of navigation, 1847; not including goods landed here and taken to the interior; compiled from the original invoices of merchants:—

Dry Goods,	$837,451.22	Liquors,	86,334.67
Groceries,	506,027.56	Tobacco and Cigars,	3,716.00
Hardware,	148,811.50	Ship Chandlery,	23,000.00
Iron and Nails,	88,275.00	Tools and Hardware,	15,000.00
Stoves and Hollow-ware,	68,612.00	Furniture Trimming,	5,564.07
Crockery,	30,505.00	Glass,	8,949.24
Boots and Shoes,	94,275.00	Scales,	4,044.55
Hats, Caps, and Furs,	68,200.00	Coaches, etc.,	1,500.00
Jewelry, etc.,	51,000.00	Looking Glasses, etc.,	2,500.00
Books and Stationery,	43,580.00	Marble,	800.00
Printing Paper,	7,284.11	Oysters,	2,500.00
Presses, Type, and Printing Materials,	7,432.50	Sportsmen's Articles,	2,000.00
		Musical Instruments,	6,426.00
Drugs and Medicines,	92,081.41	Machinery, etc.,	30,000.00
Paints and Oils,	25,460.00		

Total value of imports of merchandise, $2,259,309.83

Imports of miscellaneous articles:—

Salt, barrels,.. 24,817 Coal, tons,......... 15,782
Salt, sacks, ... 5,537   Water Lime, bush., 1,618 } Value, $117,210.29

And numerous other articles not here enumerated, such as pig-iron, whitefish and trout, fruit, grindstones, cider, etc., the precise quantity not known, but in considerable amount.

Table showing the amount of lumber, etc., received at Chicago from the opening of navigation to Nov. 1st, 1847:—

Plank, Boards, etc., feet, . 32,118,225   Shingle-Bolts, cords, ... 328
Shingles, M, ... 12,148,500   Tanner's Bark, cords, ... 600
Lath, M, ... 5,655,700   Staves, ... 50,000
Square Timber, feet, ...   24,000   Spokes,................... 100,000

Total value, $265,332.50.

Table exhibiting the exports from the port of Chicago from the opening of navigation, 1847, to Nov. 1st, 1847:—

Wheat, bushels,.......... 1,974,304   Flax Seed, bushels, ... 2,262
Flour, barrels, ...   32,598   Mustard "   "   520
Corn, bushels, ...   67,315   Timothy "   "   536
Oats,   "   38,892   Hay, tons,................   415
Beef, barrels, ...   26,504   Cranberries, bushels,.......   250
Pork,   "   22,416   Buffalo Robes, bales, ...   60
Hams and Shoulders, lbs..   47,248   Dry Hides,................. 8,774
Tallow, pounds,..........   208,435   Deer Skins, pounds,........ 28,259
Butter,   "   47,536   Sheep Pelts, ... 1,133
Beans, bushels,..........   430   Furs, packages, ...   278
Wool, pounds, ...   411,088   Ginseng, pounds,........... 3,625
Tobacco, "   28,243   Ashes, barrels, ...   16
Lard,   "   139,069   Bristles, pounds,.......... 4,548
Leather, "   2,740   Glue,   "   2,480
Beeswax, "   5,490   Brooms,................... 3,168
Oil, gallons, ...   8,793   White-fish, barrels, ... 1,229
Lead, pounds,...........   10,254   Barley, bushels, ...   400
Hemp,   "   6,521   Value, $2,296,299.

Besides a large amount of merchandise, produce, provisions, grain, horses, cattle, salt, and supplies of all kinds sent to the lumber and mining regions, and different ports on the upper and lower Lakes.

Table showing the aggregate quantity of public land subject to entry, in the Chicago land district, on the 29th day of May, 1835—when the public sale commenced—amount reserved from sale, and the amount sold, and subject to sale, up to the 1st of Nov., 1847:—

Total amount in the District, May 29th, 1835,					3,626,536
School lands,			acres,	104,520	
Canal lands,			"	228,580	
Selected by Commissioners for State purposes,			"	93,782	
Sold to individuals in 1835,			"	370,043	
"	"	1836,	"	202,364	
"	"	1837,	"	15,697	
"	"	1838,	"	87,881	
"	"	1839,	"	160,635	
"	"	1840,	"	137,382	
"	"	1841,	"	138,583	
"	"	1842,	"	194,556	
"	"	1843,	"	229,460	
"	"	1844,	"	235,258	
"	"	1845,	"	220,525	
"	"	1846,	"	198,849	
"	to Nov. 1st,	1847,	"	98,569	2,780,640
					743,895

Balance unsold land in the district, Nov. 1st, 1847.

[NOTE.—For the last two years, a large proportion of the sales were in tracts of forty acres, and to actual settlers who had improved farms in the vicinity.]

The foregoing is as correct a view of the commercial transactions of the City as it is possible to obtain. It is believed to be generally correct. Perfect accuracy can not, under existing circumstances, be attained. Results have been arrived at circuitously, and have been attended with considerable labor. Not having the benefit of custom-house regulations, and consequently no official record of imports and exports received and discharged from this port, the only resort for information has been to the invoices of our merchants, the shipping books of forwarders, and the books of lumber and other dealers in miscellaneous articles. These have been carefully examined, and our results compiled from them.

It is quite supposable, and indeed certain, that articles, both of export and import, have escaped us. We know that many shipments have been made from this port to the lumber regions, and the mining regions of Lake Superior, consisting of merchandise of various kinds, provisions, produce, salt, etc., of which no record has been kept. Steamboats and vessels have obtained supplies here, amounting to a large figure in the course of the season. Horses constitute a considerable item of export the past year.

On the other hand, goods, in some instances, perhaps entire stocks, have been introduced into the place and disappeared without leaving any trace by which their amount and value can be ascertained. We have given no account of the merchandise landed here for the numerous towns in the interior. Heavy shipments of goods have been made through this place, the present year, for Galena, Springfield, and St. Louis. These are legitimate portions of our commerce, and should be considered with it. We may safely estimate the value of this business at $1,500,000.

MARINE OF LAKE MICHIGAN.

Table showing the vessels owned at Chicago, and at the several ports on Lake Michigan, with their tonnage; also, the vessels built at Chicago for owners here, during the present year, 1847, and the whole number built at this place to the present time:

CHICAGO.

Prop.	Lady of the Lake,	tons,	326	Schr.	New Hampshire,...	tons,	100
Schr.	W. G. Buckner,...	"	100	"	Margaret Allen,....	"	80
"	Henry Norton,....	"	150	"	John C. Spencer,...	"	86
Brig	Ellen Parker,......	"	332	"	J. C. Davis,.......	"	97
Schr.	J. Young Scammon,	"	191	"	Warren,..........	"	65
"	Maria Scammon,...	"	194	"	Jas. R. Hugunin,...	"	65
"	Ottawa,..........	"	153	"	Henry Clay,.......	"	59
"	Vermont,.........	"	124	"	Erastus Bowen,....	"	52
"	Laurin P. Hilliard,.	"	175	"	Ark,-------------	"	50
"	A. Wilcox,........	"	130	"	Western Trader,...	"	53
"	Whig,.............	"	97				

The following have been, or are now being built at Chicago, in 1847, for owners here, *viz.:*

Brig	Stephen F. Gale,...	tons,	266	Prop.	A. Rossetter,.....	tons,	200
Schr.	Minnesota,........	"	181	Schr.	John Lillie,.......	"	100
"	Tribune,..........	"	276	"	Now on the Stocks,	"	300
"	Buena Vista,......	"	174	"	Contracted to be finished in the spring of 1848,.........	"	200
"	Chas. Walker, rebuilt,	"	164				
"	Samuel Hale, built at Southport,....	"	293		Total Tonnage, 4833.		

MILWAUKEE.

Schr.	Lawrence,........	tons,	284	Schr.	Joseph Ward,......	tons,	102
"	Gallinipper,.......	"	144	"	M. Dousman,......	"	137
"	L. R. Rockwell,...	"	115	"	Juniatta Patten,....	"	260
"	Mary L. Bonesteel,.	"	156	"	A. C. Mitchell,....	"	51
"	John Davis,.......	"	125	"	Manitowoc,........	"	52
"	Jesse Smith,......	"	110	"	Traveller,.........	"	74
Brig	Helfenstein,.......	"	330	"	Henderson,........	"	115
Schr.	Crook,...........	"	50	"	Baltic,............	"	120
"	Cramer,..........	"	200		Total Tonnage, 2425.		

RACINE.

Brig	W. T. Richmond,..	tons,	225	Schr.	Bolivár,...........	tons,	46
Schr.	Col. T. H. Benton,.	"	159	"	Justin Butterfield,...	"	43
"	Diamond,.........	"	68		Total Tonnage, 541.		

SOUTHPORT.—[Now Kenosha.]

Brig	C. I. Hutchinson,..	tons,	341	Schr.	Cayuga,...........	tons,	60
Schr.	Cleopatra,.........	"	104	"	Samuel Hale,......	"	300
"	Toledo,...........	"	215	"	Helena,...........	"	80

Total Tonnage, 1100. Three schooners building for 1848.

LITTLE FORT.—[Now Waukegan.]

Schooner J. B. Patten, ... 73 tons.

NEW BUFFALO.

Schooner New Buffalo, ... 35 tons.

GRAND RIVER.

Schr. Hiram Pearsons, ...	tons,	94	Schr. Amanda Harwood, .	tons,	200
" Dexter, ...	"	115	" Caroline, ...	"	80
Brig Enterprise, ...	"	150	" Lucinda	"	90
Barque Morgan, ...	"	380	" Constitution, ...	"	90

Total Tonnage, 1199.

Total Tonnage of Vessels on Lake Michigan, 9366.

So far as the same has been enrolled in the Collector's Office at this port. Some considerable amount has not yet been transferred from the district at Detroit, and is not included here. It will be safe to add one-third to the above, making 12,000 tons.

The tonnage on this Lake is increasing rapidly. It has been ascertained that vessels can be built as cheap and as well here, as on the lower Lakes. Another controlling reason is, that the shipping interest, and the command of freights here, have so far increased, that owners are not compelled to build their vessels East to secure the interest of forwarders, as was formerly the case. The domestic carrying-business of this Lake is increasing most wonderfully, requiring large additions of tonnage every year; in fact, faster than it has been possible heretofore to supply it.

Table showing the principal vessels built at Chicago from 1843 to the present time, and their tonnage:—

1843	Propeller	Independence, (now on Lake Superior), ..	tons,	268
1845	Schooner	Maria Hilliard, ...	"	184
"	"	J. Young Scammon, ...	"	184
"	"	Ark, ...	"	42
1846	Barque	Utica, ...	"	334
"	Brig	Ellen Parker, ...	"	334
"	Schooner	N. C. Walton, ...	"	127
1847	Brig	Stephen F. Gale, ...	"	266
"	"	Minnesota, ...	"	270
"	Propeller	A. Rossetter, ...	"	203
"	Schooner	Laurin P. Hilliard, ...	"	174
"	"	Tribune, ...	"	181
"	"	Buena Vista, ...	"	174
"	"	Amanda Harwood, ...	"	170
"	"	John Lillie, ...	"	100
"	Two schooners now building for 1848, the two about		"	500
		Total, ...		3511

Besides a number of small craft during the same period.

SHIPPING-LIST OF CHICAGO, 1846.

	No.	Arrivals.	Entries.	Clearances.	Departures.	Tonnage.	Persons employed.
Steamboats,	19	352	160	158	358	14,351	380
Propellers,	19	111	111	82	109	5,170	204
Brigs,	36	94	94	62	94	8,781	324
Schooners,	120	837	157	134	835	16,443	720
Total,	192	1,394	522	436	1,396	44,745	1,628

The tonnage of the Lakes in 1846 was 62 Steamers, 18 Propellers, 1 Barque, 58 Brigs, 313 Sloops and Schooners, with an aggregate tonnage of 91,250 tons.

The number of vessels now in commission on the Western Lakes is, Steamers, 64; Propellers, 26; Barques, 3; Brigs, 65; Schooners, 213; Total, 307. Aggregate tonnage, 113,000 tons. Value at $30 per ton, $3,390,000.

Table showing the number of vessels lost on Lake Michigan; their value and the value of their cargoes when known; and the number of lives lost, from 1824 to 1837:—

1824 Schr. Lawrence, ... $3,000 | 1826 Schr. Red Jacket, ... $2,000

Here follows an interval of seven years, during which vessels must have been lost, but the record is not to be found.

Dec., 1833,	Schooner Erie Packet,		$1,500
Oct., 1834,	" Prince Eugene,		27,000
" "	Steamboat Newburyport,		15,000
Aug., "	" Pioneer,		10,000
1835,	" (at Green Bay), name forgotten, about		2,000
" "	" Utica,		7,000
Nov., "	" Chance,	7 lives,	2,000
" "	" Bridget,	16 "	5,000
" "	" Sloan,	6 "	3,000
April, "	" Delaware,		20,000
Nov., 1836,	Sloop Clarissa,		1,500
Oct., "	Schooner Chicago,		8,000
" "	" Austerlitz, (vessel and goods),		12,000
" 1837,	" Ohio,		6,000
" "	Steamboat Mason,		4,000
" 1838,	Schooner Laporte,		3,000
" "	" Thomas Richmond,		6,000
" "	" Lafayette,		3,000
Nov., 1839,	" White Pigeon,		3,000

Nov., 1839,	Brig John Kinzie,			$3,000
Aug., "	Steamboat Detroit,			20,000
Nov., "	Schooner Virginia, (wheat),			7,000
Oct., 1840,	Steamboat Taylor,			8,000
May "	" Champlain,			10,000
Nov., "	Schooner Neptune, (goods),	24 lives,		15,000
Oct., "	" Cincinnati,			1,500
April "	" Jefferson,			1,800
Oct., "	" Huron,			2,000
". 1841,	" Post-Boy, (goods $1000),	13 lives,		2,500
" "	Sloop Spitfire,			500
Nov., "	Schooner Oneida, (wheat),			20,000
" 1842,	" Bancroft,			4,000
" "	Ship Milwaukee,	9 lives,		10,000
" "	" Florida,			4,000
" "	Brig Columbus, (wheat),			12,000
May, 1843,	" Hummingbird,	6 lives,		1,000
" "	Schooner Harriet,	8 "		2,500
" 1844,	" Minerva Smith,			1,000
Mar. "	" Wave,	5 lives,		1,000
" "	" Victory,	7 "		2,000
Aug., "	" Whitney,	6 "		1,000
Sept., 1845,	Ship Superior,			5,000
Nov., "	Schooner Jacob Barker,			2,000
" "	Brig Oliver,			6,000
April, "	Schooner Ocean,	6 lives,		1,000
" "	" Savannah,			5,000
" "	" Jefferson,			4,500
Oct., "	Brig Indiana,			4,000
" "	Schooner Swift,			600
" "	Brig Rosa,			8,000
Nov., "	Schooner Margaret Helm,			1,500
" 1846,	Steamboat Boston,			70,000
" "	Sloop James K. Polk,			1,000
" "	" Rodolph,	4 lives,		400
" "	Schooner ———,			4,000
Apr., 1847,	" St. Joseph,			1,000
" "	" Solomon Juneau,			4,000
" "	" Mary Elizabeth,			2,000
" "	" Wisconsin,			1,500
Oct., "	" Outward Bound,			2,000
Nov., "	" Illinois, Green Bay,			5,000
" "	Propeller Phœnix,	250 lives, [?]		80,000
" "	Schooner Champion,			15,000
" "	" Erastus B. Wolcott,			10,000
" "	" H. Merrill,			10,000
	Total value,			$512,000
	Lives lost,			367

The above account is not to be taken as strictly authentic, not being compiled from any record official or otherwise, but from the recollection of persons conversant with the Lakes during the period named. A large number of small craft, it is presumable, have escaped the recollection of every person living. For these, together with the value of cargoes, not given in the above statement, it will be fair to double the amount, making the total loss of property, in consequence of the loss of vessels, $1,000,000. The loss of life may be increased to 500.

In connection with the above, should also be included vessels that have gone ashore almost every week, at different places on our lake coast. The damage the vessels themselves have sustained in this way; the expense of getting them afloat; repairing them; damage of cargoes; and loss of time, can not be estimated at a less sum than $740,000, giving in round numbers a total of $1,740,000.

Up to the present time, Chicago has been merely the centre of a local retail trade of a few hundred miles of extent of country; and even that trade cramped by the recent settlement of the country; the poverty of the farming community; and the limited capital of her merchants, mechanics, and manufacturers. She has been merely the end of a route, and having no means of communication with the interior, but over poor and, at some seasons, nearly impassable roads. The trade of the place, though large and profitable under the circumstances, has yet been forced and unnatural. The carrying and depositing trade of the West, except a small portion, she has never enjoyed.

But opening new channels of communication—the completion of the Canal, connecting, by only one hundred miles of this navigation, the Lakes with the navigable waters of the Mississippi, and the construction, at an early day, of our lines of railroads, turnpikes, and plank-roads, already projected, chartered, and commenced, will at once, and by magic, change the condition and prospects of our City; increase its population; introduce capital to operate in our staples, produce, provisions, lumber, etc.; enlarge every avenue of commerce, and promote the growth of manufactures. The arteries of trade will then be opened and commerce will flow freely through them.

The numerous works of improvement, upon which the prosperity of Chicago and the amount and value of its commerce depends, deserve consideration in this connection.

THE HARBOR AT CHICAGO.

The harbor at this place has been constructed by running piers from Chicago River into the Lake. The work on the harbor was commenced in 1833, and has been continued ever since, so far as appropriations have been made by Congress. The amount of appropriations so far made are as follows: In 1833, $25,000 was appropriated; in 1834, $30,000; in 1835, $30,000; in 1836, $25,000; in 1837, $30,000; in 1838-9, $40,000; in 1842, $30,000. Total, $210,000. This money has all been expended, and the result is, two piers running into the Lake at right angles with the shore. One of them, the north pier, a distance of 3900 feet, and the south pier, 1800 feet.

Chicago River and its branches, with the channel between the piers, constitute the harbor. The main portion of the River is three-fourths of a mile in length, sixty yards wide, and about twenty feet deep. The north and south branches, which unite with the River from opposite directions, in the heart of the City, and have about the same width and depth, are navigable, the former three and the latter five miles. These streams are, properly speaking, bayous, having very little or no current, and being on a level with the waters of the Lake. At the junction of the branches, in the heart of the City, is a natural basin, which it is designed to enlarge by excavation. It will be a source of great convenience.

The principal difficulty in the way of constructing harbors on the western shore of Lake Michigan, proceeds from the deposition of large quantities of sand at their mouths. A strong and almost constant current, it is to be observed, passes along the shore of the Lake, from the north toward the south, carrying with it large quantities of sand, which it deposits, forming bars wherever an obstacle, in the shape of a river, or piers, or any object of sufficient force to change, in any degree, the attraction of this current is met with.

The effect of this is observable in all the streams discharging into Lake Michigan on the west. The current along the shore coming in contact with the rivers passing out, the latter are diverted from a direct passage, and taken a new direction for a longer or a shorter distance, along the shore, until the influence of the current ceases to operate, when they discharge, generally in a south-western direction, and a long bar or peninsula of sand standing at the diverging point, and terminating at the new point of entrance, is invariably formed between the Lake and the River.

Such was Chicago River before the construction of the piers. It discharged half-a-mile below the present harbor. The harbor was commenced by cutting through this bar, and forcing the River straight through into the Lake. No sooner was the north pier projected into the Lake, than the effect of the current coming in contact with it became apparent. It deposite sand along the shore of the Lake, north of the pier, extending the same farther and farther into the Lake, and passing around the end of the pier, formed a bar extending in a south-western direction across the mouth of the harbor.

To remedy this evil, two plans were suggested some years ago. One proposed the construction of false piers, half-a-mile north of the harbor, projected into the Lake parallel with the harbor. The latter recommended the further extension of the north pier into the Lake, and the abandonment of the farther extension of the south pier. The latter was adopted, and the north pier, diverging at first slightly to the north, but ultimately returning, in the shape of a circle, into a line with the original pier, was extended about nine hundred feet into the Lake. This had the desired effect until the spring of the present year, when it was discovered that the sand had found its way around the end of the extended pier, and had formed a large bar or mound two hundred feet by one hundred. About two hundred and seventy feet to the south-east, another bar, much larger, had previously formed. Some distance inside of the north pier, about two hundred feet south, still another bar, and a very troublesome one, had formed along the south side of the north pier, commencing considerably inside of the old part, and extending some distance inside of the new projection. The quantity of water had also diminished. The deepest soundings inside the bars being only ten feet, and generally scant nine and three-fourths, and nine.

These evils, previous to the present year, have found a partial remedy in dredging. But this year, that poor consolation has been denied us; the government machine, heretofore used for that purpose, having been removed last season to a northern port, and subsequently sunk. The consequence has been that our harbor has been exceedingly difficult to enter, even in favorable weather, and in storms, when its protection is especially needed, almost effectually closed. Our commerce has suffered greatly, and been subjected to the risk of almost total ruin.

Such a state of things demands a prompt and effectual remedy, particularly at a time when our Canal is on the eve of completion, and a consequently great augmentation of our commercial interests about to take place. The completion of the Canal will divert a large share of the carrying-trade of the West in this direction, and a safe and commodious harbor at this place in 1848, will be a matter of the most urgent necessity.

Some plan ought to be devised immediately to obviate the above difficulties, and the necessary amount of money appropriated to carry said plan into execution. In the meantime, we must have a sufficient annual appropriation to dredge out the harbor, and keep at all times a sufficient channel open, for the entrance and departure of vessels of every class. This latter, until the former object is secured, is imperative. Without it, our commerce of $10,000,000, with the large increase of another year, will be jeopardized, if not ruined. The cost of a dredge, and the expense of running it, will be trifling; for the former, $5000, and the latter, some $2500 or $3000 a year.

One fact presents itself to us with startling distinctness at this time. Should the accumulation of sand in our harbor, the coming winter, equal the last, it is susceptible of the clearest demonstration that the spring of 1848 will find our harbor entirely closed, and Chicago cut off, entirely *barred*, from the general commerce of the country.

ILLINOIS-AND-MICHIGAN CANAL.

THE following is a brief statement of the history and present condition of this important work. The Canal unites the waters of the Illinois River with those of Lake Michigan:—

It commences at the Chicago River, four miles south of Chicago, and terminates at LaSalle, on the Illinois River. Its length, including the four miles of Chicago River to be used as Canal, is, in round numbers, one hundred miles.

The Canal is sixty feet wide at top water line. The locks are one-hundred-and-ten feet in length in the chambers, and eighteen feet wide at top water line. The depth of water is to be six feet.

On the 30th March, 1822, Congress authorized the construction of the Canal over the public lands; granting the right of way, and ninety feet on either side. On the 2d March, 1827, Congress granted to the State of Illinois, to aid in the construction of the work, every alternate section of land for five miles on each side.

As long ago as 1822–3, the Legislature of Illinois appointed a Board of Canal Commissioners, who made an examination of the route of the Canal, and at the same session, a company was chartered to commence operations. This act was repealed in 1826.

In 1829, a new Board was organized, with the power to make further surveys and complete the work; and by an act of 1831, the Commissioners were authorized to lay out towns, and did proceed to lay off and sell lots in the towns of Chicago and Ottawa —and also some lands. At the next session of the legislature, the office of the Canal Commissioner was abolished.

In 1835, another act of the legislature was passed, providing for the construction of the work on the sole responsibility of the State. That act was imperfect, and was repealed in 1836.

In 1836, the law was passed under which the work was commenced, and prosecuted until 1842.

The amount expended, up to the time of the suspension of the work, for want of means to prosecute it, was, independent of interest, $5,133,062.21.

In February, 1843, the law providing for a loan of one million six hundred thousand dollars to complete the Canal was passed. In the spring of 1845, the loan was effected. It was obtained by the subscription of the holders of script and bonds issued to raise the money which had been previously expended in the construction of the Canal. The bed of the Canal, the tolls, resources, and canal lands, were conveyed to the Board of Trustees appointed under the provisions of said act, in trust, until the loan, and the bonds and indebtedness which the subscribers were authorized to register, should be paid. The subscribers were authorized to register $1000 of Canal indebtedness for each $320 of the loan subscribed and paid by them.

The last instalment of the $1,600,000 loan was called in on the 20th of September last.

The amount of the new loan expended upon the work, on the 30th day of November, 1847, is about $1,150,000. The Canal lands are to be offered for sale three months after the completion of the Canal. It is expected that the Canal will be in operation at the opening of navigation in the spring of 1848.

There are three lateral canals or feeders. One from Fox River at Dayton to Ottawa, four miles; one from the Kankakee River, six miles; and one from the Calumet River, sixteen miles.

From "**A Brief Sketch of the Commerce of the Lakes**: by James L. Barton, Buffalo, 1847."

PORT OF CHICAGO, ILLINOIS.

The following are of the principal articles exported from this port during five seasons:

		1842.	1843.	1844.	1845.
Wheat,	bush,	586,910	628,965	871,805	956,860
Oats,	"	53,485	3,767	------	5,900
Flour,	bbls,	2,920	10,785	4,320	13,750
Pork,	"	15,450	11,110	7,050	7,010
Beef,	"	762	10,380	7,890	6,200
Wool,	lbs,	1,500	22,050	96,635	216,615
Lard,	"	36,720	bbls, 282	bbls, 1,630	66,220
Tobacco,	"	3,000	47,900	52,653	52,000
Hams,	"	In pork ac't.	Pork ac't.	Pork ac't.	22,925
Tallow,	"	15,130	bbls, 1,185	34,900	bbls, 1,000
Hides,	No.,	6,975	14,535	11,042	12,255
Valuation,	...	$659,300	$1,008,210	$785,300	$1,500,000

The exports and imports of the same place, in 1846, were:—

EXPORTS.

Wheat,	bush,	1,358,638	Agri. Impts.,	bbls,	11	Hay,	bales,	156
Beef & Pork,	bbls,	23,788	Furs,	lbs,	37,514	Scraps tin, cop'r, lb,		3,162
Flour,	"	19,391	" bxs and bales,		18	" " " hhds,		40
Lard & Tallow,	"	2,160	Ginseng,	sks,	58	Brooms,	doz,	896
"	lbs,	76,600	Salt,	bbls,	1,423	Leather,	lbs,	11,140
Hams,	bbls,	16	Oil,	"	128	Butter,	bbls,	36
"	pcs,	22,633	Fruit,	"	322	"	lbs,	2,765
Fish,	bbls,	1,413	Merchandise,	"	806	Flaxseed,	bbls,	487
Whiskey,	"	671	Oats,	bush,	27,308	Timothy seed,	"	29
Tobacco,	lbs,	6,152	Corn,	"	9,331	Wagons,		1
"	boxes,	19	Hides,	pcs,	9,460	Lime,	bbls,	14
Candles,	"	810	Glass,	boxes,	993	Grindstones,	pcs,	18
Beeswax,	bbls,	26	Pelts,	pcs,	1,160	Coal,	tons,	26
"	lbs,	95,000	Stearine,	bbls,	64	Merchandise,	pkgs,	429
Soap,	boxes,	51	Cranberries,	"	74	Scraps tin, etc.,	"	51
Furniture,	bbls,	909	Rags,	lbs,	2,164	Leather,	"	34
"	boxes,	31	Coal,	"	8,900	Flax seed,	"	487
Wool,	lbs,	21,806	Beans,	bbls,	1	Timothy seed,	"	29
"	bales,	116	Machinery,	lbs,	2,700	Paper,	"	28

IMPORTS.

Merchandise,	tons,	8,800	Seeds,	bbls,	7	Beans,	bbls,	10
"	bbls,	10,385	Furniture,	tons,	47	Machinery,	tons,	1
" bxs & pkgs,		1,540	"	bbls,	4,039	Threshing mach.,		37
Salt,	bbls,	13,308	"	kegs,	850	Millstones,		26
"	sks,	1,346	Agri. Impts.,	bbls,	33	Water-lime,	bbls,	4,000
Fish,	bbls,	1,800	"	pkgs,	3	Lumber, feet,		23,824,297
Butter,	"	37	Wag. & coaches,	"	307	Shingles,		8,354,000
Beans,	"	10	Ploughs,		17	Lath,		2,069,500
Oil,	"	23	Hubs and wheels,		2,000	Pickets,		24,000
Whiskey,	"	1,065	Soap,	pkgs,	246	Timber,		110,000
Fruit, cider, etc.	"	4,812	Coal,	tons,	2,150	Staves,		32,000
"	pkgs,	185	Glass,	boxes,	1,725	Mahogany,		1,852

No valuation has been reported for the exports and imports of 1846.

CONTENTS.

	PAGE
Introduction,	3
Letters from Wm. Mosley Hall, the originator of the Convention,	5
Veto of the River-and-Harbor Bill,	14
The Lake Country,	16
Who is James K. Polk?	17
Call for the New-York Preliminary Meeting,	17
New-York Preliminary Meeting, proceedings,	18
The Lakes and Western Rivers,	18
New-York Resolutions,	21
Call for the Chicago Preliminary Meeting,	21
Chicago Preliminary Meeting,	23
" Resolutions,	23
" Committee of Arrangements,	25
" " Address to the People, by Hon. John Wentworth, Chairman,	26
Buffalo Preliminary Meeting, proceedings,	30
" Resolutions,	31
" Committee of Arrangements,	33
Michigan-City Preliminary Meeting, proceedings,	34
" " Resolutions,	35
" " Committees,	37
Invitation to Daniel Webster, by Samuel Lisle Smith,	37
Signers of Invitation to Daniel Webster,	39
Delegate Meetings, Notice of	39
Delegates to form in Procession, Marshal's order	40
Marshal's order of the day for 5th of July,	40
Account of the Procession, by S. Lisle Smith,	41
Chicago in 1847,—Officers, Schools, Churches, Fire Department, Institutions, Newspapers, etc.,	45
Proceedings of the Convention,	47
Rules for Organization and Voting,	48
Committee of Nomination and Rules,	49
Report of Nominating Committee,	49
Officers of the Convention,	50
Rules of the Convention,	50
List of Delegates, Arranged by States alphabetically,	52
Committee on Resolutions,	68

CONTENTS.

	PAGE
Letter of Thomas H. Benton of Missouri,	69
" Silas Wright,	72
" Henry Clay,	75
" Martin VanBuren,	75
" Lewis Cass of Michigan,	76
" Thomas B. Curtiss of Massachusetts,	76
" Joseph Grinnell,	76
" Bradford R. Wood of New York,	77
" Alpheus Felch of Michigan,	77
" George P. Barker of New York,	78
" Washington Hunt of New York,	79
Resolutions of the Convention,	81
Letter of Daniel Webster,	87
Executive Committee,	88
Committee of the Whole,	90
Pacific-Railroad Resolutions, by Wm. M. Hall,	91
Speech of Wm. M. Hall, on a National Railroad to the Pacific—the first public speech in its favor,	92
Letter of Dr. Harwell Carver of New York, one of the early advocates of a Pacific Railroad,	104
Letter of John M. Botts of Virginia,	105
" Daniel Webster on Internal Improvements,	107
Remarks of John C. Spencer of New York, to the Convention on Internal Improvements,	122
Letter of John McLean of Michigan,	136
" John Norvell of "	136
" W. S. Archer of Virginia,	137
Abraham Lincoln, Notice of	138
Samuel Lisle Smith—Obituary,	138
Jesse B. Thomas—Obituary,	138
Horace Greeley's Report of the Convention,	139
" " on Internal Improvements and Party Politics,	143
Thurlow Weed's Report of the Convention, etc.,	147
Edward Bates, President of the Convention, sketch of,	172
Statistics Concerning Chicago, by Jesse B. Thomas,	175
Sketch of Chicago,	178
Population of Chicago for 1840, '43, and '45,	182
" Cook County for 1845,	182
Business Occupations in Chicago,	183
Trade and Commerce of Chicago from 1836 to 1847,	183
Land Sales in Chicago from 1835 to Nov., 1847.	185
Marine of Lake Michigan,	187
Vessels built at Chicago from 1843 to 1847,	188
Shipping list of Chicago for 1846,	189
Losses on Lake Michigan from 1824 to 1847,	189
The Harbor at Chicago, Historical Sketch of,	192
Illinois-and-Michigan Canal,	194
Port of Chicago: Statistics by Jas. L. Barton of Buffalo, N.Y.,	196

INDEX

Of Names of Persons, Newspapers, and Vessels mentioned.

DELEGATES NAMES may be found on pages 52 to 68 inclusive, alphabetically arranged by States.

A.

Abert, *Col.* John Jas., 101, 133, 134.
Adam, *Rev.* Wm., 46.
Adams, *Pres.* John, 28.
  Pres. John Quincy, 153–172, 173.
Admiral (steamboat), 170.
Adsit, James M., 39.
Albany Argus, 161.
  Evening Journal, 147, 162, 172.
Allen, *Miss* A. A., 170.
  Elisha Hunt, 90, 139, 143, 161.
  H. V., 170.
  J. B., 170.
  John W., 22, 47, 148, 154.
  Margaret (Schr.), 187.
  Orlando, 33.
  Thos., 69, 72, 88, 152, 161, 170.
  Rev. Wm., 48, 49, 86, 140, 151, 152, 155, 165, 170.
  Zachariah, 88.
Allyn, *Capt.* Gurdon L., 7.
Alvord, P. G., 170.
Anable, H. S., 170.
Appleby, C. W., 39.
Archer, Charles G., 39.
  W. S., 138.
Ark (schr.), 187, 188.
Arnold, Isaac N., 23, 25, 30.
Atkinson, John, 46.
Atwater, George M., 20.
  Samuel T., 30, 33.
Austerlitz (schr.), 189.
Avery, Charles E., 39.

B.

Babcock, Geo. R., 21, 33.
Backus, *Senator*, 166.
Baird, Zebulon, 88.
Baker, David J., 68, 89.
Ballard, *Mr.* C. J. and *Mrs.* Adaline W., 45.
Ballingall, Patrick, 25, 45.
Baltic (schr.), 187.
  (steamboat), 151, 163.
Bancroft (schr.), 190.
Barker, Geo. P., 33, 78, 152.

Barker, Jacob (schr.), 190.
  Ward, 170.
Barnum, Mr. 169.
Barnes, Hamilton, 26.
Bartholomew, 148.
Barton, Benjamin, 170.
  James L., 11, 22, 33, 34, 47, 48, 49, 139, 151, 170, 196.
Bascom, *Rev.* Flavel, 9, 45.
Bates, *Hon.* Edward, 9, 12, 50, 68, 86, 88, 89, 90, 142, 152, 153, 160, 161, 170, 172, 173, 174.
  Jacob R., 26.
  Morgan, 20.
Beardsley, Levi, 170.
Bebb, *Gov.* Wm., 50, 88, 90, 139, 141, 142, 143, 148, 151, 154, 161.
Beers, Cyrenius, 26, 39.
Bemis, James, 170.
Benton, *Col.* Thos. H. (schr.), 187.
  Senator Thomas Hart, 69, 72, 140, 147, 152, 153, 173, 174.
Better Covenant, 46.
Biddle, John, 49, 152.
Bidwell, Benjamin, 33.
Bigham, T. J., 69, 88, 158.
Bills, George R., 46.
Bishop, James E., 39.
Blackburn, H. C., 69.
Black Hawk (Indian Chief), 179.
Blackwell, Robert S., 69, 86.
Blaikie, Andrew, 39.
Blair, Chauncey B., 34.
  Wm., 39.
Blake, *Com.* Chelsey, 149.
Blaney, *Dr.* Jas. V.Z., 46.
Bloomer, T. T., 163, 164, 169.
Blossom, I. A., 34.
Bogy, Lewis V., 170.
Bolivar (schr.), 187.
Bonesteel, Mary L. (schr.), 187.
Boone, *Dr.* Levi D., 26, 45.
Boston (stmr.), 190.
Botsford, Jabez K., 26.
Botts, John M., 105, 107, 140.

Bourland, Benj. L. T., 46.
Bowen, Erastus (schr.), 187.
Bowles, *Rev.* S., 45.
Boyce, Leroy M., 26, 39.
Boyer, *Dr.* Valentine A., 26.
Brady *Guards*, 164.
Bradley, Cyrus P., 46.
    David M., 26.
Brainard, *Dr.* Daniel, 26, 46.
Brand, Alexander, 26, 39.
Brayman, J. O., 33.
Breese, Sidney, 154.
Bridget (schr.), 189.
Brinkerhoff, *Dr.* John, 39, 45.
Bristol, Cyrenius C., 33.
    Miss C. N., 170.
    Harrison, 170.
    Capt. Robert C., 26.
Britain, Calvin, 69.
Brittain, J. P., *jr.*, 39.
Brock, *Gen.* Isaac, 171.
Brockway, John H., 50, 90.
Bronson, Alvin, 69, 139, 172.
Brooks, James, 147.
Brown, *Judge* Henry, 26, 89.
    John A., 20, 39.
    Joseph E., 25.
    Wm. H., 26, 39, 45.
Bryant, Geo. H., 169.
Buchanan, R., 170.
Buckner, W. G. (schr.), 187.
Buena Vista (schr.), 187, 188.
Buffalo Com. Advertiser, 143, 161.
    Express (newspaper), 30, 147, 173, 174.
    Journal, 168.
Bugbee, Oliver, 34.
Bull, G. W., 34, 169.
    John (Great Britain), 159.
Burch, Isaac H., 26, 39, 88.
Burdsall, E. H., 39.
Burger, Wm., 170.
Burley, Arthur G., 39.
    Charles, 39.
Burlingame, Anson, 11, 69, 90, 143, 161.
Burr, Edwin C., 147, 170.
    E. D., 5, 18, 22.
Butler, Charles, 153.
Butterfield, Justin, 26, 39, 88.
    Justin (schr.), 187.
    Justin, *jr.*, 39.
Buttles, A. B., 170.
    Joel, 170.
Butts, Isaac, 89.

C.

Calhoun, John, 26.
    John Caldwell, 10, 116, 134, 160.
Camp, Enoch E., 9, 161, 170.
    H., 170.
    John G., 49, 50, 68, 89, 90, 170.
Cann, Thomas, 46.
Carney, James, 26.
Caroline (schr.), 188.
Carson, Kit, 104.
Carver, *Mr.*, 80.
    Dr. Hartwell, 12, 96, 97, 99, 102, 104, 143.
Carter, Thos. B., & Co. (firm), 39.
Cary, *Miss* Lucinda, 170.
    Trumbull, 154, 162, 170.
    Dr. Walter, 169.
Cass, *Gen.* Lewis, 76, 140, 145, 152, 153, 168.
Cataract (steamboat), 147, 171, 172.
Cathcart, C. W., 36.
Cayuga (schr.), 187.
Chambers, A. B., 10, 12, 47, 48, 50, 90, 151, 161, 170.
    David, (should be A. B.) 22.
Champion (schr.), 190.
Champlain (stmr.), 190.
Champlain, *Capt.* Stephen, 168.
Chance (schr.), 189.
Chandler, M. A., 49, 50, 69, 90.
Chapin, *Hon.* John P., 6, 26, 39.
Chappel, Delos N., 46.
Chicago (schr.), 189.
Chicago American, 181.
    Commercial Advertiser, 46, 161.
    Democrat, 46, 138, 181.
    Democratic Press, 138.
    Evening Journal, 15, 16, 17, 18, 22, 23, 37, 39, 41, 46, 138.
    Lyceum, 46.
    Tribune, 46.
Christy, Edwin P., 168.
Church, Thomas, 39.
Cincinnati (schr.), 190.
Clarissa (sloop), 189.
Clark, *Gov.* William, 71.
    Lewis W., 26, 39.
Clarke, Henry B., 26, 45.
    Wm. Hull, 39.
Clay, Henry, 75, 140, 152, 172.
    Henry (schr.), 187.
Clement, *Miss* M. E., 170.
Cleopatra (schr.), 187.
Cleveland, I. T., 69.

Cleveland Light Artillery, 42.
   Plain Dealer (newspaper), 16.
Clinton, Geo. W., 154, 161, 163, 169.
Clybourn, Archibald, 39.
Clymer, George, 124.
Cobb, *Rev.* Jacob, 45.
   Silas B., 26, 39.
Coe, Bela D., 34, 169.
Coit, George, 33.
Colfax, Schuyler, 9, 50, 90.
Collins, James H., 26, 138.
   Samuel B., & Co. (firm), 39.
Colt, Roswell L., 69, 154, 162, 170.
Colton, Wells, 88.
Columbus (brig), 190.
Columbus, Christopher, 92.
Conklin, H. H., 170.
Constitution (schr.), 188.
Convention (vessel), 42.
Converse, Joseph M., 88, 170.
   L. P., 170.
Cook, John D., 69.
Corning, Erastus, 50, 90, 162.
Corwin, Thomas, 49, 50, 89, 139, 140, 142, 144, 148, 151, 152, 154, 157, 160, 161, 164, 165, 166, 168, 170.
Couch, Ira, 26.
Cowles, Alfred, 26, 39.
Coxe, H. S., 170.
Cramer (schr.), 187.
Cramer, Wm. E., 162.
Crawford, T. H., 49, 69.
Crocker, Hans, 48, 151.
Crogan, *Col.* George, 164.
Crook (schr.), 187.
Cross, *Dr.* Thomas L. Halsey, 49.
Crosswell, Edwin, 162.
Crow, 69.
Curtiss, *Hon.* Jas., 6, 26, 45, 47, 150.
   Peter, 34.
   Thomas B., 76, 152.

D.

Daily Wisconsin, 162.
Darrow, H. P., 30, 31, 33.
Davies, E. W., 170.
Davis, Chas. A., 170.
   George, 26.
   G. W., 161.
   Gen. Geo. R., 147.
   J. C. (schr.), 187.
   John (schr.), 187.
   Samuel Edward, 39.
Day, *Miss* Anna M., 45.

Deane, Robert L., 170.
Dearborn *School*, 45.
Delaware (schr.), 189.
Detroit (stmr.), 190.
   Advertiser, 161.
Dexter (schr.), 188.
Diamond (schr.), 187.
Dickinson, Daniel S., 152.
Dodge, Chas. V., 46.
Dole, Geo. W., 22, 23, 26, 39, 47, 87.
Douglas, Stephen Arnold, 154.
Dousman, M. (schr.), 187.
Drew, George C., 39.
Dryden, John, 146.
Duffy, Patrick, 26.
Duncan, Alex., 88.
Dunham, John H., 26, 39.
Dunlevy, A. B., 170.
   Miss F., 170.
Durant, *Miss* Martha C., 45.
Durfee, Philo, 33.
Dutch, Alfred, 39, 46.

E.

Eastman, Zebina, 25, 46.
Eaton, W. W., 8.
Edwards, Nelson G., 50, 90.
   W. R., 170.
Egan, *Dr.* Wm. Bradshaw, 11, 26.
Elbert, J. N., 170.
Eldridge, *Dr.* John W., 26.
Ellis, Erastus W. H., 50, 90.
Empire (steamboat), 147, 148, 149, 150, 151, 169.
Enterprise (brig), 188.
Erie Packet (schr.), 189.
Eugene, Prince (schr.), 189.
Eustis, Wm. T., 50, 90.
Evans, *Miss*, 170.
   C., 170.
   George, 89, 170.
   James C., 34.
   Dr. John, 46.
Ewing, Wm. B., 88.
Excelsior (fire-engine), 46.

F.

Falstaff, *Sir* John, 167.
Felch, Alpheus, 77, 78, 140, 153.
Fennerty, James, 26.
Fenno, Francis Upton, 50, 90, 158.
Fergus, Robert, 5, 6, 7, 10, 11, 13, 18, 37.
Ferguson, *Miss*, 45.
Field, David Dudley, 48, 80, 81, 84, 85, 141, 146, 151, 152, 153, 158.

Field, Joseph, 10.
Filkins, *Capt.*, 171.
  John, 39.
Filmore, *Pres.* Millard, 11, 31, 33.
Fire King (fire-engine), 43, 46.
Fiske, Francis S., 49, 50, 90.
  John, 171.
Florida (ship), 190.
Follansbee, Charles, 26.
Follett, Oran, 168.
Folsom, E., 34.
Foote, *Dr.* Thomas M., 30, 33, 154, 161, 169.
Ford, Elijah, 33.
Forrest, *Rev.* Joseph K. C., 45, 46.
Foss, Robert H., 45.
Foster, George F., 26, 46.
Francis, John, 34, 37.
Frink, John, 26.
  (John) & Walker (M. O.) (firm) 10.
Fremont, *Col.* John C., 93.

G.

Gage, John, 26.
Gale, Stephen F., 26, 39, 42, 46.
          (brig), 187, 188.
Gallagher, James H., 8.
Gallatin, Albert, 159.
Gallinipper (schr), 187.
Gamaliel, 13.
Garay, Don José, 7.
Gardner, Daniel, 69, 72, 80, 84, 152, 158.
Garrett, Augustus, 26.
Geer, Nathan C., 25, 26, 39, 46.
Gem of the Prairie, 46.
Getzler, Anton, 26.
Gibbs, *Dr.* Aaron, 39.
  Gibbs, George A., 26.
Gilbert, Ashley, 46.
Gold, Charles R., 169.
Goodhue, W. H., 34.
Gooding, Wm., 39.
Goodrich, Grant, 25, 30, 46.
Goss, Samuel W., 39.
Graham & Phillips (firm), 70.
Granger, Elihu, 45.
Gray, Chas. M., 26.
  John, 26.
  Joseph H., 26.
  Joseph W., 69.
Gregg, David L., 23.
Greeley, Horace, 49, 51, 90, 139, 140, 141, 143, 147, 152, 154, 157, 161, 166.

Green, Wm., 86, 158, 161, 170.
Greene, Thomas L., 147.
Griffith, John M., 34.
Grinnell, Joseph, 76, 77, 140, 152, 153.
Gurley, Jason, 26.
Gurnee, Walter S., 26.
Gustine, Ebenezer M., 46.
Gutherie, James, 88.

H.

Hadduck, Edward H., 26, 39.
Haight, Fletcher M., 69.
  Dr. Nathaniel D., 104.
Hale, Samuel (schr.), 187.
Hall, E. Allan, 8.
  James, 88, 161, 170.
  Nathan K., 30, 31, 33, 161, 169.
  Wm. Mosley, 5, 6, 7, 8, 9, 10, 13, 18, 34, 69, 81, 88, 90, 91, 92, 104, 143.
Hamlin, R., 39.
Hancock, *Gen.* Winfield Scott, 9.
Haraszythy, A., 21.
Hardy, Isaac, 39.
Harkinson, W. S., 39.
Harriet (schr.), 190.
Harrison, *Miss*, 170.
  Pres. Wm. Henry, 35.
Harwood, Amanda (schr.), 188.
Hastings, B. B., 170.
Hatch, I. T., 34.
  Junius H., 170.
Hathaway, Isaac G., 170.
Hawley, Seth C., 34, 139, 148, 154, 161, 169.
Helena (schr.), 187.
Helfenstein (brig), 187.
Helm, Margaret (brig), 190.
Hempstead, Chas. S., 50, 90.
Henderson (schr.), 115.
Henry, Alexander, 163, 164.
Herald of the Prairies, 46.
Heywood, R. H., 34.
Higgins, W. W., 34.
Hilliard, Laurin P., 26.
  Laurin P. (schr.), 187, 188.
  Maria (schr.), 188.
Hinman, John E., 139.
Hoadley, George, 8.
Hoard, Samuel, 26, 45.
Hobart, Aaron, 50, 90.
  Rev. C., 45.
Hobbie, Albert G., 26.
Hodson, Wm. B., 68, 89.
Hoeffgen, Robert B., 46.

Hook-and-Ladder Comp'y, No. 1, 43.
Hooker, Joseph W., 39.
   & Sons (firm), 170.
Hollister, J. J., 170.
   John, 11, 33.
   Robert, 11.
   William, 11.
   Messrs. (Jno.,Wm.& Rob't), 169.
Holmes, *Maj.* Andrew Hunter, 164.
Hone, *Miss* M., 170.
   Philip, 152, 161, 162, 170.
"*Hope*" *Hose Co.*, 42.
Hoppin, Hamilton, 50, 69, 90.
Hoyne, Thomas, 25, 121.
Hubbard, Gurdon Saltonstall, 26, 46.
Hubbell, Levi, 90, 143, 161.
Hudson, Hendrick (steamboat), 147.
Hugunin, Jas. R. (schr.), 187.
Hulburt, Eri B., 26.
Humming-bird (brig), 190.
Humphreys, David, 26, 39.
Hunt, Washington, 79, 80, 152, 153.
Huntington, Alonzo, 26.
Huron (schr.), 190.
Hutchinson, C. I. (brig), 187.

I.

Illinois (schr.), 190.
   (steamboat), 149.
   Med. and Surg. Journal, 46.
Independence (prop.), 188.
Indiana (brig), 190.
Ingalls, Albert W., 45.
Ingersoll, Joseph R., 151.

J.

Jackson, Albert, 49.
   Gen. and Pres. Andrew, 9, 28, 125, 126, 141, 159, 167, 172.
Jacobus, Augustus L., 39.
Jarvis, Charles, 89.
Jefferson (schr.), 190.
   Pres. Thomas, 28, 156.
Jernegan, Thomas, 34, 35, 37.
Jewett, S. S., 33.
Johnson, J., 46.
   John B., 88, 139.
   Sanford, 46.
Johnston, Anthony, 26.
Jones, Tarleton, 39.
   William, 170.
   Wm., 26, 45.
   Wm. E., 26, 45.
Joy, C., 170.
Judd, Norman B., 23, 25, 51, 75, 121,
136, 138, 152.
Juneau, Solomon (schr.), 190.

K.

Kasson, Arche, 39.
Keemle, Chas., 10, 161, 170.
Keen, Joseph, *jr.*, 39.
Keene, James Wilson, 89.
Kellogg, Dwight, 170.
   Rev. Ezra B., 46.
   N. O., 68.
Kelly, James, 46.
Kennedy, W., 169.
Kent, *Miss* Mary A., 45.
Kercheval, Louis C., 26.
Ketchum, Wm., 34.
Kilbourne, Byron, 22, 47.
Kimberly, John L., 33.
King, Charles, 21, 50, 69, 81, 89, 141, 152, 161.
   Charles B., 39.
   John, *jr.*, 26, 39.
   Gen. Rufus, 89, 162, 176.
   Thomas Butler, 12, 49, 50, 68, 86, 89, 90, 139, 141, 151, 159, 160, 161, 166, 170.
Kingman, Mahlon, 34.
Kingsland, J. D., 69.
Kinne, Henry M., 11, 30, 33.
Kinsella, *Rev.* Jeremiah A., 46.
Kinzie, John (brig), 190.
   John H., 26, 39, 46.
   School, 45.
Kirkpatrick, Littleton, 49, 50, 89, 90.
Knowles, Sheridan, 13.
Knox, Milton, 170.
Kuhn, George Horatio, 69.

L.

Lacy, *Miss* A. E., 170.
Ladue, P. A., 170.
Lady of the Lake (prop.), 187.
Lafayette (schr.), 189.
Lamb, *Mrs.*, 45.
Lane, James, 45.
Langdon, James J., 46.
Laporte (schr.), 189.
Laporte-County Whig, 34, 37.
Larned, Samuel, 170.
Larrabee, Charles H., 26.
Laverack, Wm., 169.
Lawrence (schr.), 187.
   Abbott, 88.
   H. C., 39.
Lee, Artemas, 49.

Lee, David S., 39.
Liberty-Tree (newspaper), 46.
Lille, John (schr.), 187, 188.
Lincoln, Abraham, 81, 138, 141.
Link, John, 46.
Long John (*Hon.* John Wentworth), 9, 145.
Loomis, Andrew W., 50, 90, 143, 161, 170.
   C. O., 170.
   Horatio G., 26.
Love, George M., 165.
   Miss Julia, 169.
   Thomas C., 33, 34, 86, 154, 161, 169.
Lovell, Frederick S., 50, 90.
Lowe, J. G., 170.
   Oscar F., 46.
   Samuel J., 25, 121, 136.
Loyd, Alex., 26.
Lucinda (schr.), 188.

M.

Macduffie, George, 173.
McArthur, *Dr.* E., 45.
McClelland, R., 153.
McConnell, Fleix Grundy, 154.
McCurdy, Theo. F., 170.
McDonald, Michael, 45.
McDonnell, Chas., 26, 45.
McKay, Jas., 31, 33, 34.
McLean, John, 136.
McMartin, Peter, 50, 90, 170.
Mace, Daniel, 68.
Madison, *Pres.* James, 28.
Madisonian (newspaper at Washington, D. C.), 161.
Magie, Haines H., 26.
   & Co. (firm), 39.
Maid of the Mist (steamboat), 147, 170.
Manierre, George, 25, 30.
Manitowoc (schr.), 187.
Marcy, *Gov.* Wm. L., 117.
Marsh, Jason, 81.
Marsh, Joshua L., 9.
Marshall, James A., 9.
   J. C., 69.
   O. H., 30.
Martell, John B, 170.
Mary Elizabeth (schr.), 190.
Mason (stmr.), 189.
Mathews, Stanley, 170.
Maynard, Elisha A., 31, 33.
   R. H., 34.
Maxwell, *Dr.* Philip, 26, 40, 47.

Meeker, George W., 23, 25, 39, 45, 78, 121, 136, 137.
Merrill, H. (schr.), 190.
Merritt, Jacob D., 26.
Merryman, *Dr.* E. H., 170.
Metamora (fire-engine), 43, 46.
Michigan (U. S. steamer) 168.
Michigan-City News, 37.
Miller, Wm. T., 39.
Mills, *Capt.*, 167.
   John, 88.
Milwaukee (ship), 190.
   Sentinel, 161.
Minnesota (schr.), 187, 188.
Mitchell, A. C. (schr.), 187.
Missouri Republican, 10, 18, 19, 161.
Mix, John, 170.
Monroe, *Pres.* James, 28.
Montgomery *Guards*, 42.
Morehead, James T., 88.
Morehouse, D. B., 170.
Morgan (barque), 188.
Morris, Buckner S., 39.
   Gouverneur, 124.
Morrow, *Ex-Gov.* Jeremiah, 139, 151.
Morton, Chas., 46.
Moseley, John H., 170.
Mosley, Wm. A., 33, 161, 169.
Mowbray, Mortimer M., 22.
Mueller, 46.
Murphy, John, 25.

N.

Neely, Albert, 26.
Neff, Michael A., 39.
Neptune (schr.), 190.
New Buffalo (schr.), 188.
New Hampshire (schr.), 187.
Newberry, Oliver, 11, 149.
   Walter L., 26.
Newburyport (stmr.), 189.
Newton, Isaac (steamboat), 147.
New-York Courier & Enquirer, 143.
   Express (newspaper), 143.
   Herald, 9, 17, 18.
   Police Reporter, 161.
   Tribune, 9, 139, 157.
Niagara (fire-engine), 43, 46.
Nickerson, Samuel, 39.
Niles, O. F., 170.
Noble, David A., 50, 89, 90, 176.
Norton, Henry (schr.), 187.
Norvell, John, 137.

www.ingramcontent.com/pod-product-compliance
Lightning Source LLC
Chambersburg PA
CBHW020908230426
43666CB00008B/1356